SPIRIT LIFE

SPIRIT LIFE

EXPERIENCE
THE POWER,
EXCITEMENT,
AND INTIMACY
OF GOD'S
SHAPING HAND

JERRY VINES

BROADMAN
&HOLMAN
PUBLISHERS
Nashville, Tennessee

0–8054–1651–X

Published by Broadman & Holman Publishers, Nashville, Tennessee
Acquistions and Development Editor: Leonard G. Goss
Page Design: TF Designs; Mt. Juliet, Tennessee

Dewey Decimal Classification: 231
Subject Heading: Holy Spirit
Library of Congress Card Catalog Number: 98–9547

Unless otherwise noted, Scripture quotations are from the
Holy Bible, New International Version, copyright © 1973, 1978, 1984
by International Bible Society, used by permission. Quotations
marked NKJV are from the Holy Bible, New King James Version,
copyright © 1979, 1980, 1982, Thomas Nelson, Inc., Publishers. Quotations
marked TLB are from The Living Bible, copyright © Tyndale
House Publishers, Wheaton, Ill., 1971, used by permission.

Library of Congress Cataloging-in-Publication Data
Vines, Jerry
SpiritLife : experience the power, excitement, and intimacy of God's shaping hand
/ Jerry Vines.
p. cm.
Includes bibliographical references.
ISBN 0–8054–1651–X
1. Holy Spirit. 2. Christian life.
I. Title.
    BT121.2.V56   1998
    231'.3—dc21
        98–9547
    CIP

1 2 3 4 5 02 01 00 99 98

*This book is lovingly and gratefully dedicated to four men
who have shown me what it means
to be Spirit-filled men of God.*

*R. L. Caswell
Carl Tapley
Horace Wilson
Charles Williams*

Contents

PREFACE

"What's up with that?" the girl said as she listened to her friend's story at the steak restaurant that day. I overheard only the one statement, but it spoke volumes to me. Most people today are confused, wondering what is up in their lives and in our world.

Have you ever been confused? Have you ever wondered where to find the truth? Many Christians today are confused too. They're interested in all kinds of spiritual matters, but they don't always find the answers to their questions. Adding to the confusion is the poor teaching which exists. What *is* up with all of this?

My friend John Phillips says the best way to spot a counterfeit hundred-dollar bill is to set a genuine bill beside it. An FBI agent told him the way they learn to recognize fake bills is to know the genuine so thoroughly that they can instantly recognize a counterfeit.

This is true when it comes to the subject of the Holy Spirit and his work today. So I have written this book for "plain Christians" like you and me. In most of my previous books, preachers were my primary audience. This book is different. I hope it will be helpful for preachers, but, quite honestly, I am writing from the top of my head and the bottom of my heart for Christians who are seeking to live spiritual lives each day. The outlines are not as prominent as in my other books. I have included more illustrations. I have tried to word the chapters in easy-to-understand language.

It is impossible to thank everyone who has helped me put this book together. Some, however, have been especially helpful. Nancy Smith, who was a vital part of our media ministry for several years and is now coordinator of media services at Converse College, was extremely helpful. She helped me get my language into a more contemporary, down-to-earth style. Thank you, Nancy.

Shirley Cannon, my secretary for more than fifteen years, has faithfully worked with me in getting the material in manuscript form. She always does an excellent job. Jacki Raulerson also assisted in this. Thank you, Shirley. Thank you, Jacki.

I am also indebted to Len Goss, my editor at Broadman & Holman, who has made helpful suggestions and guided me through the project. I'm also grateful for Bucky Rosenbaum, Broadman & Holman's director and managing editor. Bucky has been a friend for many years. He is the one who agreed to publish the book. Thank you, Bucky.

I would be remiss if I did not thank the wonderful members of First Baptist Church of Jacksonville. They are the greatest congregation of Christians I have ever known. They have listened patiently to my messages and have put the truths of those messages into their daily lifestyles. Thank you, First Baptist Jacksonville family.

I want to thank Navpress for their permission to quote from Eugene Peterson's most helpful *The Message*. I found this modern paraphrase very good in presenting New Testament truth in easy-to-grasp terminology.

INTRODUCTION

R. R. and I were inseparable. We did everything together. He was my best friend. I've always remembered R. R. because his initials were the same as my favorite cowboy's, Roy Rogers!

My heart broke the day R. R. told me he was moving away. My friend and my closest companion was leaving, but he promised he would come back and visit me. He never did.

I met a new friend, and he is still my Friend. He has never left me. I have written this book to tell you about my Friend and to share what I've learned about him over more than fifty years of my Christian life and more than forty years as a pastor and preacher.

This book has several sections. The opening chapters give you a little background information about my Friend based on what the Bible teaches about him. I share with you from the Old Testament and the New Testament what Scripture says about Him. I believe we must always base what we believe on any subject from the Bible.

My Friend has changed me on the inside and on the outside. A few of the chapters in this book explain these changes. He is a very generous Friend. He has provided me with wonderful gifts. He has also helped me learn how to live the Christian life successfully and serve Jesus Christ effectively.

Sometimes my Friend is misunderstood. At other times he is blamed for actions or events that he does not cause. I have tried to talk about several areas where these misunderstandings occur.

Finally, I have written a few chapters that explain how to be in fellowship with this Friend every day.

I have written this book because my Friend can be your Friend too. Maybe he already is. If so, my prayer is that this book will help you get to know him better and let him do more of his wonderful work in and through your life. Who is my Friend? He is the Holy Spirit. The Spirit of Jesus. The Spirit of God. The Spirit of glory. The breath of God. And on and on I could go. But most especially, he is the Comforter. He is my *Friend!*

CHAPTER 1

YOU HAVE
A FRIEND

Driving down the highway one day, I hit the seek button on my car radio (yes, I'm a TV channel surfer too!) and I heard a pleasant voice, singing a familiar lyric,

> Winter, spring, summer or fall,
> all you have to do is call and I'll be there.
> You've got a friend[1]

Appealing, wouldn't you agree? All of us need a friend. Life is too lonesome and the journey is too treacherous to travel without a friend.

Many of you have probably had the frightening experience of traveling to a strange land. You are in a land where the language is completely different and the scenes are unfamiliar to you. You do not know exactly how to get where you want to go. The customs are different; the people are different. This experience could be unnerving, especially if you are in this country alone. But if you go to a strange land and are met by a guide who knows the land, the journey could be a great deal more interesting and more beneficial to you. A guide who understands the language, who knows the right hotels to select, who knows the foods for you to avoid, who takes you to all the places you need to go and shows you all of the pleasures you need to experience—a guide like this makes the journey more desirable.

Now, suppose the guide who is going to lead you on this journey is not only an expert in that land, but is also your very best friend! Wow! What a difference!

That's sort of the way it is in the Christian life. Perhaps you have recently received the Lord as your personal Savior. You find yourself in a very different atmosphere. You have now received the Lord Jesus and you have come into his family and his kingdom. Although you are living in this world, you are aware that you are also in another world. The language is different. The customs are somewhat strange. The patterns of thought and the habits of life you are now experiencing are new. Wouldn't it be helpful in the Christian life if you had someone who could guide you? What if that someone who guides you could also be your friend? Even better, huh?

The Lord Jesus Christ walked with his disciples in the land of Israel for about three and one-half years. He was constantly with them. If you had asked any one of those disciples, Who is your best friend?—there is no question in my mind—every one of them would have said, "Jesus is my best friend." He's a friend who stays closer than a brother. It's wonderful to have someone like Jesus to be with us.

When the disciples had questions about perplexing matters, they could go to Jesus and ask him. He had the answers. When they wanted to know about prayer, they went to Jesus and said, "Lord, teach us to pray." Jesus taught them how to pray. When the disciples got stressed out about their lives, they could call on Jesus. Peter got in a jam—he jumped out of the boat and walked on the water. His eyes shifted to the storm instead of staying on the Savior, and he began to sink. He cried, "Lord, save me." In an instant, his best friend—the Lord Jesus—took him by the hand and delivered him. It was wonderful for these disciples to have a friend like Jesus! He was there to guide them through the experiences of their new lives.

John 13 and 14 present the closing words of the Lord Jesus before he left the earth. In a few hours, he would die on the cross. In John 13:33, Jesus declared, "My children, I will be with yo u only a little longer. You will look for me, and just as I told the Jews, so I tell you now: Where I am going, you cannot come." Jesus wanted his friends to know he was getting ready to leave them.

Have you ever had the experience of a good friend moving away? When I was a little fellow, I had a good friend named Ray Riggs. He was my "most best-est friend." Ray and I were constantly together. One day Ray came to me and said, "We're moving. My dad has a job in another town and we're moving away from Carrollton, Georgia." I remember how it hurt my little heart to think that my best friend was going to move away. He did move away, and I have never seen him again.

We can only imagine how it must have been for these disciples who had been with the Lord Jesus for more than three years. They had been constantly by his side. He had meant so much to them and now he was leaving them. That's why I think Jesus said in John 14:1, "Do not let your hearts be troubled." Their hearts were troubled. Their best friend was going away.

In that uncertain atmosphere, Jesus made a promise to his disciples in John 14:16: "And I will ask the Father, and he will give you another Counselor to be with you forever." In three chapters of John's Gospel (14, 15, and 16) Jesus made four references to "the Counselor." Four times in three chapters, he promised them he would send to them another Counselor after he left.

The word is also used in 1 John 2:1: "But if anybody does sin, we have one who speaks to the Father in our defense—Jesus Christ, the Righteous One." The phrase "one who speaks to the Father in our defense" is the same word translated "counselor" in the Gospel of John. The Greek word for "counselor" is *paracletos*, which is really two Greek words put together. It is the word *kaleo*, which means "to call"; and *para* which means "alongside of." Put the two together and you get our English word *paraclete*. A paraclete is one who is called alongside to help. That's why in 1 John 2 we are told about "the one who speaks to the Father in our defense"—our Advocate.

In New Testament times, citizens sometimes needed someone who could stand with them in a court of law. Today, we call such a person a lawyer. A lawyer is one who comes alongside us in court and defends us against a charge. He or she pleads our case. Jesus declared, "I'll send you another Counselor. I'll send you someone who will stand beside you in your defense." In 1 John 2:1, our Advocate with the Father is "Jesus Christ, the Righteous One."

We actually have two Comforters, two Advocates. One of our Advocates is in heaven. The Lord Jesus Christ is our divine attorney who is pleading our cause before the heavenly Father. But the Bible also says we have another Advocate who is pleading the Father's cause in our hearts. Who is this other Advocate? In John 14:16 Jesus said, "The Father will give you another Counselor." Then, in verse 26, he stated, "But the Counselor, the Holy Spirit . . ." So, Jesus was talking about sending them another Comforter. He was sending them an Advocate. This Advocate is the Holy Spirit.

I have spent many years studying the Bible's teaching about the Holy Spirit. I have wrestled with how to translate this word. The King James Version uses the word *Comforter*. That's a good word. The Holy Spirit is the Counselor or Comforter. Or, we may just transliterate the Greek word into English—*Paraclete*. The Holy Spirit is the Paraclete. Others prefer to translate it as "Helper." But to me, there is another word which is better. As you continue reading you may see more clearly why this word is so attractive to me.

"Comforter" is found only one time in the entire Greek version of the Old Testament. Job was going through all of his agonies and afflictions. His friends came to him and, instead of comforting him, only increased Job's agony and despair. Job said to them, "Miserable comforters are you all" (Job 16:2). They were supposed to be friends to him—they were to be comforters to him—and yet they became "miserable comforters."

A friend is someone who sticks with you in the bad times as well as the good times. That radio singer was right to sing, "I'll come running. You've got a friend." A friend is someone who walks in when everybody else walks out. A friend is someone who knows all there is to know about you—but loves you anyway. The Bible says there is a Friend who knows all about us and who still loves us. This Friend is the Holy Spirit. We have a Comforter, we have a Helper, we have a Friend.

If you have received Jesus Christ as your personal Savior, the Bible teaches that you have a Friend who is a friend forever. You have a Friend who not only walks with you; you have a Friend who lives inside you. He is the Holy Spirit. When we come to understand that and when we come to view the Holy Spirit as our very best Friend, we can live transformed lives! I have three very simple signposts for the journey.

Our Friend the Holy Spirit Is a Definite Person

You are a person. I am a person. Jesus Christ is a person. The Comforter, our Friend, the Holy Spirit, is a definite person. Sometimes people refer to the Holy Spirit as "it." In fact, the King James Version creates a little confusion on this point. Romans 8:16 in the King James Version says, "The Spirit itself beareth witness with our spirit." The King James translators put it this way because in 1611; they did not make the distinction between the gender of words like we do today.

Words have gender. There are masculine words; there are feminine words; there are neuter words. The word translated "Spirit" in our Bible is a neuter word. So, the King James translators were grammatically correct when they translated, "the Spirit itself." But it is inaccurate to refer to the Holy Spirit as an "it." Some people look upon the Holy Spirit as an "it"—just some kind of influence or an impersonal force in the world. No, that's not what the Bible says. The Bible teaches that the Holy Spirit is a definite person. He is not an "it."

Look at the personal pronouns Jesus used when referring to the Holy Spirit. "And I will ask the Father, and *he* will give you another Counselor to be with you forever" (John 14:16). Verse 17 continues, "the Spirit of truth. The world cannot accept *him*, because it neither sees *him* nor knows *him*. But you know *him* for *he* lives with you and will be in you (italics added)." All these words are definite personal pronouns. Jesus was referring to a real person. It is an insult to refer to any person as an "it." Suppose you are at the mall with your little boy. Somebody comes up and says, "Is that your son?" "Yes, that's my boy," you reply. "Well, what a pretty little *it* you have there." I have a feeling this statement would offend you. The Holy Spirit is not an "it." The Holy Spirit is a person.

This concept can be confusing. We often think a body is essential to personality—that one must have a body to be a person. There will come a day (if Jesus doesn't come before then) when you and I will die. To die is to be absent from the body and to be present with the Lord (2 Cor. 5:8). You are not going to cease to be a person when you are absent from the body and present with the Lord, are you?

Personality does not demand visibility. The real me is invisible. There is more to me than just hands and feet and eyes and ears and a nose. The real me is the person inside of me! My body is only the vehicle which expresses my personality. So, you don't have to have a body to have a personality. Because the Holy Spirit does not have a physical body as we do does not mean the Holy Spirit is not a person. The Holy Spirit is a person.

In fact, the Holy Spirit possesses all the essentials of personality. What are the essentials of personality? We as persons can think, feel, and act. Another way of putting it is that a person has intellect, emotion, and will. In the Bible, all of these attributes of personality are ascribed to the Holy Spirit—your best Friend.

For instance, the Holy Spirit can think. Romans 8:27 refers to the "mind of the Spirit." The Bible states that the Holy Spirit searches the deep things of God (1 Cor. 2:10). The Holy Spirit has the ability to think. Our best Friend has intellect.

The early church sought the mental ability of the Holy Spirit in making decisions. In the book of Acts, the church was deliberating, praying, and debating about a decision: "It seemed good to the Holy Spirit and to us" (Acts 15:28). In other words, they sought the mind of the Holy Spirit. The Holy Spirit has a mind. The Holy Spirit can pray; the Holy Spirit can make decisions; the Holy Spirit can search; the Holy Spirit can teach; the Holy Spirit can call. He possesses intellect. He can think. He's a person.

The Holy Spirit has feeling. Romans 15:30 tells us about the love of the Holy Spirit. Your Friend, the Holy Spirit, is a loving Friend. If the Holy Spirit is capable of love, then the Holy Spirit is capable of being grieved. That's why Ephesians 4:30 says, "Do not grieve the Holy Spirit of God." You can grieve someone who loves you. Your mother loves you. You can grieve her. You can break her heart. You can sin against your mother's love. You have a Friend who loves you far more than your mother loves you. This Friend is the Holy Spirit.

Because of his great love for you, he can be grieved, too. The Holy Spirit possesses emotion just like any other person, and the Holy Spirit is capable of feeling just like us or just like James Taylor singing his song!

The Holy Spirit is capable of doing. The Holy Spirit possesses will. The Holy Spirit gives gifts to individual believers. Some believers have gifts of preaching. Others have gifts of teaching. Others have gifts of helps. There is quite a variety of gifts. First Corinthians 12:11 says, "All these are the work of one and the same Spirit, and he gives them to each one, just as he determines." He can carry out actions. So, we have a Friend, the Holy Spirit. Jesus said the Comforter is the Holy Spirit. And he is a person.

Does this make any difference? Does this matter to us on our journey? It makes a great difference! The Holy Spirit is a person, so that means when you receive Jesus as your Savior, the Holy Spirit, as a person, comes into your life. Possessing the Holy Spirit is not like purchasing a car or a house through an installment plan. Many well-meaning people make this mistake. They say you get a little of the Holy Spirit when you are saved. Then, on down the road, you receive a little more of the Holy Spirit. That's a violation of the teaching of the personality of the Holy Spirit.

When you enter a building, how do you come in? Do you stand at a door and say, "I think I'll put a leg in first." Then after a little while do you say, "I think I'll bring my head in next." No, when you enter a building, you enter in your fullness. You enter in your totality. You are a person. When you receive Jesus Christ as your Savior, the Bible says the Holy Spirit of God enters your life in his totality. He is a person—a real definite person.

Viewing the Holy Spirit as a *person* rather than an *it* makes all the difference in the world. If the Holy Spirit is just an *it*, then the question becomes, How can I get *it*? How can I use *it* to do what I want to do? This appeals to pride. "I've got IT. How can I use IT?" But if the Holy Spirit is a person, then the question is not how can I get *it*, but how can he possess me. It causes not pride, but humility.

We don't have anything to brag about as Christians because everything we do is accomplished in the power of the Holy Spirit. The Spirit takes possession of our lives. He is the One who provides the power. Our Friend works through us. It is the Holy Spirit who gives us victory. It is a blessed and humbling experience to know that the Holy Spirit takes charge of our lives and leads us through our journey.

There is something else this truth means. It means you have a Friend—the Holy Spirit—and that your Friend—the Holy Spirit—is just like Jesus. In John 14:16 Jesus said, "I will ask the Father, and he will give you another Counselor." There are two words in the Greek language that are translated "another." A word frequently used is *heteros*. Our English word *heterosexual* is built on *heteros*. In our language, the meaning of this word is "another of a different kind."

A person may say, "I'm going to trade cars. I'm going to trade my Toyota for a Chevrolet." You are trading for another car of a different kind. *Heteros* is used in 2 Corinthians 11:4, where Paul warned about people who were preaching *another* Jesus, *another* Spirit, and *another* gospel. He was referring to "another of a *different* kind." It was not the right kind of gospel, not the same kind of spirit.

That's not the word Jesus used in this passage. The word he used here is *allos*. *Allos* means "another of the *same* kind." When Jesus said "I will give you another Comforter," He meant "I'm going to give you another of the same kind; one just like me." So we have a Friend in the Holy Spirit who is just like Jesus Christ—someone who is a friend to us just like Jesus Christ was to his disciples two thousand years ago.

In fact, what you and I possess with the indwelling presence of our Friend the Holy Spirit is better than what the disciples had when Jesus walked on this earth. In his days of earthly life, Jesus voluntarily limited himself to time and space. When Jesus was over here in this spot, he was not over there in that spot in his flesh. We have another Comforter just like the Lord Jesus Christ. But the good news is that he's with us all the time. The Holy Spirit is a definite person. In your times of loneliness, sorrow, temptation, and decision—you have a Friend! To realize that Jesus is in our midst today just as he was with his disciples should transform us all! Use this truth and let the Holy Spirit transform your life for the journey ahead.

Your Friend the Holy Spirit Is a Divine Person

The Holy Spirit is God. Most people understand that the Father is God and that Jesus Christ is God, but many people fail to understand the truth that the Holy Spirit is God. Yet, when you read the Bible, you will find that there are different attributes ascribed to the Holy Spirit that can only be ascribed to God. In Hebrews 9:14, the Holy Spirit is referred to as "the eternal Spirit."

Genesis 1:2 presents the Holy Spirit as omnipotent or all-powerful. First Corinthians 2:10–11 indicates the Holy Spirit is omniscient or all-knowing. In Psalm 139:7, his omnipresence or presence everywhere is declared.

The Holy Spirit manifests the attributes of God. The Holy Spirit does things that only God can do. For example, he inspired humans to write the Bible. Only God could do that. The Holy Spirit conceived the Lord Jesus Christ in the womb of the virgin Mary. Only God could do that. The Holy Spirit regenerates people and births them into the family of God. Only God can save a human soul. The Holy Spirit is a divine person.

The titles of the Holy Spirit let us know he is God. The Comforter is only one title for the Holy Spirit. There are many others. For instance, in the Old Testament eighteen titles are given for the Holy Spirit. In the New Testament, there are thirty-nine titles for the Holy Spirit. A careful study of these makes it very apparent that they are, in fact, titles for God. He is referred to as the Spirit of God (Gen. 1:2). Exodus 28:3 refers to him as the spirit of wisdom (KJV). In Zechariah 12:10, he is the spirit of grace. John 14:17 indicates He is the Spirit of truth. John 15:26 uses the same terminology, "I will send to you from the Father, the Spirit of truth who goes out from the Father." John 16:13 uses the title again: "When he, the Spirit of truth, comes." The Holy Spirit is the Spirit of truth. Only God can be the Spirit of truth. Such a beautiful title tells us how God works in our lives as believers.

In contrast, the devil works on the human mind by trying to feed us lies. This is why great care and caution should be given to what enters our minds. What you read, the kind of music you hear, the kind of television you watch, and the types of movies you rent all feed your mind. So much of it is filled with the lies of the devil. The devil wants to destroy your life with error. Many people today are hopeless and depressed or confused and miserable. The misery of our time is often due to the incorrect thinking established by Satan's deceit and error.

Remember, God works in our lives by means of truth. I need truth today for my mind. God the Holy Spirit helps me know the truth. I need truth now for my heart. The Comforter, the Holy Spirit, helps me love the truth. I need truth now for my will. My Friend, the Holy Spirit, helps me carry out the truth. Only God can be the Spirit of truth.

The Bible also teaches the doctrine of the Trinity. Although there is only one God, he reveals himself in three ways. God the Father is God. God the Son is God. God the Holy Spirit is God. They are all God.

To prove this, read Matthew 28:19. Jesus gave us the baptismal formula. When we baptize people, we use this formula: "Therefore go and make disciples of all nations, baptizing them in the name [singular] of the Father and of the Son and of the Holy Spirit." One God—but he reveals himself as Father, Son, and Holy Spirit.

Second Corinthians 13:14 says, "May the grace of the Lord Jesus Christ, and the love of God, and the fellowship of the Holy Spirit be with you all." God the Son, God the Father, and God the Holy Spirit—all are present.

What a mystery! How one God reveals himself in three persons is beyond our human comprehension. Yet, this shouldn't prevent us from accepting this Bible truth. I don't understand how a brown cow can eat green grass and produce white milk, which can be churned into yellow butter. But I drink milk and I eat butter!

Water exists in three forms—liquid water, ice, and fog. Yet all three are water. I am a son, a husband, and a father. I am three persons; yet I am one. The Holy Spirit, our Friend, is just as much God the Father and the Son. How do these three members of the Trinity work together? How does the Holy Spirit function in the work of the Trinity? God the Father is the originating cause. God the Son, the Lord Jesus, is the mediating cause. God the Holy Spirit is the executing or administering cause.

For instance, there are three professions involved in providing a remedy or a medicine to cure someone who is sick. There is the doctor who prescribes the remedy. There is the pharmacist who prepares the remedy. Then, there is the nurse who administers the remedy.

It's just the same with our salvation. God the Father originated the great plan of salvation. God the Son, the Lord Jesus, came down, died on the cross, and paid the price to make possible this great salvation. But God the Holy Spirit administers the great work of salvation in the heart of any believer. What the Father devises and the Son accomplishes, the Holy Spirit communicates.

Right now, we are living in the day of the Holy Spirit. To some extent, the Old Testament was the age of the Father. The New Testament was the age of the Son, and from the days of the apostles until now, we are in the age of the Holy Spirit. You can put it this way: God thought it, Jesus wrought it, and the Holy Spirit brought it!

I trust you are convinced that your Friend the Holy Spirit is a divine person. So, what does this mean to us and how can we use this on our journey? It means that we should worship the Holy Spirit. Do you worship the Holy Spirit? When we worship, we offer praise and adoration to God. I was brought up in a fine church, but its members had a tendency to get hung up on one song—the Doxology. We sang it every Sunday morning! By the time I was a teenager, I was so weary of it I thought I would never want to hear it again. But the truth is, it is a great, powerful hymn. Here's the way it goes:

> Praise God from whom all blessings flow.
> Praise him all creatures here below.
> Praise him above ye heavenly hosts.
> Praise Father, Son and Holy Ghost.

When you get up in the morning, do you worship God? I hope you have a quiet time—a time when you read your Bible, letting God talk to you; a time for prayer when you talk to God. Do you have a little chapel in your heart where you worship the Lord? Do you worship God the Father and thank him for his love and grace? Do you worship God the Son and thank him for dying on the cross for you? Do you worship God the Holy Spirit and thank him for bringing this great salvation and coming to live in your life? Do you yield your life to him? It will change your life and guide your journey if you begin your day worshiping your best Friend, the Holy Spirit.

Your Friend, your Comforter, is a definite person. He is a divine person. That means if you are a born-again child of God, the Holy Spirit dwells in you. Your best Friend is God! God is your Friend. What an astounding, awesome fact. Kids like to sing, "Friends are friends forever." That may or may not be true, but God is your Friend. He loves you. God the Holy Spirit dwells in your heart. All you say, all you do, everywhere you go in a day, your Friend, the Holy Spirit, is right there with you as you continue on your journey.

The Holy Spirit Is a Dynamic Person

I am using the word *dynamic* purposely. Acts 1:8 says, "You shall receive power when the Holy Spirit has come upon you" (NKJV). The Greek word is *dunamis*, from which we get the words *dynamite* and *dynamic*. Your best Friend, the Holy Spirit is a dynamic person. There is empowerment available in the Holy Spirit. We need the Holy Spirit's *dynamite* in our daily lives! Our own strength is insufficient to cope with temptations, to grapple with problems, or to deal with our inner needs.

Let me show you how this power works. The Holy Spirit comes to dwell in you. In John 14:17 Jesus said, "But you know him, for he lives with you and will be in you." Add to that two other statements: "Don't you know that you yourselves are God's temple and that God's Spirit lives in you?" (1 Cor. 3:16). "Do you not know that your body is a temple of the Holy Spirit, who is in you?" (1 Cor. 6:19). The word *dwell* means he makes his home in you.

If you are saved, your heart is not a motel where the Holy Spirit comes, stays a few nights, and moves on. Your heart is his permanent residence. The Holy Spirit has come to make his abode in your heart and to live with you forever. John 14:16 says, "He will give you another Counselor to be with you forever." He will never leave us. We may ignore, grieve, quench, or neglect our Friend, but he is there—ready to bless, encourage, and strengthen us. He will be with us forever.

Are you lonely? Here is your cure. You have a Friend in your heart. He will never let you down. He will be with you all the time. This is a remedy for low self-esteem. Do you feel you are worth very little? Do you feel unimportant and insignificant? Remember that your best Friend, the Holy Spirit lives in your heart. You are so important that God himself has come to live in your heart. That's dynamite; that's empowerment!

Your Friend, the Holy Spirit, has also come to be your teacher. In John 14:26, Jesus said, "The Holy Spirit, whom the Father will send in my name, will teach you all things." Do I hear a high school student say, "He's going to teach me all things. Great! I have an algebra test in the morning"? No, he doesn't mean algebra, chemistry, biology, and computer things. Jesus means the Holy Spirit will teach you all *spiritual* things. He'll teach you how to live the Christian life. He'll teach you how to have victory over temptation. He'll teach you what to do when heartache, sorrow, and death come.

Bill Gates's book, *The Road Ahead*, is a fascinating read. While I was reading the book, I thought, *How great it would be if Bill Gates would just come to spend a few days with me and explain certain parts of his book to me.* That is exactly what is available for you and me as we study the Bible. The same Holy Spirit who inspired people to write the Bible is in your heart. As you read your Bible, if you will ask him, he will help you understand it.

A little boy in school grew frustrated with a math problem. "It won't come out right," he complained. His teacher came to his aid and showed him how to find the right answer. The power of the Holy Spirit and his teaching is a cure for our ignorance. In a thousand situations we need wisdom. Our Friend, the Holy Spirit, is in our life to be our Teacher. D. L. Moody once said, "The Holy Spirit makes real *in* me what Jesus did *for* me." That's empowerment!

The Holy Spirit will enable us to be witnesses for Jesus. John 15:26 says, "When the Counselor comes, whom I will send to you from the Father, the Spirit of truth who goes out from the Father, he will testify about me." As the Holy Spirit comes into your life, changing your language and your habits, you become more and more like the Lord Jesus Christ. People begin to see Jesus in you and wonder why this change for the better. Then, the answer dawns: "It's Jesus. He has given his life to Jesus."

A changed life calls attention to Jesus. John 16:14 declares the primary purpose of the Holy Spirit is to call attention to Jesus. So, the Holy Spirit provides the power to be a witness for Jesus. I believe most Christians want to be witnesses for Jesus. I accepted Jesus at nine years of age. I have tried to witness along the way. Sometimes I have made such a mess of it that it discouraged me and I would get embarrassed. Matthew 10:20 changed witnessing for me. Jesus said, "For it will not be you speaking, but the Spirit of your Father speaking through you." That changed my whole outlook on witnessing. Now I ask the Holy Spirit to give me the right words and help me say the right things.

The Christian journey can be an exciting adventure because you have a divine, dynamic Friend in your heart. You can be a witness for the Lord Jesus and reach somebody for Jesus because you have this divine, dynamic personality in you. That's empowerment for witnessing!

Imagine a little girl standing on a street corner in New York City. She has a bundle under her arm and cars are whizzing back and forth on the street in front of her. In a moment a tall gentleman in a uniform comes up to her and says, "Little girl, what's the matter?" She's almost crying. "I can't get across. It's too busy and crowded." The friendly policeman says, "We'll fix that." He reaches down and takes her by the hand and leads her safely across the busy intersection. Your Friend, the Holy Spirit, wants to take you by the hand and lead you into victory on your Christian journey.

By the way, the singer on the radio was James Taylor, singing his hit, "You've Got a Friend." I think it is wonderful that he is willing to be a friend to someone. I wonder—does James Taylor have *the* Friend? I wonder—do you?

Tips for the Journey

1. The journey of life is too treacherous to risk it alone. Invite the Holy Spirit, your Friend, to be your personal guide.

2. As you begin each day's journey, begin by acknowledging your Friend's presence and yielding your all to him.

3. As you encounter daily problems and decisions along the road, ask your Friend for wisdom to do the right thing, power to be able to do the right thing, and love to do the right thing in the right way!

4. Although you may feel lonely at times, talk to your Friend, the Holy Spirit, who will never leave you alone.

CHAPTER 2

BREATHE ON ME

"And with that he breathed on them and said, 'Receive the Holy Spirit'" (John 20:22). Is this puzzling to you? It is to me.

We aren't told how the disciples reacted to this. In coliseums and churches around the country, pastors and evangelists are breathing on people. Some are falling down. Others try to fall, but don't. It's all a part of the modern activity of being "slain in the Spirit." Is this similar to what took place when Jesus blew on his disciples?

Jesus died on the cross. He rose again from the dead, and he prepared to go back to heaven. Before his departure he gave the disciples their marching orders. He told them what they were to do after he went back to heaven (John 20:21).

At different times God the Father has dealt with people in a variety of ways. There are three distinct periods of time for believers. Since Jesus returned to heaven, believers have been living in what has been referred to as the age of the Holy Spirit. The Old Testament period might be called the age of the Father. In the New Testament Gospels, there was the age of the Son, the Lord Jesus. During that time the Lord Jesus made the Father real to people. He spoke often of the heavenly Father and taught us to pray, "Our Father." From the New Testament era until now, we could well say that believers are living in the age of the Holy Spirit. The purpose of the Holy Spirit in the present era is to make the Lord Jesus real to us.

Sometimes we get the idea that the Holy Spirit was not present in the world until he came to live in the lives of the early disciples on the day of Pentecost. We do know that the heavenly Father had promised the Holy Spirit would come (Acts 1:4). In fact, a mighty outpouring of the Holy Spirit was promised. Look at two Old Testament predictions: "I will pour out my Spirit on your off-spring, and my blessing on your descendants" (Isa. 44:3). "I will pour out my Spirit on all people" (Joel 2:28).

The heavenly Father had promised that there would be a time when the Holy Spirit would be given in a special and unusual way. Jesus said this to the disciples before he went back to heaven: "I am going to send you what my Father has promised; but stay in the city until you have been clothed with power from on high" (Luke 24:49).

In Acts 1 the Lord's disciples were waiting for this promise of the Father, and it was fulfilled on the day of Pentecost (Acts 2). The Lord Jesus said he would pray the Father and the Father would send the Holy Spirit (John 14:16). So on the day of Pentecost the Holy Spirit of God came. John the Baptist also predicted a time of baptizing with the Holy Spirit and with fire (Matt. 3:11).

These statements might lead one to think that the Holy Spirit did not appear or do any work on the earth until the day of Pentecost. But a careful study of the Bible makes it clear that the Holy Spirit of God was present and active even from the very beginning of the earth's existence. The Holy Spirit has always been present and active on the earth. He's been a part of people's lives.

The Old Testament has much to say about the Holy Spirit. The Spirit of God is mentioned eighty-eight times in the Old Testament. He is mentioned in twenty-two of the thirty-nine Old Testament books. There were times when the Holy Spirit was present at several places. When the tabernacle was constructed and then when the more permanent temple was constructed, the Spirit of God came as a cloud hovering above these places of worship (Exod. 40:34–35; 1 Kings 8:10–11). Sometimes the Holy Spirit came to bless particular individuals, equipping them for specific work. The workmen selected to construct the temple were filled with the Holy Spirit in order to do the work of craftsmanship which God intended (Exod. 35:31; 36:1).

The book of Judges tells us about people who received a special outpouring of the Holy Spirit for specific purposes in their lives. Gideon knew all about this. The Bible says the Spirit of the Lord came upon Gideon (Judg. 6:34). Literally it means the Spirit of the Lord clothed himself with Gideon. Gideon was "wrapped up" around the Holy Spirit like a garment. Samson is another example. He had a mighty filling of the Holy Spirit (Judg. 14:6). Samson was strong not in his physical strength, but strong because the Spirit of the Lord would come mightily upon him from time to time. The Spirit of God would come upon different people for different purposes and in different ways in the Old Testament. The Holy Spirit is still entering the lives of real people.

Today, the Spirit deals differently with Christian believers. In the Old Testament, the Holy Spirit could come upon individuals, but his presence could also be withdrawn. King Saul had an experience like this. The Spirit of the Lord did come upon him, but when Saul disobeyed and displeased the Lord, the Spirit of the Lord departed from him (1 Sam. 16:14). Similarly, when David confessed his sin of marital infidelity, he pleaded with the Lord, "Do not cast me from your presence or take your Holy Spirit from me" (Ps. 51:11). You and I need never pray that prayer in this age, as we shall see.

Today, the Spirit of God lives in the hearts of believers and he stays there forever. When you receive the Lord Jesus Christ as your personal Savior, the Holy Spirit comes into your heart to live there as a part of your life. He can never be withdrawn. Money can be withdrawn from your banking account, but the Holy Spirit will never withdraw from your heart. Jesus said in John 14:16, "And I will ask the Father, and he will give you another Counselor to be with you forever."

We may quench the Holy Spirit. We may refuse to let him use us in the Lord's service. We may grieve the Holy Spirit. We may say or do things that hurt him. We may bring bitter agony to the Holy Spirit. But the Holy Spirit will never be withdrawn from believers. He abides—he lives with us—forever. If you are saved, you have the indwelling of the blessed Holy Spirit of God.

What does the Bible mean when it describes Jesus as "breathing" on his disciples? It ties back to the Old Testament work of the Holy Spirit. Jesus gave his disciples their commission. He assured them that his peace was there for them and then he said, "As the Father has sent me, I am sending you" (John 20:21). A similar description of this commission says, "Therefore go and make disciples of all nations" (Matt. 28:19). Wow! What overwhelming feelings of inadequacy they must have felt as they realized their tremendous responsibility.

Jesus "breathed" upon them precisely at this time. The Greek word used here is a word that means "to blow." Jesus said, "Receive the Holy Spirit" (John 20:22). Sometimes, in the King James Version of the Bible, you will find the word for "spirit" translated "ghost." That is not a good translation for modern times. The better translation here is "spirit." When you talk about the "Holy Ghost" today, people think about some horror figure, some frightening personality. The Holy Spirit is not a scary, horrible ghost.

The Lord Jesus said, "Receive the Holy Spirit." The word *Spirit* here is the translation of a Greek word (*pneuma*) used in several different ways in the New Testament. This New Testament word is parallel to the word *ruach* in the Old Testament. From this Greek word, we get such words as pneumonia, pneumatic, etc. These two Bible words are rendered in three different ways— sometimes translated "wind" or "breath" or "spirit." Considering the context explains the reference.

The concepts of wind and breath are both beautiful pictures of the Holy Spirit. The Holy Spirit's work is like the blowing of the wind or the breathing of breath. Many times in the Old Testament, the Spirit of God is called the "breath of God." The Lord Jesus connected what was soon to happen on the day of Pentecost to what took place in the Old Testament as the holy breath of God moved and breathed with mighty, life-giving power. Soon the Spirit would come "like the blowing of a violent wind" (Acts 2:2).

Like wind or breath, the Holy Spirit cannot be seen. Jesus declared, "God is spirit, and his worshipers must worship in spirit and in truth" (John 4:24). Some people don't believe there is a Holy Spirit because they cannot see the Holy Spirit. I heard about a cynic who was talking to a Christian one time about this. He said, "I don't believe there is a Holy Spirit. I can't see any Holy Spirit." He then said to the Christian, "Have you ever seen the Holy Spirit?"

The Christian said, "No."

"Have you ever tasted the Holy Spirit?"

"No."

"Have you ever smelled the Holy Spirit?"

"No."

Then he said, "Then, how do you know there is a Holy Spirit?"

The Christian said to the skeptic, "Well, have you ever seen your brain?"

The skeptic said, "No."

"Have you ever tasted your brain?"

"No."

"Have you ever smelled your brain?"

"No."

"Then, how do you know you have a brain?"

We cannot see the Holy Spirit, but this is not a reason to deny the existence of the Holy Spirit. The Holy Spirit is the great wind of God. The Holy Spirit is the great breath of God. And the Holy Spirit can be with us in real life.

There are some instances of God breathing in the Old Testament. Let's explore this concept.

The Holy Spirit Created a World

His Work of Creation

The Holy Spirit, the breath of God, acted in the creation of the world. The Genesis account of creation says, "In the beginning God created the heaven and the earth. And the earth was without form, and void; and darkness was upon the face of the deep, And the Spirit of God moved upon the face of the waters" (Gen. 1:2).The second verse of the Bible has a reference to the Spirit of God—the breath of God. The Spirit of God moved. The Hebrew word can be translated as "brooded." Picture a mother bird *brooding* or hovering over the nest of her young. Deuteronomy 32:11 depicts a similar image. The Spirit of God *brooded* or hovered over the deep.

Here is a picture of chaos. The earth was without form and void. Isaiah 45:18 specifically says that is not the way God created it. Could this be a reference to the fall of Satan and the world becoming chaotic? I think so, although interpreters take different views of this. But in the midst of the chaos, the sweet breath of God blew upon the creation. *Out of chaos came order and beauty.* So the Spirit of God was present at creation.

God said "let us" many times in the creation account. "Let us make man in our image." To whom was the Lord referring? Many believe the reference is to the Trinity. "Let us"—God the Father. "Let us"—God the Son. "Let us"—God the Holy Spirit. The Spirit of God was present at the creation of this universe, working with the Father and the Son.

Psalm 104:30 states the Spirit's participation in creation: "When you send your Spirit, they are created, and you renew the face of the earth."

Psalm 33:6 adds, "By the word of the LORD were the heavens made, their starry host by the breath of his mouth." What a beautiful statement—by the breath of his mouth. The breath of God blew upon chaos and then came order. The Spirit of God moved like a bird hovering over its nest and this universe came into existence.

Job 26:13 makes an interesting statement. "By his breath the skies became fair." What happens after a storm? The blue is restored to the skies and the sparkle is returned to the trees and the flowers. God transformed the heavens by his Spirit. Every bit of the beauty we find in our universe is the result of the creative activity of the breath of God. Every beautiful leaf on every tree has been touched by the breath of God. All the beautiful stars were created and made beautiful by the breath of God. Every bit of beauty we see in our physical world is the work of the Holy Spirit. All the variety and color and shape and design in the world is a result of the breath of God!

Wonder at the beauty and vastness of this universe which the Spirit of God took part in creating. Think of all the stars and their beauty. We are just beginning to learn the true scope of the stars. A century and half before Jesus Christ, the Greek philosopher Hipparchus estimated there were 1,022 stars. Two centuries after the Lord Jesus Christ, Ptolemy had the number up a little higher—1,026 stars. Three hundred years ago, with the invention of the telescope, Galileo estimated there might be millions of stars. Then, in 1921, one astronomer estimated there were three hundred billion. The stars are innumerable. No one is able to count them all.

One astronomer said the stars in the universe are more numerous than all the grains of sand on all the seashores on all the earth. Man is unable to number all the stars (Ps. 147:4). Yet the Bible says that God knows the number of the stars and has given a name to every one. All of this comes as result of the creativity of the breath of God. Wherever the breath of God blows, light and beauty are brought into existence.

There is universal life when the Spirit of God begins to blow and there is human life. Genesis 2:7 says, "The LORD God formed the man from the dust of the ground [man's physical nature], and breathed into his nostrils the breath of life [his spiritual nature), and the man became a living being [his psychological nature]." Job 33:4 teaches, "The Spirit of God has made me." When God created humanity, the Bible says that he took formless clay and breathed upon it. This life-giving breath of God brought physical life into existence. Man is just dust until God breathes upon him, putting life in him. Our very existence is due to the life-giving work of the Holy Spirit.

Psalm 139:7 contains a remarkable statement: "Where can I go from your Spirit? Where can I flee from your presence?" The psalmist is saying he can't go anywhere the Spirit of God is not present. Psalm 139 talks about the creation of a baby in the womb of its mother. When conception occurs, the sperm cell from the male and the egg cell from the female come together.

This is only an illustration, but I like to imagine that when a birth occurs, the breath of God blows the sperm cell toward the egg cell and life occurs. Life begins at conception. That's why I am opposed to abortion. Abortion is the taking of a human life, and it is a snuffing out of the breath of God.

We owe universal existence to the Holy Spirit, the breath of God. We owe our very human existence to the Holy Spirit, the breath of God. Our new birth, as well as our physical birth, is due to the breath of God. When Jesus was talking to Nicodemus in John 3, he said, "Flesh gives birth to flesh, but the Spirit gives birth to spirit. The wind blows wherever it pleases. You hear its sound, but you cannot tell where it comes from or where it is going. So it is with everyone born of the Spirit" (John 3:6, 8). He was using the physical wind as an illustration. The physical wind can't be seen, but its effects are very visible!

Think of the wind and what it can destroy in a hurricane! But while hurricane wind works destructively "spirit" wind works creatively. The same is true of spiritual birth. The actual conception of the new life in Christ may be unseen as the wind, but the changed life as a result is seen. The drug user becomes clean. The wife abuser becomes gentle. At the moment of our new birth in Christ, we are made partakers of the divine nature (2 Pet. 1:4). The Spirit of God moves believers and produces beauty, design, and purpose. He is conforming us to the beautiful image of Christ (Rom. 8:29).

The Holy Spirit Composed a Book

His Work of Revelation

Without question some of the great books of literature have been inspired. Who could question that Milton's *Paradise Lost* or Bunyan's *Pilgrim's Progress* were inspired? Some of the great poets have been inspired. Think of Dante's *Inferno* or Longfellow's *Paul Revere's Ride*. But there is one book that is inspired like no other book in all the earth. I'm referring to the Bible. The word *inspire* means "to breathe in." The Holy Spirit, the breath of God, has breathed life into one book—the Bible. This sets it above all other books.

The inspiration is explained in 2 Timothy 3:16: "All Scripture is God-breathed." That phrase is the translation of one Greek word, *theopneustos*. It is a compound Greek word. It is made up of the word for God, *theos*, and the word for spirit, *pneumos*. Put them together and you have *theopneustos*. This means all Scripture is "God-breathed." This Bible is a God-breathed, living book. In John 6:63 Jesus declared, "The Spirit gives life; the flesh counts for nothing. The words I have spoken to you are spirit and they are life." First Peter 1:23 affirms, "For you have been born again, not of perishable seed, but of imperishable, through the living and enduring word of God."

The people who wrote the Bible were inspired to do so. Second Peter 1:21 says, "For prophecy never had its origin in the will of man, but men spoke from God as they were *carried along* by the Holy Spirit." The Old Testament writers who gave us our Old Testament were moved by the Spirit of God. The word *carried along* is the picture of the wind blowing the sails of a ship and guiding it along its course. Over and over again the Old Testament writers say, "thus saith the Lord"; "God spoke to me"; "God said this." They claimed that their words did not originate from their own ability or intellect. The words came from the Spirit of God.

In that light, Acts 1:16 is interesting: "Brothers, the Scripture had to be fulfilled which the Holy Spirit spoke long ago through the mouth of David concerning Judas." This refers to a psalm David had written. David said it, but he said it through the influence of the Holy Spirit.

What about the New Testament writers? Were they inspired by the Holy Spirit? In John 14:26 Jesus promised, "But the Counselor, the Holy Spirit, whom the Father will send in my name, will teach you all things and will remind you of everything I have said to you." How is it that the Bible writers could remember everything that the Lord Jesus said and record it in the Scriptures? Jesus told us exactly how it happened. He said the Holy Spirit would bring it all to their remembrance. So the Gospels were inspired by the Holy Spirit.

Jesus expanded the picture in John 16:13: "But when he, the Spirit of truth, comes, he will guide you into all truth. He will not speak on his own; he will speak only what he hears, and he will tell you want is yet to come." Now, the Gospels, the book of Acts, and the epistles are indicated. The final statement is, "And he will show you *things to come*." Things to come. Future things. The book of the Revelation.

Each Bible book is the result of dual authorship. The dual authorship of the Bible may be compared to the birth of Jesus. When Jesus was born, he had a human nature and also a divine nature; yet he was without sin. The Bible has human authors and a divine Author, yet, without error.

There is the human author and the divine Author. The personalities of the human authors are evident in the writing—the pathos of Jeremiah, the logic of Paul, the philosophy of John. As you read, you become aware of another Author who was inspiring and revealing and moving through all of Scripture. The Holy Spirit of God has composed a book for us. It is the Bible—the Word of God.

The very words of the Bible are inspired—not just the thoughts. How are thoughts possible without words? Have you ever had a thought without a word? Take about three seconds right now and think a thought without a word attached to it. Can you do it? You can't think a thought without a word. Words are vehicles of thought.

First Corinthians 2:13 indicates the words of the Bible were inspired by the Holy Spirit: "This is what we speak, not in words taught us by human wisdom but in words taught by the Spirit, expressing spiritual truths in spiritual words." Where do you find the words the Holy Spirit teaches? In the Bible. That's why Jesus said, "The words I have spoken to you are spirit and they are life" (John 6:63).

The Holy Spirit composed a book. He inspired men to write the Scriptures. But the same Holy Spirit who inspired men to write the Scriptures is the Holy Spirit who enables us to read and understand the Scriptures. We can't understand the Bible apart from the Holy Spirit. The Bible is a spiritual book. You have to have spiritual help in order to understand it. First Corinthians 2:10 says, "But God has revealed it to us by his Spirit. The Spirit searches all things, even the deep things of God." Then verse 14 says, "The man without the Spirit does not accept the things that come from the Spirit of God, for they are foolishness to him, and he cannot understand them, because they are spiritually discerned." The Holy Spirit provides us the text—the Bible. He also provides the Teacher—himself! This is why the Bible is a closed book to an unsaved person. The Holy Spirit must guide a person into the truth of Scripture. It's the only way we can understand it.

A skeptical professor in a college classroom was making fun of the Bible. He said, "I've read the Bible and I can't make any sense out of it. That's why I don't believe the Bible is the Word of God. I don't understand it." A Christian student had had about as much as he could stand. "Well, sir," he said, "that's what you get for reading somebody else's mail!"

The Bible is a book inspired by the Spirit of God for the people of God. The Holy Spirit will help you understand the Scriptures. You say you can't understand the Bible. Do you mean you don't understand the words of the Bible? Perhaps you need a version with more current wording.

There may be another reason. Many times whether you understand something has to do with how motivated you are. A teenage boy has his eyes on a girl in his class. She's so cute and he thinks he would like to get to know her better. One day after school she tells him, "We are having a little party at my house Friday night and I'd like you to come. Here's a map to my house." He takes the map and opens it up and it's upside down. What's he going to do? Because he doesn't understand it, will he drop it? No. He will turn it around. He may see some streets he's never seen before. He will find where the streets are. Why? Why is he so interested in understanding that map? A cute young thing has motivated him!

A letter arrives in the mail. "Dear Mr. and Mrs. Woods, We are happy to inform you that you have inherited ten million dollars. We have enclosed in this letter a form we would like you to fill out." The form is rather complicated. Some of the words are unfamiliar. Will this couple throw the form away? No. They will get a dictionary and find the meanings of the words. They will get all the help they can. They will study the form. They will learn how to fill it out and understand it. They have been motivated!

I want to motivate you about understanding the Bible. The good news is that the same One who gave you the text, the Bible, is the Teacher who can help you understand the Bible. If you are willing to allow the Holy Spirit to put you in his school, he'll teach you the Word of God. He will not merely guide you into truth to increase the number of facts for your notebook. No, he will take those truths and change your life. Keep in mind that the Holy Spirit's purpose in the Bible is to exalt Jesus (see John 15:26; 16:14). The Bible is all about Jesus. He is coming; he has come; he is coming again!

The Holy Spirit Conceived a Savior

His Work of Incarnation

The Holy Spirit has a special relationship to the Lord Jesus. The Holy Spirit is called the Spirit of Christ (Rom. 8:9). In Philippians 1:19, he is called the Spirit of Jesus Christ. A study of the life of the Lord Jesus Christ reveals that the Holy Spirit was active at every crucial juncture in the life of the Lord Jesus.

For instance, the virgin birth. Matthew 1:20 says, "What is conceived in her is from the Holy Spirit." Luke was a medical doctor. His account is even more extensive. In Luke 1:34–35, Dr. Luke says about the virgin Mary that the Holy Spirit would come upon her, that the Spirit of God would overshadow her—or envelop her—and that Holy Thing which would be born of her would be the Son of God. Dr. Luke knew he was in the presence of a miracle.

When the Lord Jesus Christ was born, he already had a divine nature. He existed before Bethlehem. But when the breath of God breathed upon Mary, there was added to the divine nature of the Lord Jesus Christ a human nature. But because he was conceived of the Holy Spirit, his was a sinless body. Just in passing, note that at our new birth, the Holy Spirit adds a divine nature to our human nature (see 2 Pet. 1:4).

All through the ministry of Jesus, the Spirit of God was present. When Jesus was baptized, the Spirit of God, like a dove, came down upon him, anointing him for his ministry (Matt. 3:16). When we are saved, we are baptized by the Holy Spirit (1 Cor. 12:13). We serve by the anointing of the Holy Spirit (see 2 Cor. 1:21). He went into the temptation led by the Holy Spirit (Luke 4:1). After the temptation, he returned in the power of the Holy Spirit (Luke 4:14).

He conducted his ministry in the power of the Holy Spirit. He said, "I drive out demons by the Spirit of God" (Matt. 12:28).

Jesus died on the cross by the Holy Spirit. Hebrews 9:14 says, "How much more, then, will the blood of Christ, who through the eternal Spirit offered himself unblemished to God." The question is sometimes asked, Who killed Jesus on the cross? Some say the Jews killed Jesus on the cross. In a sense, they took part in the circumstances that brought it about, but that's not the ultimate answer. Others say the Roman government killed Jesus on the cross. They did arrange the political circumstances, but that's not the final answer. The Bible says that the Lord Jesus Christ was the Lamb slain before the foundation of the world (Rev. 13:8). It was foreordained by God the Father that the Lord Jesus would die on that cross. When Jesus Christ was on the cross, the Bible says he offered himself up by the Holy Spirit. The Spirit of God was the divine executioner when the Lord Jesus died at Calvary.

Jesus Christ was raised again from the dead by the Holy Spirit. Romans 8:11 tells us the Spirit raised Jesus from the dead. The breath of God blew on that third day and Jesus came out of that tomb alive.

In a sense, the believer parallels the experience of the Lord Jesus in his own life. Just as Jesus had a miracle birth, you become a Christian by a miracle birth. You must be born of the Spirit of God. The Christian life is lived in the power of the Spirit. God's Spirit has come into your life. You serve the Lord and overcome temptation. All is done in the power of the Holy Spirit.

The only way to die to the old you is through the power of the Holy Spirit. Paul says in Galatians 2:20, "I have been crucified with Christ." The Bible says you and I are to live a crucified life. Actually, living the Christian life is an impossibility. Have you ever tried it? "I'm going to live it today. I'll get rid of this profanity. I'll conquer these habits today." You set out to live it today and before the day is out, you've blown it again. You don't have enough self-will, self-determination, or self-power to live the Christian life in your own strength. Self-crucifixion isn't possible. Yes, taking your life can be done several ways—a gun, poison, a rope. But not crucifixion. Take a hammer and drive a nail in your right hand, then drive a nail in your feet. There is still an uncrucified hand. Someone else has to put you to death by crucifixion.

Romans 8:13 says, "For if you live according to the sinful nature, you will die; but if by the Spirit you put to death the misdeeds of the body, you will live." Who puts you to death? The Spirit of God. The Holy Spirit puts you on the cross and enables you to die to self.

Romans 8:11 says, "And if the Spirit of him who raised Jesus from the dead is living in you, he who raised Christ from the dead will also give life to your mortal bodies through his Spirit, who lives in you." When the Holy Spirit kills the old you, then the spirit will raise you up and you can live a resurrected life in the Lord Jesus.

In Ezekiel 37 the prophet Ezekiel saw a valley of dry bones. The Lord told Ezekiel to prophesy to those bones. He did, and the toe bone connected to the foot bone and the foot bone connected to the ankle bone, and so forth. All he had then was a bunch of organized bones. The Lord said to Ezekiel, "Prophesy to the breath; prophesy, son of man, and say to it, 'This is what the Sovereign LORD says: Come from the four winds, O breath, and breathe into these slain, that they may live'" (Ezek. 37:9). When the breath of God came, there was life and beauty. That's what we need. We need to come to the Lord and say, "O, Lord, breathe on this dead life of mine that I may live." Our churches, for all their programs and organization, are just valleys of dry bones. We need to say, "O Holy Spirit, come breathe on us." In the Bible, breathing on someone or something is an act of deity. When God breathes, there is not a slaying, but a coming to life.

A hymn we used to sing when I was a young Christian meant a great deal to me. Let these words be our prayer.

> Holy Spirit, breathe on me
> Until my heart is clean;
> Let sunshine fill its inmost part
> With not a cloud between.
> Holy Spirit, breathe on me,
> My stubborn will subdue;
> Teach me in words of living flame
> What Christ would have me do.
> Holy Spirit, breathe on me,
> Fill me with power divine;
> Kindle a flame of love and zeal
> Within this heart of mine.
> Holy Spirit, breathe on me
> Till I am all thine own;
> Until my will is lost in thine
> To live for thee alone.

Breathe on me, breathe on me,
Holy Spirit, breathe on me;
Take thou my heart, cleanse every part,
Holy Spirit, breathe on me.[1]

CHAPTER 3

WHAT A DIFFERENCE A DAY MAKES

December 7, 1941. Japanese aircraft attack Pearl Harbor, wiping out American air units. World War II begins.

October 31, 1517. A German monk, Martin Luther, nails his Ninety-Five Theses on the door of the Castle Church in Wittenberg, Germany. The Protestant Reformation is launched.

July 16, 1942. At Los Alamos, New Mexico, a tremendous blast rushes out across the desert. A huge, mushroom-shaped cloud lifts heavenward. Nuclear weaponry becomes a reality.

September 22, 1937. I see the light of day in a country house in rural Georgia. Life starts for me.

The day of Pentecost. The age of the Holy Spirit is inaugurated. What a difference a day makes!

What do you know about the Holy Spirit? Early in my life I found a series of statements. They helped me understand this complex topic better. Some of these were:

- The average Christian is bogged down somewhere between Calvary and Pentecost.

- Christians have been to Calvary for pardon, but they have not been to Pentecost for power.

- Bethlehem means "God with us"; Calvary means "God for us"; but Pentecost means "God in us."

Those statements greatly aided my concept of the Holy Spirit's person and work.

The average Christian today is much like the Ephesian believers when the apostle Paul asked them in Acts 19:2, "Did you receive the Holy Spirit when you believed?" They replied that they didn't even know there was a Holy Spirit. Christians simply do not understand the role of the Holy Spirit. Because of this, they have not "harnessed" his power in their personal lives. In John 14–16 Jesus had much to say about the Holy Spirit. He promised to send the Holy Spirit to believers.

In John 14:20 Jesus made special reference to "that day." The Lord had a specific day in mind when he made that statement—the day of Pentecost (Acts 2). Soon afterward the Lord Jesus went to the cross of Calvary where he died for our sins. He was buried in a tomb, and three days later he rose from the dead. Then, before he ascended back to heaven, he gave his disciples a commission, an assignment. The Lord Jesus said to his disciples in Luke 24:46–48 that repentance and remission of sin should be preached in his name among all nations beginning in Jerusalem, and he told them that they were to be witnesses of these things.

I have a feeling that when the disciples realized the Lord had given them the job of telling the story of the good news of salvation to the whole world, they were pumped up. They were ready to get out and get at it.

Then, Jesus said in Luke 24:49, "I am going to send you what my Father has promised; but stay in the city until you have been clothed with power from on high." Jesus has just said to go into all the world. Now, he said, tarry in Jerusalem until you are given power from on high. The word *tarry* actually means to sit down. Jesus said, in effect, "I'm sending you out to the whole world, but before you go, sit down in Jerusalem and wait there until you are endued with power from on high." The Lord was indicating to them they must have a specific experience which would equip them for their assignment of carrying the gospel to the end of the age. When was this to happen? "At that day"—a specific day. The Lord Jesus was referring to the day of Pentecost. This definite day is recorded for us in the second chapter of Acts.

Acts 2:1 tells us of the arrival of this great, difference-making day. "When the day of Pentecost came, they were all together in one place." What an amazing, astounding day. No ordinary, average day—but one of the greatest days in the history of the world. This day completely changed the Christian enterprise. If the day had not occurred, then the gospel of the Lord Jesus Christ would not have gone forth with such power and with such great effectiveness.

According to the Old Testament, the day of Pentecost had been going on for a long time. For over 1,500 years, there was an annual celebration of the day of Pentecost. In the Old Testament, God gave the children of Israel a series of festival or feast days, religious holidays that had particular meanings. There were about seven of these special days. Each day had some unique detail to add to the depiction of the coming of the Lord and his salvation work.

For instance, on the day of the Feast of Firstfruits, the Lord Jesus was raised from the dead. The feast celebrated the outpouring of God's blessings upon the harvest. But it also anticipated the resurrection of Jesus. The day was symbolic in these two ways. He became the firstfruits of those who were dead as a foreshadowing of what he was going to do in raising born-again believers. After his resurrection, the Lord Jesus did not go back to heaven immediately. Jesus remained on the earth for a period of forty days. Then he ascended back to heaven. In Acts 1 we are told that the disciples tarried just as Jesus said to do. They prayed and waited in the upper room for a period of ten days. Then Acts 2:1 says, "When the day of Pentecost came."

From the resurrection of Jesus to the day of Pentecost there were fifty days. This is exactly what the word *Pentecost* means. It is important to understand that the day of Pentecost would have come regardless of what the disciples did. Don't get the idea that the ten days of praying by the disciples in the upper room caused the day of Pentecost. The day was divinely appointed by God. On day fifty, Pentecost came. But because the disciples prayed and waited in obedience to the Lord, they knew what God was going to do on the day of Pentecost. For ten days they waited, prayed themselves into spiritual cleanness and spiritual unity, and readied themselves for God and his will on that day.

The day of Pentecost was obviously an earth-shaking day. It was a day that makes all the difference in the world to us. In the Old Testament, God predicted there would be a special day when he would pour out his spirit on all flesh (Joel 2:28). The day came.

Acts 2 tells us about this unique day. The people in the city of Jerusalem were startled and stunned by what took place. In Acts 2:12, they asked, "What does this mean?" Simon Peter answered the question in verse 16 when he said, "This is what was spoken by the prophet Joel." Then he quoted from Joel 2, where God had promised that he would pour out his spirit on all flesh. So according to the Bible, the day of Pentecost was to be a special day—a day when God would pour out the Holy Spirit upon his people.

What a difference this one day made! These disciples were transformed on the day of Pentecost. Have you ever been fearful about the events you face? The disciples began the day of Pentecost weak, fearful, and ineffective. I remember vividly how inadequate I felt as I stood to preach for the first time. I truly was as "a lamb led to the slaughter!" Standing before the altar on my wedding day was no "piece of cake" either. The disciples walked away from the day of Pentecost filled with the Holy Spirit of God, anointed to carry the gospel of the Lord Jesus and equipped to shake up the Roman Empire.

The disciples! The Roman Empire! Paul! All of that happened almost two thousand years ago! You may feel it doesn't relate to you! What difference does that make to Christians today? The day of Pentecost makes a tremendous difference because it tells us about several important truths.

The Reality of the Holy Spirit's Presence

On Pentecost day, the Holy Spirit's presence came in a real and personal way. This presence was new. I read about Ronald Reagan. I saw him on the nightly news. But the night I talked with him for two hours at a White House dinner, he became real and personal to me.

Jesus said in John 14:17, "You know him, for he lives with you and will be in you." When was that change going to occur? When would these disciples move from the experience of having the Holy Spirit *with* them to an experience of having the Holy Spirit *in* them? Jesus told them in verse 20, "at that day." This means that since the day of Pentecost, the church of the Lord Jesus Christ collectively and Christians individually have been empowered by the Holy Spirit's presence. The Holy Spirit is now a permanent resident in our lives.

He is now present—in your church, in your life. Sometimes at church we sing this chorus: "He is here, hallelujah. He is here, amen." It's more than a memorable melody. It's really true!

As you begin your day, do you acknowledge his presence? In prayer, do you invite him to direct every activity and decision of your day? At church, do you welcome him into your worship? "Holy Spirit, thou art welcome in this place" is another appropriate chorus.

Think about the Spirit's presence in the church. Can we hear him or see him or touch him? No, but we can feel him. First Peter 2:5 says the church is a spiritual house. Ephesians 2:22 teaches we are the temple of God, the habitation of God through the Spirit. First Corinthians 3:16 adds, "Don't you know that you yourselves are God's temple and that God's Spirit lives in you?" The Holy Spirit is present in the services and in the fellowship of your church.

Do you like birthdays? I don't! Well, the day of Pentecost records the birthday of the church. As Acts 1:5 indicates, the believers were baptized by (not with) the Spirit. The body (the church) came into existence from a historical perspective. In a sense, the Lord Jesus Christ had two bodies. He had a physical body, but he also has a spiritual body. Luke 2 gives the account of the birth of the Lord's physical, material body. In Acts 2 we have the record of the birthday of the spiritual, mystical body of the Lord Jesus—the church.

Historically, Pentecost will never be repeated. But what a difference a day makes! Before Pentecost day the church was an empty shell. The disciples were powerless and fearless, behind closed doors. After Pentecost day, after the Holy Spirit came in power, the church came alive.

Let's get a little closer to this truth. Pentecost means that the Holy Spirit dwells in Christians individually. Jesus said in John 14:17, the Spirit "lives with you." This means if you have received Jesus as your personal Savior, the Holy Spirit has come to live in you. First Corinthians 6:19 says, "Do you not know that your body is a temple of the Holy Spirit, who is in you?" God's Holy Spirit lives in you. You, individually, are the temple of the Holy Spirit of God.

So, how many Pentecosts can you have? Historically, there can be only one. There was only one occasion when the Holy Spirit of God baptized believers into the body, and the body of Christ, the church, came into existence. The day of Pentecost can never be repeated, just like the miracle at Bethlehem can never be repeated. But, in a real and personal way, every time a soul is saved, every time an individual Christian receives Jesus Christ as his or her Savior, he or she is baptized by the Spirit into the body of Christ.

Baptism is more than just being baptized in water. First Corinthians 12:13 says, "For we were all baptized by one Spirit into one body—whether Jews or Greeks, slave or free." This means that so far as your salvation is concerned, the moment you accepted Jesus, the Holy Spirit baptized you, identified you, made you a part of the body of the Lord Jesus Christ. Baptism by the Spirit into the body of Christ is a divine work. From our viewpoint, it is also a personal experience.

Since you are a Christian, God's Holy Spirit *resides* in your heart, but does the Holy Spirit *preside* in your heart? The Holy Spirit of God is *present* in your heart, but is he *president* in your heart? You and I have the presence of the Holy Spirit dwelling in us. What a difference!

God intended for people to be inhabited. God never meant for us to be a vacuum. Think of a black hole in outer space. Without God in your life, there is an emptiness, a black hole. That's why people who do not know the Lord try all kinds of things to bring happiness and contentment and peace into their lives. "It's like I have a hole in my heart," some may say. Simply put, you do have a hole in your heart. It is a triangle-shaped hole, and a round world cannot fill a triangle-shaped heart. Only the triune God can. It's a perfect fit! Only Jesus, in the person of the Holy Spirit, can fill that emptiness in the human heart.

Every human heart is filled with some kind of spirit. You may be filled either with the Holy Spirit or an unholy spirit. In Ephesians 2:2 the Bible talks about "the spirit who is now at work in those who are disobedient." That's an unholy spirit. But with Jesus in your heart, God the Holy Spirit comes in and his presence becomes a reality in your life.

This is an exciting reality because the Holy Spirit brings tremendous potential into any life. Jesus described it as a river of living water flowing out of one's innermost being (John 7:38). What potential! Power beyond our own to live for Jesus, to overcome temptation, to be a blessing to others, and to be a witness for Jesus.

Let me illustrate the truth in this way. Suppose that a crew clears the lot down the street where you live. Soon men are digging a foundation. Then other men pour the foundation. The frames goes up. Windows are set in place and a roof is added. Sheet rock, paint, and carpet are installed. There it sits. It's pretty, but there's something missing; it's not complete. One day a moving van rolls up. Soon a car drives up. Children jump out of the car and begin running around in the yard. The furniture is unloaded. A family moves in. An empty house suddenly comes alive. Why? This is similar to what happens in your life when Jesus comes in. Before Christ, life is empty and hollow. But when the Holy Spirit comes in, your heart comes to life. That's the difference a day makes!

The Availability of the Holy Spirit's Power

One cannot read about what happened on the day of Pentecost without realizing that a new kind of power became available. Jesus promised this power to the disciples. He promised they would be "clothed with power from on high" (Luke 24:49). In Acts 1:8 he said, "But you will receive power when the Holy Spirit comes on you." If there was anything those disciples needed, it was power! They came to Pentecost powerless; they walked away filled with power.

After Jesus Christ was crucified, they went into a room and slammed the doors shut. They were frightened by the possibility they might be the next ones to die on a cross. They had no peace, no contentment, no power. But Jesus had promised them they would be filled with power from on high. What a difference a day makes. The power came on the day of Pentecost.

Several symbols of this power were visible on the day of Pentecost. Acts 2:2 says, "Suddenly a sound like the blowing of a violent wind came from heaven and filled the whole house where they were sitting." Do not understand this to mean it was the wind. It was not the wind, but a sound *as of* a mighty wind. The language is symbolic. The wind can be heard. It makes a sound. The wind is a beautiful symbol of the power of the Holy Spirit.

What do you know about the wind? Well, the wind is invisible; we can't see it. Jesus said that to be born of the spirit is like the wind blowing (John 3:8). We can't tell where it comes from; you can't tell where it's going. Meteorologists who try to predict the wind have a hard job. They try to forecast the unpredictable movements of the wind. For all their accessibility to sophisticated technology, they still often miss the changing currents of the wind. (Did you hear about the weatherman who left town for health reasons? The weather didn't agree with him!)

The Holy Spirit of God is like the wind. The movement of the Holy Spirit can't be predicted. The Holy Spirit is sovereign. He will move when and where he chooses. His power is irresistible, just like the wind's power. "The Spirit blows wherever it pleases" (John 3:8). When the wind of heaven begins to blow, things are moved. What our churches and cities need is a fresh flow of the wind of God blowing with freshness and saving power. Like the wind, the Holy Spirit is influential. Things are changed when God's spirit blows. Without the Holy Spirit, we are like Ezekiel's valley of dry, dead bones (Ezek. 37:9–11). Ah, but when the wind of God blows, death becomes life; disorder becomes order.

There is a second symbol of the power of the Holy Spirit in Acts 2:3: "They saw what seemed to be tongues of fire that separated and came to rest on each of them." This verse doesn't say it was fire, it *seemed to be* fire. Again, the language is symbolic. Fire is a symbol we can see just like the wind is something we can hear. Fire is another beautiful symbol for God. Moses discovered, at the burning bush, that God was in the bush. God said, "I am who I am" (Exod. 3:14). When Elijah prayed on Mt. Carmel, the fire of God fell (1 Kings 18:38–39).

Fire is a beautiful symbol of the Spirit of God. What do we know about fire? Fire cleanses. It has a purifying effect. Put gold in the fire and it purges the dross from the gold. The Holy Spirit of God does this when he takes over in a church. A cleansing effect occurs. Sin can't exist when the fire of the Spirit of God is burning. For example, in the early church, the fire of the Holy Spirit was so real and consuming that if a person lied in the church, he or she was struck dead. This happened to Ananias and Sapphira (Acts 5). If the Spirit of

God killed all the liars in the church today, there wouldn't be enough ushers to haul them out and bury them!

Which characterizes your Christian experience—ice or fire? Fire brings warmth. Ice brings coldness. Which one is characteristic of your relationship to God and your openness to the power of God? I heard about a Christian who got all worked up in a worship service and prayed, "O Lord, if there's a spark of fire among us, water that spark." Many want to water the spark. Instead, we ought to stir up the fire. Let's ask the Holy Spirit to set us on fire for Jesus. We ought to be open to the fire of the Spirit of God as he moves in our midst— not wild fire, but Spirit fire, cleansing and consuming.

These symbols of power have spectacular aspects, but they also have sub-stance. The wind and the fire are just the symbols of the power. What they signify is what really matters.

The sensational aspects of life surround us today—as exemplified in tabloid journalism and "tell all" television shows. But even when Jesus was born, man-kind dealt with the sensational. Remember the star that guided the wise men? Angels appeared to the shepherds. Stars and angels weren't the significant things. The central fact was the birth of a Savior. Even so, on the day of Pen-tecost there were some sensational aspects—the wind and the fire—but the central significance was the coming of the Holy Spirit in power upon the early believers.

What was the purpose of this power? The central purpose for the power of the Holy Spirit is revealed in the second chapter of Acts. The purpose was to make power available so believers would tell other people about Jesus. The dis-ciples spoke other tongues and languages, so that people from many national-ities heard the gospel, and three thousand people were saved. What a difference a day makes.

These disciples couldn't convince anybody about Jesus before Pentecost. They couldn't get anybody to believe in the Resurrection. They couldn't even get their fellow disciple, Thomas, to believe that Jesus had risen. When the Lord Jesus appeared to them after his resurrection, Thomas was not present. He was unmoved by their testimonies. Ten other disciples did their best, but they couldn't convince one man of the reality of the resurrection. Now, on the day of Pentecost, three thousand were convinced and were saved on a single day! What a difference a day makes when the power of the Holy Spirit is in your witnessing!

That's what God's Holy Spirit is for—to give you power to witness. Could those early believers ever witness! These disciples were transformed into bold witnesses. They witnessed with unbelievable boldness. The Holy Spirit gives us power to speak a good word for Jesus.

Let's follow these Spirit-empowered disciples. They witnessed with courage. In Acts 4 they were warned not to speak the name of Jesus or to witness in the name of Jesus. So, they had a prayer meeting and they prayed to overcome these threats. "Now, Lord, consider their threats and enable your servants to speak your word with great boldness" (Acts 4:29). The Bible says the place where they prayed was shaken and that they were all filled with the Holy Spirit. They spoke the word of God with boldness (Acts 4:31). That's exactly what God will do for us. He'll help us become courageous witnesses for the Lord.

As you go about your work today, you ought to pray for the power of the Holy Spirit and say, "Holy Spirit, give me boldness, give me courage to speak a word for Jesus." Often, we allow ourselves to be intimidated into silence. We let people of power or prominence frighten us and stifle our witness. Our doctor needs Christ. We let his professional status silence us. The wealthy city leader intimidates us and closes our lips. The conscious presence of the Holy Spirit will give us courage to witness faithfully.

The disciples were also given unusual wisdom as they witnessed. Acts 6:10 tells us about Stephen's witness: his opponents were not able to resist the wisdom and the Holy Spirit in his speaking. The same wisdom is available to us and will often amaze us as we tell others about the Lord. Jesus promised, "I will give you words and wisdom that none of your adversaries will be able to resist or contradict" (Luke 21:15).

I've had this happen to me. I've been in witnessing situations when people asked difficult questions and I surprised myself at the statements I made. I remember well the night a young agnostic asked about some of the "contradictions" in the Bible. My answers could have only come from the Holy Spirit. It is exciting what God will do if you have the power of the Holy Spirit in your witness. Surrender yourself to the indwelling Holy Spirit and say, "O Spirit of God, speak through me." He'll say things through you that will surprise you.

There is also spiritual power available for the preaching of God's word in worship services. Simon Peter preached before thousands of Jerusalem citizens and people from many distant lands. *Who?* Simon Peter, standing up in front of that crowd preaching? *The* Simon Peter who was by the fire the night Jesus was arrested? Yes. You talk about fear! Do you remember what happened? One little servant girl totally intimidated the rugged fisherman. Three times he denied he even knew the Lord Jesus Christ.

But after Pentecost, Peter looked these people right in the eye and declared, "You crucified the Lord Jesus." They were pierced in their hearts, and three thousand of them were saved! Preach before thousands without fear? What a difference a day makes!

Why such a difference? Why such a service? There is only one explanation—the power of the Holy Spirit. That's what we need in our church services. Every time the pastor stands to preach, prayer for the power of the Holy Spirit to convict the hearts of individuals with his words should be made. It doesn't mean he will be preaching louder. A loud voice doesn't translate into being filled with the Holy Spirit!

A preacher wrote on the margin of his notes, "Weak point, yell loud." Good preaching is not noise. If you think it's sound level, you've missed the whole point. I'm talking about power that takes the "spoken" word of God and brings it with conviction to the hearts of lost people so they are convicted and brought to understand their need for the Lord Jesus Christ. We have too much "painted fire" in today's church services.

The late revivalist Vance Havner used to say that some churches are wired to produce their own fireworks. Too many are running on their own batteries. They have so much imitation and manipulation that it reminds me of Cheese Whiz—the processed cheese spread that tastes so good on crackers or bread! It's not really cheese, but it looks like cheese. Look at the ingredients the next time you're at the store and you'll see that it's really fake cheese. Attempts can be made to imitate a sincere church service, but an imitation is just that—it's Cheese Whiz church.

Vance Havner told of Leonardo da Vinci, who attempted to reproduce Pentecost. He got a group of actors and costumed them like the disciples. He had wind blowing and fire falling from the roof. Things went haywire. The drapes caught on fire. Several of the actors were burned. The stage set ignited and nearly burned the building down. There is too much whipping up our own wind and producing our own fire. But Pentecostal power can work in your life today if you will yield your life to the wind and fire of the Spirit. There's a meaningful old hymn we used to sing:

> Brethren, we have met to worship
> And adore the Lord our God.
> Will you pray with all your power
> While we try to preach the Word.
> All is vain unless the Spirit
> Of the Holy One comes down.
> Brethren, pray, and holy manna
> Will be showered all around.[1]

Do you pray for the services of your church? Or do you put your mind in neutral and idle through the service—like the man whose mind wandered in church one Sunday morning? The pastor said, "Is there anyone here who wants to go to hell?" No one stood. The pastor, in a louder voice, repeated, "Is there anyone?" The man heard the second statement. Standing, he declared, "Well, preacher, it looks like you and I are the only ones voting for it!"

We ought to be praying, "Lord, take the word. Lord, take the music. Spirit of God, set it on fire." The choir can't sing in a way that helps anyone if they are not anointed with the power of the Holy Spirit of God. There's nothing worse than a singer who is singing in the flesh. The only thing worse is a preacher preaching in the flesh. We need the power of the Holy Spirit. What a difference a day makes!

The Continuity of the Holy Spirit's Permanence

Jesus promised in John 14:16, "I will ask the Father, and he will give you another Counselor to be with you forever." How long? Forever. The day of Pentecost had been repeated many times. It had come and gone—once a year, every year. Then, it was "fully come" (Acts 2:1 KJV). The Holy Spirit had come to stay. That's the difference Pentecost made.

Before Pentecost, the Holy Spirit came upon special people at special times for special purposes. But the Spirit of God could be withdrawn. He was withdrawn from Saul (see 1 Sam. 16:14). The Spirit was withdrawn from Samson (Judg. 16:20–21). That's why David begged God when he had sinned, "Do not cast me from your presence or take your Holy Spirit from me" (Ps. 51:11). But what a difference a day makes. On the day of Pentecost, the Spirit of God came to dwell in his church and in Christians, and Jesus said, "He'll be with

43

you forever." His presence is now permanent instead of temporary—eternal instead of external. He is available for all, not just the few.

As you read through the rest of Acts, you will see the continuity of the Spirit's permanence. In the next twenty-six chapters, the Spirit of God is mentioned in sixteen of them. The disciples were filled with the Holy Spirit on several occasions (4:8, 31, etc.). People weren't just filled one time. They were filled many times. The Holy Spirit of God gave wisdom (Acts 6:10). The Holy Spirit called people into service (13:2, 24). The Holy Spirit encouraged people. They experienced the encouragement of the Holy Spirit (Acts 9:31). The Holy Spirit guided people (Acts 11:12). In Acts 16 the Holy Spirit said to Paul, "Paul, you can't go that way. Go this way." The Holy Spirit will guide you in your life. He's right there. He'll be with you forever. If you will ask him, he will guide you and lead you in your decisions.

Not only will the Holy Spirit guide you in your own life; he will also lead you to lost people. Acts 8 tells of Philip in a great revival meeting in Samaria. The Spirit of God said, "Go to a desert." He went to the desert, not knowing why. A man riding along in a chariot came by and the Spirit said to Philip, "Join yourself to that chariot." Philip led the man to Christ. He will lead you to lost people. When you get up in the morning, do you pray and ask the Holy Spirit to lead you to lost people? He's here. He's in your heart. He's given you the power. He is with you permanently. He'll never leave you.

If the Holy Spirit of God is not leading or blessing and is not at work, why not? Although the Holy Spirit dwells in us permanently and will never leave us, it is possible for us to grieve, to quench, or to ignore the Holy Spirit. Be very careful. Some sin—some secret area of your life—may stifle the Spirit's presence and power.

Historically, the day of Pentecost happened only one time. There will be no repeat performance. But a church can have a Pentecostal blessing. Our daily prayer should be, "O God, let the fire fall and let the wind blow over our wonderful congregation." A personal Pentecost can be yours.

Now, let's talk about how we can have the power of the Holy Spirit and have the Holy Spirit move in our lives. It's the same way you became a Christian. How did you do that? By simple faith. The Bible says, "Everyone who calls on the name of the Lord will be saved" (Acts 2:21). Simple faith. By simple faith we claim the presence, power, and permanence of the Holy Spirit.

The transaction is similar to getting married. As you stand at the altar on your wedding day, the preacher says, "Who gives this woman to be married to this man?" An emotional father says, "I do." Then the preacher looks at you and says, "James, do you take this woman to be your lawful wedded wife?" "I do." By that simple act your life is never again the same. What a difference a day makes! You are into a brand new relationship. Your life is changed. But the wedding day is just the beginning. Marriage is a lifelong experience of understanding this new relationship with another personality.

To experience the permanence, presence, and power of the Holy Spirit means a lifelong love relationship with a new person—the Holy Spirit—who has changed your life forever. What a difference a day makes!

This Can Be the First Day of Your Journey

1. Will you yield your life to the control of the Holy Spirit?

2. Will you ask him to work his changes in your life?

3. Will you begin to look for opportunities to allow the Holy Spirit to touch others through you?

4. Will you live out another chapter of the book of Acts?

If you will, what a difference *this day* will make in your life!

CHAPTER 4

SPIRIT BORN

Physicals are no fun! Bill was certainly not looking forward to his annual exam. But it helped a little that Dr. Carter was a personal friend. Dr. Carter had often given him words of encouragement when minor problems had become major in Bill's mind. But on this occasion, Bill's doctor friend was not his comforter. He was his convincer. After the examinations were all done and the test results were back, Bill learned that he had cancer. It was serious but operable. Surgery was scheduled immediately. Bill readily complied. After successful surgery, Bill thanked Dr. Carter for not only being a friend who comforted him in his fears, but also a competent physician who convinced him of serious danger.

The Holy Spirit not only has a relationship to a Christian as the Comforter. he also confronts the world of all mankind as the convicter. In this role, the Holy Spirit plays a crucial part in bringing a person to know God in what the Bible presents as being Spirit-born.

You might think that the Holy Spirit of God is present only in the lives of believers. But the Holy Spirit is present and active in our world in general. The Holy Spirit is *in* believers; therefore, he is also present wherever believers go.

This ever-present Spirit is busy and active. For example, the Holy Spirit restrains evil. Isaiah 59:19 says, "From the west, men will fear the name of the

LORD, and from the rising of the sun, they will revere his glory. For he will come like a pent-up flood that the breath of the LORD drives along." This means that the Holy Spirit restrains evil in the world. You're probably thinking, *If that is true, what is the Holy Spirit doing, because I see evil everywhere every day?*

The Bible predicts there will be a time when the restraining work of the Holy Spirit will be withdrawn from the world. In 2 Thessalonians 2:6–8 Paul made a fascinating prediction about this. In verse 7 he said, "For the secret power of lawlessness is already at work; but the one who now holds it back will continue to do so till he is taken out of the way." The Bible predicts that just as the Holy Spirit of God was injected into human history in a special way on the day of Pentecost, there will come a time in the future when God's Holy Spirit—so far as his current activity is concerned—will be drawn out of the world like drawing blood from a human body.

So, you think there is evil in the world right now? You ain't seen nothing yet! Wait until the Restrainer, the Holy Spirit, is taken out of the way. Right now, the Holy Spirit is holding back the worst effects of the evil that started with Adam and Eve. His restraining work keeps the world from plunging into total depravity and ruin.

In John 16:7–11, the Lord Jesus introduced the work of the Holy Spirit in relation to an individual. In this regard, the Holy Spirit functions much like Dr. Carter did with Bill: He diagnoses the cancer and prescribes the radical surgery. He is called the Comforter, the Friend, the One who has been called alongside. But, in contrast, to a sinful world, the Holy Spirit is the Convicter; the Friend who tells us the truth about our condition. The Lord Jesus said, "When he comes, he will convict the world" (John 16:8).

This isn't an ideal world. In fact, it is in serious need of spiritual surgery. Wouldn't it be tragic to know a treatment for a deadly disease, yet not use it as a cure? In the same way, being Spirit-born cures mankind of our sin disease. The Holy Spirit has the cure. Let's examine the remedy.

Conviction

The Bible makes it very clear that only the Holy Spirit can convict us that we are sinners. Think of a trial in a courtroom. The Spirit of God is much like heaven's prosecuting attorney. He brings an unsaved person face-to-face with his need for Jesus. No person will ever receive Jesus as Savior unless he or she has first been convicted of sin by the Holy Spirit. No other power, no other person in the universe can do this. I can't convict anybody of their need for Jesus. There is no way any person can cause any other individual to be convicted and convinced that he or she is a sinner in need of a Savior. The first work of God in the human heart is to make the need for salvation evident.

Jesus specifically indicated that the Holy Spirit is the agent of conviction. Conviction is his primary job. At times people gather in a worship service and the message is preached by the pastor. An invitation is given and no one or perhaps a few people respond. At other times, the response is different. The music, preaching, and the praying might seem identical. But when the invitation is given, many come forward. What made the difference? The Holy Spirit did. He has worked with convicting power in the service in a special way. It is not our human logic, eloquence, or psychology that brings people to Jesus. People come because of the convicting work of the Holy Spirit.

Why are more people not saved? Most don't feel any need to be saved. A man has cancer, but he does nothing about it. He schedules no visit to the doctor's office. Why? He has cancer, but he is not aware of it. Those without Christ have spiritual cancer, but they don't know it. A person traveling late at night in a fog crashes over an embankment to his death. Why doesn't he hit the brakes before he crashes? He is not aware of the danger. Without Christ, people are in a spiritual fog, blind to the dangers around them.

When Jesus was on the earth, he made people aware of their sin. Early in his ministry he encountered Simon Peter. As you recall, he produced a miraculous catch of fish. As Simon Peter saw the power of the Lord displayed before him, he fell to his knees and said, "Go away from me, Lord; I am a sinful man!" (Luke 5:8). Jesus convicted Simon Peter of his lost, sinful condition.

On another occasion a poor, sinful woman was brought into the presence of the Lord Jesus (John 8). She had been caught in the act of adultery. (Why wasn't the guilty man also brought?) The Lord Jesus stooped down and began to write on the ground. Then he said, "If any one of you is without sin, let him be the first to throw a stone at her" (verse 7). The account says they all walked out "being convicted in their own conscience" (verse 9 KJV).

After the Resurrection, the disciples sought to convince Thomas that Jesus was alive. Thomas was not present when Jesus appeared to them the first time. They failed to convice Thomas. He insisted, "I will not believe" (John 20:25). Ten disciples couldn't convince one. Just a few days later, Peter preached on the day of Pentecost. The people were "cut to the heart" (Acts 2:37), and three thousand were saved. What made the difference? The Convicter had come! On that day, one disciple convinced thousands.

This convicting work is targeted to the unsaved person. The Lord indicated that the Holy Spirit would reprove the world in three ways by bringing three charges against the lost soul. First, he will convict the world of sin. The Holy Spirit makes the human heart aware: "You are a sinner." John 16:9 says, "in regard to sin, because men do not believe in me."

There is not much consciousness of sin in contemporary society. Most people are not aware of the fact that they are sinners. The existence of sin is often denied. Multitudes are unconscious of the reality of sin. However, the tragedy of sin's consequences continue. These results are apparent—in broken homes, scarred lives, and shattered relationships—everywhere we look. Christians are aware that sin is a reality. Sin is to blame for it all! But only the Holy Spirit can convict people and convince them of their sin.

Jesus did not say the Holy Spirit will convict a person of *sins* (plural), but *sin* (singular). He did not refer to sins in general, but to one sin in particular. In verse 9 Jesus told us what that sin is: "Because they believe not on me" (KJV). There is one sin that is the root of the others—failure to believe in the Lord Jesus Christ. Yet, often people like to brag about this. Talk to people about their need of Christ and some say, "I don't believe in that stuff." They are proud of themselves because they don't believe. They think they don't need that "religious stuff."

Think about it for a moment: Jesus Christ left heaven's glory, came down into this world, died on a cruel Roman cross, and suffered like no one ever suffered. All for sinners. Now he is standing before a lost person with tears in his eyes, pleading for his soul, wanting him to let him come into his life. That lost person can just sit there with no feeling, no tear in his or her eyes, no love in his or her heart—and totally reject the Lord Jesus Christ.

This is the greatest sin any person will ever commit—the sin of all sins. *The sin that can never be forgiven is rejecting the Lord Jesus Christ.* If you dismiss Jesus Christ, God has no other way of salvation. As long as the sin of refusing Jesus Christ is in a human heart, God can't deal with any other sins and he can't have fellowship with this person.

How many people think they are wrong? Do you ever get frustrated driving in traffic? I'll bet you always think the other driver is wrong—not you! Well, I'm the same way. Most people don't think there is anything wrong with them and that they are doing pretty well. People are fairly pleased with themselves. The average guy says, "I'm good to my family, I pay my bills on time, I give to worthy causes. I'm a whole lot better than that Bob down the street. And I'm a whole lot better than that hypocrite Harold, who goes to church all the time."

But the reason most people don't know they are wrong—the reason why they feel so good about themselves—is that they are making the wrong comparison. They compare themselves to other people. In comparison to others, they look good. But this comparison is wrong. It's like a man who appears before a king at an official state occasion. He feels confident. He dresses in his J. C. Penney best. When he arrives at the palace, however, he experiences a growing uneasiness. He looks at the other people who are gathered. In comparison to them, he still feels like he is dressed fairly well. Then the king comes out in all of his royal splendor. When the man sees the king's royal robes, he knows he is not as well clothed as he thought. Once he makes this comparison, he realizes how shabbily he is dressed.

Jesus also said that the Holy Spirit "will convict the world of guilt in regard to sin and righteousness . . . because I am going to the Father, where you can see me no longer" (John 16:8, 10). The Lord Jesus is the righteous one. When the Holy Spirit makes the Lord Jesus Christ real to the heart, showing the Lord's perfect righteousness and beauty, it is then, and only then, that a lost person is aware of the fact that Jesus is righteous while he is unrighteous. Jesus is holy; I am unholy. Romans 3:23 says, "For all have sinned and fall short of the glory of God." God's perfect glory is revealed in Jesus. When the Holy Spirit shows us ourselves compared to Jesus, there is no comparison.

The Holy Spirit also convicts the world of judgment. Jesus said in John 16:11, "In regard to judgment, because the prince of this world now stands condemned." The first charge is that we are sinners, while the second charge is that Jesus is righteous. The third charge which the Holy Spirit brings to bear upon a human soul is the accusation that we are on the losing side. Jesus said, "The prince of this world is judged." The battle has already been fought, and the outcome has already been determined. When the Lord Jesus went to the cross, the decisive battle of the ages was waged. God and the devil did battle at Calvary. Jesus won! The devil and his demons lost.

The Spirit will convict the world of judgment because the prince of this world is judged. Adolph Hitler almost brought the world to its knees. It seemed Hitler's diabolical scheme would succeed. He decided to conquer the world. By his mesmerizing words, he actually inflamed the prejudices and pride of a nation. Millions of people were deceived by an insane man. The masses followed him into the terrible, tragic Second World War. But Hitler did not succeed. As the end of the war approached, Hitler retreated like a mole into a bunker, where he committed suicide.

Before he ended it all on April 30, 1945, Hilter sent a wire instructing that Marshal Goring, his second in command, was to be replaced by General Admiral Doenitz. Doenitz wired back these words, "My Fuhrer! My loyalty to you will be unconditional." The fool didn't even know that Hitler was already defeated and dead.[1]

Doenitz had chosen to follow a loser, and he didn't even know it. Choosing evil over the goodness of Christ is similar. Many have chosen the loser. The battle is over. The prince of this world is judged. It's just a matter of time. Thankfully, the Holy Spirit convicts an unsaved person that he is on the wrong side and that he needs to choose the victory side. Get on the winning team!

Well, how does the Holy Spirit do this? How does he convict? Why are there times when conviction seems to be present in a church service and other times when it doesn't? Some worship services are filled with an atmosphere of conviction; others are not. Just how does this work of conviction take place? A study of the word *convict* can help.

Convict means "to convince" or "to reprove." Ephesians 5:11–13 says, "Have nothing to do with the fruitless deeds of darkness, but rather expose them. For it is shameful even to mention what the disobedient do in secret. But everything exposed by the light becomes visible, for it is light that makes everything visible." The word *expose* is the same as *convict*, used by Jesus in John 16. Notice that this exposing or convicting has to do with turning on the light. How does the Holy Spirit convict? He turns on the light.

Jesus used another light illustration in John 3:19–21, "This is the verdict: Light has come into the world, but men loved darkness instead of light because their deeds were evil [same word used in John 16]. Everyone who does evil hates the light, and will not come into the light for fear that his deeds will be exposed. But whoever lives by the truth comes into the light, so that it may be seen plainly that what he has done has been done through God."

The Bible says that "God is light" (1 John 1:5). But humanity does not like the light of God. People hate the light. So man has turned away from God. But God loves this fallen world. He loves all humanity and wants every person to experience life in the light. Therefore, God has deposited the light in several places. He put the light in his Son, the Lord Jesus. Jesus said, "I am the light of the world" (John 8:12). What did mankind do with the Lord Jesus Christ? They put him on a cross. They didn't want the light. They wanted to stay in darkness.

God the Father also deposited light in the Scriptures. The Bible says, "Your word is a lamp to my feet and a light for my path" (Ps. 119:105). It further says, "The unfolding of your words gives light" (Ps. 119:130). But how many people read the Bible? Most people never open the Bible to get light from the Word of God. Most people don't know where their Bibles are. They're kept on shelves gathering dust. Do you know where your Bible is?

For the most part, an unbelieving world has turned its back on God, who is light. It has rejected the light manifested in God's Son, the Lord Jesus. It doesn't seek the light revealed in his Word, the Bible. So, you may ask, how does the Holy Spirit turn on the light? God has deposited the light in another place. His light shines in the saints, the children of God. He says to us, "You are the light of the world" (Matt. 5:14). What is God's way of convicting the world? As believers allow the light of God to shine out of their hearts, unbelievers realize their desperate need for Jesus Christ.

First Corinthians 14:24–25 presents a fascinating concept of a worship service. It depicts a person coming into a public service where the word of God is preached. When a lost person comes into a place where believers are prophesying (that is, sharing the word of God), that unbeliever is "convinced by all." The same Greek word, *elegcho*, is used here. The secrets of his heart are revealed.

For this reason, Christians should be very prayerful when we come into a worship service. We should pray especially for those present who do not know Christ. This is the reason our singing should be Spirit-inspired. The preaching should be delivered in the power of the Holy Spirit. When a lost person comes in, if the light is turned on—if the light is shining—the Holy Spirit uses that light to bring this unbeliever to realize his need for Jesus Christ. Like a searchlight in the night sky, the Holy Spirit uses God's Word to guide people to Christ.

There is more. Return to Ephesians 5. The Holy Spirit must be involved in a Christian's personal witness, his daily testimony for Jesus. Look at verse 8: "For you were once darkness, but now you are light in the Lord. Live as children of light." Verses 11–14 continue, "Have nothing to do with the fruitless deeds of darkness, but rather expose them. For it is shameful even to mention what the disobedient do in secret. But everything exposed by the light becomes visible, for it is light that makes everything visible." Paul is saying that Christians are to let their lights shine. The light is in you as a Christian. As God's light shines though you, you have a part in reproving the world.

The obedient Christian lives a life very different from most people. How do we as Christians bring lost people to conviction? By beating them over the head with a big family Bible? No. A condemnatory, holier-than-thou attitude is not the right approach. To rebuke people for smoking, drinking, or filthy language might make a Christian feel better, but this won't reach the non-Christian. Mankind does what it does because it represents human nature. They are merely expressing their fallen nature through the lives they live. People are rarely convinced by condemnation.

A far more positive method is to turn on the light! Do what Jesus said. Every day as you live your life, let your light shine by the words you say, the things you do, and the attitudes you display. As you let the Holy Spirit live through you, the light shines out and lost people are brought to the point of conviction like ships tossing and turning at sea when they see the light shining from a lighthouse on shore. They may not be saved right then, but the Holy Spirit, God's lighthouse, is doing his work. The lost will be brought to a realization that there is a better, happier way to live.

A second word leads us on in the process toward being Spirit-born.

Regeneration

Salvation is explained by many words. One of them is regeneration. Regeneration is God imparting divine life to the person who receives Jesus as personal Savior. The word is used in Titus 3:5: "He saved us, not because of righteous things we had done, but because of his mercy. He saved us through the washing of rebirth and renewal by the Holy Spirit." Regeneration is the more theological term. The simpler term is "born again." This is the term Jesus used in the greatest sermon ever preached. John 3 tells us of the occasion and the substance of this glorious experience of being born again. Jesus spoke these words to one person—Nicodemus.

Nicodemus came one night to talk with Jesus. After Nicodemus opened the conversation with complimentary words to Jesus, the Lord shocked Nicodemus when he said, "I tell you the truth, no one can see the kingdom of God unless he is born again" (John 3:3). Nicodemus was mystified and raised the question, How? In response Jesus replied, "I tell you the truth, no one can enter the kingdom of God unless he is born of water and the Spirit" (verse 5). He continued by saying, "Flesh gives birth to flesh, but the Spirit gives birth to spirit" (verse 6). Then, in verse 8 he said, "So it is with everyone born of the Spirit."

There it is—Spirit-born. What does Jesus mean by "born of the Spirit"? This term *born of God* is used in other Bible verses. Notice that "born of God" and "born of the Spirit" are both used. This is an incidental proof that the Holy Spirit is God.

Jesus also used the term *born again*. The word *again* could be translated "from above." To be Spirit-born is to experience a heavenly birth. In one sense, the Holy Spirit is the agent of our physical birth. Job 33:4 says, "The Spirit of God has made me; the breath of the Almighty gives me life." This corresponds to the creation of man in Genesis 2:7. As the Spirit of life blows, biological conception occurs. What a humbling thought! When you were conceived in your mother's womb, the Holy Spirit was there. (This is beautifully presented in Psalm 139. The language is astonishingly consistent with what modern science tells us about the conception and development of the human embryo.)

But in an even more special sense, the Holy Spirit is responsible for our being "born again," "born of God," "regenerated."

In Jesus' remarks to Nicodemus, he spoke in terms of necessity. He said, "You *must* be born again." Why did Jesus say that? Well, for one reason, because you and I were born incorrectly the first time! This is what Jesus referred to when he said, "Flesh gives birth to flesh, but the Spirit gives birth to spirit" (verse 6). Our first birth is a flesh birth. By means of that first birth, we received our physical, fleshly, earthly nature. People do the things they do because they were born with this nature.

Psalm 51:5 says, "Surely I was sinful at birth, sinful from the time my mother conceived me." The act of conception is not sin, but the fact that we are born with a sinful nature is described here. Psalm 58:3 explains it further: "Even from birth the wicked go astray; from the womb they are wayward and speak lies."

Little babies are so sweet and precious. They appear so innocent. Before long, the baby begins to utter syllables: "Goo, goo; mama; dada." Then the precious one starts putting sentences together, and comprehensible speech occurs. It won't be long before the sweet, innocent one tells a lie. It's natural. It's a result of the flesh birth. We need to be born the second time because we were born incorrectly the first time.

Jesus discussed Spirit birth in terms of "must." This is the only way to get a brand new life. Second Corinthians 5:17 says, "Therefore, if anyone is in Christ, he is a new creation; the old has gone, the new has come!" God gives a brand new life! It is so new, in fact, that it takes another birth to accomplish it. Second Peter 1:4 describes it as becoming a "partaker of the divine nature" (KJV).

Obviously, what Jesus was talking about is in the realm of mystery. Two times Nicodemus asked, "How?" (John 3:9). It was mysterious to him. He didn't understand it. He was thrilled at the possibility. But "How?" Just because you don't understand something doesn't mean it's not true. There are countless things which are true, but they are beyond our comprehension.

I don't understand television. I have read the technological explanations. I still don't understand it! But I enjoy watching television from time to time. I don't understand electricity. It is a mystery to me. But I am careful to keep my thumb out of wall sockets. I believe in electricity, even if I don't understand it!

I don't understand the mystery of being Spirit-born. This is puzzling to me. Evidently, Nicodemus didn't understand it either. Just because you don't understand the new birth shouldn't cause you to miss out on it.

Jesus compared the new birth to physical birth: "That which is born of the flesh is flesh; and that which is born of the Spirit is spirit" (John 3:6 KJV). Physical birth is a mystery, too. A gynecologist friend of mine tried to explain how a baby is born. He had delivered several thousand babies. He eloquently described the miracle of birth. But when he finished, we were both aware that he was discussing a mystery. It's a birth—a brand new life. That's what salvation is.

When God saved you, when the Spirit of God birthed you into the family of God, he didn't try to change the old you into a new you. He didn't try to improve you or patch you up. "That which is . . . flesh is flesh" (John 3:6). That's all flesh will ever be. The old nature is still the old nature. But when you receive Christ as your Savior, you are Spirit-born. You get a brand new life—a totally new you. You've had a birth. Like your physical birth, it is never repeated. Jesus didn't say, "You must be born again and again and again!" Being Spirit-born is never repeated. And your past is washed away. It no longer exists. There is only a bright future!

An old man got up one morning and read his name in the obituary column. He immediately called the newspaper office. He chewed out the editor for several minutes. Finally, the editor said, "Cheer up, mister! I'll put your name in the birth column in the morning and give you a brand new start!" A new start! That's what being Spirit-born can give you.

Jesus said the new birth is like the breeze blowing. He declared, "The wind bloweth where it listeth, and thou hearest the sound thereof, but canst not tell whence it cometh, and whither it goeth: so is every one that is born of the Spirit" (John 3:8 KJV). The wind is a mystery. In spite of all our knowledge, the movement of the wind is still a mystery to us. We can't see the wind or predict its movements. But we can see its effects! The wind can uproot trees and work an ocean into a frenzy. The Holy Spirit often moves mysteriously, but we can see the changed lives which result from this movement.

Jesus explained how to be Spirit-born to Nicodemus. In John 3:12 he said, "I have spoken to you of earthly things and you do not believe; how then will you believe if I speak of heavenly things?" Then, he proceeded to tell him heavenly things! He talked about the Savior's part—Jesus died on the cross. In verses 13 and 14, he declared, "No one has ever gone into heaven except the one who came from heaven—the Son of Man. Just as Moses lifted up the snake in the desert, so the Son of Man must be lifted up." Then in verse 15 he talked about our part: "that everyone who believes in him may have eternal life." Jesus did the hard part. He gave his life on the cross of Calvary. Our part is simply to receive by faith what he did for us.

In John's Gospel we read, "Children born not of natural descent, nor of human decision or a husband's will, but born of God" (1:13). John tells us how this new birth comes about. "Yet to all who received him, to those who believed in his name, he gave the right to become children of God" (1:12). Now add 1 Peter 1:23, which states, "For you have been born again, not of perishable seed, but of imperishable, through the living and enduring word of God."

Here's the way it happens. The Holy Spirit convicts a person of his lost condition. As the word of God is preached in a service or as a Christian witnesses to a lost person, the Spirit of God convicts the unbeliever of his need for Christ. The word of God, the plan of salvation, is given. The seed of the word goes forth. The Spirit of God takes the word of God and makes it real to the unsaved person. When he repents of his sins and by faith receives the Lord Jesus Christ, he is born of the Spirit! That's what the Holy Spirit does. This is why we sing:

> Blessed assurance, Jesus is mine.
> O, what a foretaste of glory divine.
> Heir of salvation, purchase of God.
> Born of His spirit, washed in His blood.

The work of the Holy Spirit is a work of regeneration. Yet, there is a third word to consider.

Protection

Many spiritual realities take place when a person is Spirit-born: the believer is baptized (1 Cor. 12:13); filled (Rom. 8:9); adopted (Rom. 8:15); anointed (2 Cor. 1:21). In addition, two other spiritual realities are available to the new believer. These show us how the Holy Spirit provides protection for Christians.

The first of these two symbols is the earnest. This is mentioned three times in the Bible (2 Cor. 1:22; 5:5; Eph. 1:14). At our Spirit birth, God gives us an earnest. Ephesians 1:13 says, "And you also were included in Christ when you heard the word of truth, the gospel of your salvation. Having believed, you were marked in him with a seal, the promised Holy Spirit." Then verse 14 says, "Who is a deposit guaranteeing our inheritance until the redemption of those who are God's possession—to the praise of his glory."

A deposit is a down payment promising that full payment will be made. Have you ever shopped for a car? After browsing through a few lots, you find a car you like. You want that car, but you have some other errands to run and you must come back later. The salesman says, "There are several other people who have been looking at this car." You really want the car, so you say, "I'm going to give you $100 as a deposit." This means you are serious enough to put down partial payment to guarantee full payment later. That's what a deposit is—a down payment. A deposit says, "I mean business. I'm not going to back out."

Or, perhaps you've moved to town and you're looking for a house. The real estate agent takes you out and shows you many homes. Your wife finds one she really likes. "That's the one I like. That's our dream home. It would be wonderful to live in that house." The agent says, "You are going to have to make your decision quickly because several people are looking at this house." So you put down some earnest money because you are serious about that house. The earnest money is a promise that the full amount is on the way.

It's kind of like an engagement ring. Mortimer gives Millie an engagement ring. The diamond is his way of saying to her, "I love you. I want you. I'm going to take you to live with me." The Holy Spirit is our earnest. It is God's promise to us: "I love you. I want you. One of these days I'm going to take you to live with me." When you, by faith, receive the Lord Jesus into your heart, you are saying, "I love you, too. I want to live with you forever." We receive Jesus as our Savior. God slips on the ring (the Holy Spirit in our hearts). This is his powerful promise and pledge that he will protect us until he comes again for us.

Look at a second beautiful picture. We are also sealed by the Holy Spirit. The seal is also mentioned three times in the Bible (Eph. 1:13; 4:30; 2 Cor. 1:22). Look at Ephesians 1:13: "And you also were included in Christ when you heard the word of truth, the gospel of your salvation. Having believed, you were marked in him with a seal, the promised Holy Spirit." Note that we are sealed *when*, not after, we believe. We are sealed at the moment of our salvation.

What is a seal? The word *seal* means different things to different groups. Most children tend to think of a funny little animal that bounces a ball on its nose. Women think about something you do with a fruit jar. Men think about something that belongs in an automobile engine. But in the Scriptures, the word *seal* includes the idea of ownership. To put a seal on something means it's yours. In the West, ranchers put a brand on their cattle. Each has his brand, his seal, on the animal, indicating it belongs to that ranch owner. When we are Spirit-born, the Holy Spirit comes into our hearts. The Spirit's presence is God's seal which says, "That one belongs to me. I own that one. He is valuable to me!" A seal, placed on soft material, leaves a copy of itself. What is God's purpose in sealing our hearts with the Holy Spirit? His aim is to make us like Jesus!

A seal also indicates a finished transaction. Seals are used sometimes in important corporate documents. The seal means the deal is done. Salvation is like a legal document. God has drawn up the terms by which he will save a human soul. God signs it. When a person says "yes" to Jesus, the person signs the document. Then God puts his Holy Spirit in that heart. The terms of the agreement are cemented. Heaven is a guaranteed promise. It is just as much ours today by promise as it will be by experience in the future. It means we are just as much in heaven as if we had been there ten thousand years.

How long will this seal last? Ephesians 4:30 tells us we are sealed "for the day of redemption." That points to the beginning of our eternal joy. Revelation 7 tells of the 144,000 who were sealed by God. In Revelation 14:1 they appear again. How many made it from Revelation 7 to Revelation 14? Not 143,990, but all 144,000! Not one is missing. When God seals a person by the Holy Spirit, he says, "This one is eternally mine!"

A man heard a knock on his door one day. He opened his door, and a man said, "Sir, I'm here to tell you that you have received an unbelievable inheritance, a huge sum of money. It will be a while before you receive it all. I have been instructed to present you with a check." He gave the man a check for fifty million dollars! As the man left he said, "I want you to know there's far more than this."

Every blessing you and I receive, every sweet touch of God in our lives, every evidence of the movement of the Holy Spirit in our lives as believers right now is just a drop in the bucket compared to what God has waiting for us in the future. It's all part of what it means to be Spirit-born.

Some Thoughts for the Spirit—Born on the Journey

1. To be born of the flesh produces only what flesh can give you. To be Spirit-born produces what the Holy Spirit can conceive in you.

2. If you are born only once, you will die twice. If you are born twice, you will die only once.

3. To be heaven-bound, you must be heaven-born!

4. Now, do you understand why Christians sing unusual words like these?

> This is my story, this is my song,
> Born of His Spirit, washed in His blood.

CHAPTER 5

TURN OVER THE CONTROLS!

Homer Lindsay tells the gripping story of an air tragedy which occurred in his seminary days in Fort Worth, Texas. One morning at breakfast he was reading the *Fort Worth Star Telegram*. An article told of a tragic plane crash. A young student pilot was making one of his final training flights. Evidently he froze at the controls. Fear does cause people to freeze up at times. His instructor was heard yelling, "Turn over the controls! Turn over the controls!" The student pilot did not. Both were killed in the crash.

Tragedy can occur when those who are in training don't turn over the controls to the wiser instructor. In the Christian life, we must learn to turn over the controls. I learned the importance of this early in my Christian service.

I was called to preach at the age of sixteen, and I served my first church as pastor at eighteen. For the earlier years of my ministry I was known as the "boy preacher." I really didn't like that designation in those early years. As I have grown older, it certainly sounds more appealing to me! During those years as a "boy preacher," I learned so much about the Holy Spirit in the life of a Christian. One of the most important lessons I learned was to allow the Holy Spirit to work in my life through preaching and Christian service.

"How's our boy preacher?" my church members would often say. "Fine," I would say with my lips, but my heart didn't like it! Now that I'm older, I rather like the term! During these years as a "boy preacher," I learned a lot about the Spirit's work. I learned what it means to "turn over the controls."

I became a believer at the age of nine. I was "Spirit-born." At that time my Friend, the Holy Spirit, came into my life. Although I was not always what the Lord wanted me to be, I was aware of the Spirit's presence in my life. I look back on those years now and I am astounded and grateful for the patience those people had with me.

My first pastorate lasted sixteen months. Those youth sermons finished up quickly! I moved to another church. I was still in my teens. As I began to minister and to preach in my second church, I became aware that my ministry was not as effective as I wanted it to be. I was faithful to proclaim God's word as best I could. There just didn't seem to be much power. You might say I had the words to the song, but I didn't have the music.

Gratefully, the Lord brought wonderful Christians and pastors into my life in those early years. They helped me in many ways. Irving Phillips is one example. A college educated man, he served rural churches all his ministry. When he preached, there was an obvious power in his messages. It was not in the delivery, which was rapid-fire and high-geared like a machine gun, but there was something else—a sense of power and blessing.

I sought out Brother Irving and explained my desire for power and effectiveness in preaching. This humble man of God explained to me the filling of the Holy Spirit. He showed me that only when we allow the Holy Spirit to preach through us can there be spiritual blessing produced. As a result of his simple teaching and encouragement, I asked the Holy Spirit to fill me as I preached, as I witnessed, and as I sought to live for Jesus among my people.

I didn't hear any voices. I was not knocked over. No bells went off inside. But there was a conscious, refreshing new "touch of the Lord" upon my ministry. This was the first time I was consciously filled with the Spirit. What does that mean? Let's talk about what it means to be filled with the Holy Spirit.

A great deal of terminology is used today in Christian circles when we talk about the power of the Holy Spirit in a life. Some speak in terms of being "slain" in the Spirit. Others speak of a "baptism" of the Spirit. Still others refer to a "filling" of the Spirit. How do we work through all this confusion on this subject? I believe we must look carefully to what the Bible has to say about it. What the Bible teaches must be our final authority. One must use precise terminology when dealing with controversy and disagreement among Christians. For this reason, let's take a look at the promise of Jesus in Acts 1:4–5.

Jesus told the first disciples that they would "be baptized with the Holy Spirit not many days from now" (NKJV). Obviously, the Lord was referring to the day of Pentecost. In Acts 2, as we have seen in a previous chapter, the day of Pentecost came. On that day, "they were filled with the Holy Spirit." Jesus said they would be "baptized with the Holy Spirit"; and on Pentecost they were all "filled with the Holy Spirit." No mention is made in Acts 2 of Spirit baptism. This certainly gives the impression that the baptism and the filling are the same.

A careful examination of Scripture, however, makes it clear that the baptism and the filling of the Spirit are not the same. Perhaps you remember that we have previously stated that certain experiences take place at the moment of salvation. At salvation, every believer is filled (1 Cor. 3:16; Rom. 8:11), baptized (1 Cor. 12:13), and sealed (Eph. 4:30) by the Holy Spirit. If you are a saved person, these spiritual realities are true for you. Scripture does not state that you are filled with the Holy Spirit at the moment of salvation. A believer may be, or may not be.

What is the difference between the baptism and the filling of the Holy Spirit? We are never commanded to be baptized; we are commanded to be filled. The baptism happens to every believer (1 Cor. 12:13); not all

Christians are filled, although they should be. The baptism is a once-for-all truth; the filling may be repeated. Baptism is what we call a positional truth. It has to do with our belonging to Christ's body. The filling is an experiential truth. This means I belong to him. While it is one thing to have the Holy Spirit, it is another thing for the Holy Spirit to have me. An often-used phrase probably is helpful for us: There is one baptism; there are many fillings.

We must be very careful not to allow errors of teaching and the extremes of others to cause us to neglect or miss out on the glorious experience of being filled with the Holy Spirit. Whatever we call it, we certainly need it! I do not believe a Christian life can be lived successfully apart from the filling of the Holy Spirit. Nor do I think our witness for Jesus is effective apart from the filling of the Holy Spirit.

There is a passage which sets forth the filling of the Holy Spirit better than any other. I refer to Ephesians 5:18: "Do not get drunk on wine, which leads to debauchery. Instead, be filled with the Spirit."

A careful study of this Scripture indicates several truths about what it means to be filled with the Holy Spirit.

The Filling of the Holy Spirit Is a Real Experience

Some television shows are make-believe, like *Star Trek* or *Andy Griffith*. But others like *Cops* or *Real-TV* depict real life. To be filled with the Holy Spirit is not fiction; it is a real-life experience.

This verse is a command, "Be filled." It's not optional; it is obligatory. A Christian should never attempt to teach a Sunday school class, serve on a committee, sing a song, preach a sermon, or make a visit unless he or she is filled with the Holy Spirit. This is not a suggestion; it is a command.

In the New Testament, we find many people who were filled with the Holy Spirit. For instance, the entire family of John the Baptist knew the filling of the Holy Spirit. In Luke 1:67 we read that John's father, Zacharias, "was filled with the Holy Spirit." In Luke 1:41 John's mother, Elizabeth, "was filled with the Holy Spirit." In Luke 1:15 John himself, we are told, "will be filled with the Holy Spirit, even from birth." What a wonderful Bible family. Father, mother, and son—all filled with the Holy Spirit.

The apostles were filled with the Holy Spirit (Acts 2:4). In Acts 4:8 Simon Peter was filled with the Holy Spirit again. The first deacons were spirit-filled men (Acts 6:3). The apostle Paul knew the experience of being filled with the

Holy Spirit (Acts 9:17–18). If New Testament Christians were filled with the Holy Spirit, we can be, too. If they needed this experience then, we need it now.

Our Lord Jesus was filled with the Holy Spirit. Luke 4:1 says, "Jesus, filled with the Holy Spirit, returned from the Jordan and was led by the Spirit in the desert." Evidently, he received this filling of the Holy Spirit at his baptism. Luke 3:22 says that at his baptism, "and the Holy Spirit descended on him in bodily form like a dove." As Jesus experienced temptation by the devil, he was full of the Spirit. After the temptation was over, we read in Luke 4:14, "Jesus returned to Galilee in the power of the Spirit." Just four verses later Jesus said, "The Spirit of the Lord is on me" (4:18). If the perfect Son of God needed the filling of the Holy Spirit to face temptation, so do we! If he needed the filling of the Holy Spirit to conduct his ministry, so do we!

A study of the lives of great Christians, both past and present, reveals that they were individuals who were filled with the Holy Spirit—people such as Martin Luther, Charles Haddon Spurgeon, D. L. Moody, and more current people such as Billy Graham, Charles Stanley, and Charles Colson. These Christians have been filled with the Holy Spirit.

Now, the question: Have you been filled with the Holy Spirit? This is something the Bible commands of us. Have you obeyed this command?

D. L. Moody was an effective lay preacher. He was never ordained as an "official" preacher. He felt he was doing a good job. He was preaching in crusades and successfully serving as pastor of his congregation in Chicago. Two women in his church told him they were praying he would be filled with the Holy Spirit. He was rather irritated with them. How could they say he needed to be filled with the Holy Spirit? People were coming to Christ. There seemed to be blessing upon his ministry. Yet after Moody's remarkable experience with the Holy Spirit, he indicated he preached the same sermons, but there was a new power and anointing on these messages.

There is another truth which emerges from this verse about the meaning of being filled with the Holy Spirit.

The Filling of the Holy Spirit Is a Remarkable Experience

It should not be remarkable for a Christian to be filled with the Holy Spirit. Apparently, this is to be the normal condition of a Christian. Vance Havner, late beloved itinerant preacher from North Carolina, used to say that the average Christian is so subnormal that when one becomes normal, everybody thinks he is abnormal! But while being filled with the Holy Spirit should be the normal experience of every Christian, the experience of being filled with the Holy Spirit is remarkable. Ephesians 3:19 says, "That you may be filled to the measure of all the fullness of God." What a thought! To think that we human beings can be filled with the fullness of the God of this universe! Awesome!

The nature of the Spirit-filled experience is illustrated powerfully in Ephesians 5:18. Notice that the verse begins with a prohibition: "And be not drunk with wine, wherein is excess" (KJV). The same illustration is used two other times in connection with the Spirit-filled experience (see Luke 1:15; Acts 2:13–15).

Let's look for a moment at the words used in the statement. The word *drunk* means to be intoxicated with wine or soaked with wine. The word *excess* means to be abandoned. A person who is intoxicated has abandoned himself to alcohol's control. This totally changes a person. A man in an Armani suit begins to look like a homeless person. A shy person becomes obnoxious. "God shave the queen!" shouts a person abandoned to wine. A fearful person becomes bold.

I well remember on my high school senior trip to Washington a little guy in our class. He was short, timid, and cautious. Getting drunk on our trip, he suddenly became loud, bold, and obnoxious. Yelling like Tarzan, he jumped up and down on beds. He shouted obscenities to anyone who saw him. He burped and slurped his drinks. To be drunk with wine is to abandon oneself to the control of alcohol.

To be filled with alcohol can make you a fool. I remember seeing an elderly couple get in an argument at a college football game. Each one was drinking alcohol. The drunker they got, the louder and madder they became. Their shouting match stunned everyone around them. Don't let these illustrations frighten you. Don't get the idea that to be filled with the Holy Spirit will make you a fool or a fanatic. To be filled with the Holy Spirit is the most sane, sensible experience a person could ever have.

I believe this is the key to the illustration: It is not that a person filled with alcohol becomes a fool (though he does). The point is that a person filled with alcohol is someone who is controlled and changed. This is the key to the illustration.

Likewise, to be filled with the Holy Spirit is to be controlled by the Holy Spirit. The verb "be filled" is interesting. It is used in several ways. It can mean "to fill a vessel." Or it can mean "to cover a surface." For our purpose here, the idea is to permeate a soul. To be filled with the Holy Spirit is to be completely filled with the Holy Spirit. The idea is one of control. When an individual is absorbed with the Holy Spirit, every area of that person's life is under the control of the Holy Spirit. As a sponge absorbing water is filled with water, so a person who is filled with the Spirit is absorbed. I want to point out that we do not take control of the Holy Spirit. He takes control of us.

What a change this makes in our daily lives. What a different alternative this provides as we face temptation. If we are under the control of the Holy Spirit, we can meet temptation in the power of the Holy Spirit. Send the Holy Spirit to answer the door when you hear Satan knocking! This really helps in daily decisions. We can make intelligent decisions because we have the presence of the Spirit of wisdom himself within us. Life's struggles and battles are hard. Isn't it nice to know we have the mighty power of the Holy Spirit within to strengthen us and give us the victory.

Young Samson faced a ferocious lion. Judges 14:6 says, "The Spirit of the LORD came upon him in power so that he tore the lion apart with his bare hands as he might have torn a young goat." When the lions of life's struggles roar at you, you are not helpless. Power is available!

There is something additional to be noted in terms of the Holy Spirit's control. The verb "be filled" is passive. The subject is being acted upon. Now, the fact that we can be controlled by an outside influence is rather frightening. Scripture says a person can be filled with sin (Rom. 1:29). Also an individual can be filled with envy (Acts 13:45), confusion (Acts 19:29), even Satan (Acts 5:3). But the good news is that one can be controlled by the Holy Spirit.

The idea conveyed by the verb "be filled" also means to be changed by the Holy Spirit. The verses after Ephesians 5:18 are very instructive. After the command to be filled with the Holy Spirit, several key words are used. One is "speaking" (v. 19). The filling of the Holy Spirit in your life can have a healing, stabilizing impact upon your inner being. Picture a man living a life filled with depression and despair. Then picture him with peace and contentment. The Holy Spirit can change the picture. A sound mind, a radiant heart, and a poised spirit are all possible. Note that the speaking here is couched in musical terms. "In psalms and hymns and spiritual songs, singing and making melody in your heart to the Lord" (Eph. 5:19 KJV). This means the filling of the Holy Spirit puts a song in your heart.

Another term is "giving thanks" (v. 20). The filling of the Holy Spirit is amazing medicine. J. B. Phillips paraphrases this statement, "Thank God at all times for everything." Thankfulness remedies many illnesses. As the Holy Spirit enables us to be thankful, worries disappear, complaints diminish, courage increases, and sweet peace enters.

The next key term is "submitting" (v. 21). The idea here is to fit in with others. J. B. Phillips renders it, "Fit in with each other." The filling of the Holy Spirit takes away self-assertion, a "me-first" attitude, and replaces it with humility. It makes us more like Jesus, who humbled himself and served others.

Simply remarkable! What changes the Holy Spirit can bring into a life! These changes affect our inner being, our relationship with God, and our relationships with others. How wonderful to think that we can be controlled and changed by the Holy Spirit.

It is helpful at this point to consider the evidences of being filled with the Spirit. I was fascinated some years ago to notice that those in the New Testament who were filled with the Spirit did not say they were. The only possible exception to this is the statement of our Lord, "The Spirit of the Lord is on me" (Luke 4:18). Why did the New Testament believers fail to say they were filled with the Spirit? Jesus specifically said that the purpose of the Holy Spirit is to call attention to Jesus. In John 15:26 Jesus said, "He shall testify of me" (KJV). John 16:14 says, "He shall glorify me" (KJV). Because of this, we should be very cautious about any movement which makes more of the Holy Spirit than the Lord Jesus.

But why did those filled with the Spirit fail to say they were? The answer seems obvious. They were so caught up with Jesus and telling others about him that they did not think of themselves. Have you noticed that when people were filled with the Spirit, others noted it? For example, consider Stephen in Acts 7. He was filled with the Spirit. Rather than dwelling upon his experience, he pointed his listeners to the Lord Jesus (Acts 7:55–56).

What, then, is the evidence of being filled with the Spirit? Acts 1:8 makes it very clear. Is it speaking in tongues? No. Falling in the floor? No. Barking like a dog? No. Acts 1:8 says, "But ye shall receive power, after that the Holy Ghost [Spirit] is come upon you: and ye shall be witnesses unto me" (KJV). The main purpose of the filling of the Holy Spirit is not to call attention to ourselves, but to have Spirit power to witness to others about Jesus.

Pank was a delightful Christian. He was a member of a church in a city which placed a strong emphasis on speaking in tongues. I always saw Pank at the post office. He would ask me, "Preacher, have you been filled with the Holy Spirit?"

I would reply, "Yes, Pank, I have."

"Did you speak in tongues?" he asked.

"No, Pank, I did not."

Then Pank would say, "You haven't been filled with the Spirit."

This went on for months. Finally, one day after Pank's questions, I asked a few of my own. "Pank, have you led anybody to Jesus this week?"

Pank replied, "No, but Sunday night we prayed until midnight for several to be filled with the Spirit."

"Well, Pank, did you lead anybody to Jesus last month?"

"No," he replied.

"If what you have makes you speak in tongues and what I have helps me tell others about Jesus," I said, "I would rather have what I have than what you have!"

Pank never asked the questions again. I believe that the great evidence of being filled with the Spirit is power to win people to Christ.

The Filling of the Holy Spirit Is a Repeated Experience

The verse says, "be filled." The idea is continuous action. One could translate the command this way: "Be continuously being filled with the Holy Spirit." The indication is that the filling of the Holy Spirit is to be a daily, constant, moment-by-moment experience.

Being filled with the Holy Spirit is not a once-for-all experience. There are many Christians who would like to have one sensational experience which would solve all their problems—a one-dose cure. I do not believe the Bible teaches such an experience. I do believe, however, that the filling of the Holy Spirit may develop from a crisis which leads to a process.

In contrast, some Christians may be filled with the Holy Spirit at the time of salvation. This seems to have been the experience of the apostle Paul. Hours after Paul's phenomenal encounter with Jesus on the road to Damascus, we are told that he was filled with the Holy Spirit (see Acts 9:17). This is the exception.

Many, perhaps most, Christians are not filled with the Holy Spirit at the beginning of their salvation experiences. For most Christians, there is probably an initial time when they are filled with the Holy Spirit. But this is not an experience which is a "cure all." It should be repeated. The language is very clear. We should seek constant fillings of the Holy Spirit. The illustration of being drunk with wine fits here. There is no such thing as permanent intoxication from alcohol. For a person to continue to be under the control of alcohol, he must continue to consume alcohol.

The filling of the Holy Spirit is an experience which may be lost, but it can be restored. Scripture tells us of the encounter between Jesus and Simon Peter. Jesus asked him who people were saying he—Jesus—was. Simon Peter reached a high level of spirituality when he exclaimed, "You are the Christ, the Son of the living God" (Matt. 16:16). In response to this, Jesus declared to Simon Peter, "Blessed art thou" (Matt. 16:17 KJV). Just moments later, as Jesus began to talk about his impending death on the cross, Simon Peter took him aside and rebuked him for such talk.

Then Jesus said to Peter, "Get behind me, Satan!" (Matt. 16:23). One moment Peter was blessed; the next moment he was Satan! The same tragedy may occur to us. At one moment we may be filled with the Spirit. The next moment, we may behave more like the unholy spirit. This is a result of our human condition.

Thus, we should seek to be filled with the Holy Spirit every day of our lives. We need him. I begin my day with a quiet time. I read my Bible. God talks to me. I pray. I talk to God. I ask to be filled with the Holy Spirit each morning. Whatever fullness of God's Spirit I may have known yesterday is not sufficient for today. Just as the children of Israel had to gather manna in the wilderness each morning, I must seek a fresh filling of God's Spirit each day.

There are also times when we need a special filling of the Holy Spirit. I never try to preach unless I have asked for a new supply of the Holy Spirit's power. I do not go on visitation unless I ask the Holy Spirit to fill me and help me say the right thing. As you lead your family, or teach Sunday school, or witness on your job, ask the Holy Spirit to fill you.

As you grow in your Christian life and seek a daily filling of the Holy Spirit, you may discover areas of your life where you have never yielded control to the Holy Spirit. I read about a person who collected old books. Visiting a home one day, he ran across a battered old book. Its cover was frayed, there were cracks along the seams, and pages were loose. His friend gave him the book as a gift. He lamented that some of the pages were missing, but he was grateful for the book. A few days later, the person who gave the collector the book visited him. "Do you remember that old book I gave you?" the man said.

"Yes, I do," said the book collector. "Well, I found some more pages. If I find others, I will bring them to you also."

As we continue in our Spirit journey, enjoying adventures in the Spirit-filled life, we may indeed find "more pages" or areas of our lives which have yet to be yielded to the control of the Holy Spirit. Every day, let us turn these areas over to the infilling of the blessed Holy Spirit.

I heard a story when I was a teenager that has stayed with me through the years. One day, a little fellow came bouncing into a flower shop. He had his fist doubled up and some unsold newspapers under his arm. He walked up to the counter and said to the lady, "I want to buy the biggest bouquet of flowers you have in the store. I've been selling papers and I've already sold thirty-seven cents worth. Today is my mother's birthday, and I want to get her the biggest bouquet of flowers you have in this store with my thirty-seven cents."

This touched the heart of the lady in the flower shop. She got a huge bouquet filled with roses and orchids and carnations. Wrapping it in green paper, she brought it to the counter. The little boy, eyes wide and bulging, asked, "How much is it?" She said, "Thirty-seven cents." "Wow, that's just what I have!" He gave the thirty-seven cents to the lady, took his flowers under his arm, his papers under the other arm, and went bouncing out of the store.

In a moment the flower shop clerk heard the blaring of a horn and the screeching of tires. Rushing out, she saw the little boy under a big truck. He had been hit. The little fellow was taken to the emergency room. A Christian doctor who knew his family attended him. The situation was hopeless. The little boy looked up at his doctor and said, "Doctor, I'm not going to make it, am I?" The doctor said, "No, son, you're not." The little boy said, "I know Jesus as my Savior. When I die, I'm going to heaven. But, doctor, I want you to do something for me. Take the flowers to my mother. Today is her birthday. Tell her it's only thirty-seven cents worth, but it's all I've got. Tell her I love her."

Have you ever told the Holy Spirit that? Have you ever said, "Holy Spirit, I'm only thirty-seven cents worth. It's all I've got. But I love you, and I want you to take control of my life."

To Be Filled

1. Ask God to fill you with the Holy Spirit. Luke 11:13 says, "If ye then, being evil, know how to give good gifts unto your children: how much more shall your heavenly Father give the Holy Spirit to them that ask

him?" (KJV). In the upper room prayer meeting recorded in Acts 1, after ten days of prayer, the Holy Spirit came. God is anxious to give us the filling of the Holy Spirit. Maybe it won't take ten days, unless it takes us that long to get our hearts empty and clean!

2. By faith, claim the filling of the Holy Spirit. John 7:37–39 says, "On the last and greatest day of the Feast, Jesus stood and said in a loud voice, 'If anyone is thirsty, let him come to me and drink. Whoever believes in me, as the Scripture has said, streams of living water will flow from within him.' By this he meant the Spirit, whom those who believed in him were later to receive. Up to that time the Spirit had not been given, since Jesus had not yet been glorified." Note that *receive* and *believe* are used interchangeably. How does a person get drunk with wine? He drinks it!

3. Surrender your life to the Holy Spirit. The command is, "Be filled." Acts 5:32 says, "We are witnesses of these things, and so is the Holy Spirit, whom God has given to those who obey him." With a deliberate act of your will, hand yourself over to the control of the Holy Spirit. Say to your Friend, the Holy Spirit, "Here is my life. Here is all I have. Take control of every part of it!"

CHAPTER 6

WHAT A DIFFERENCE YOU'VE MADE IN MY LIFE

Well, I'm at it again! I'm in my car pushing the scan button on the radio. It hits a country station. Ronnie Milsap is singing one of his best sellers. The words are: "What a difference you've made in my life. What a difference you've made in my life. You're my sunshine day and night. O, what a difference you've made in my life."[1]

I turn off the radio and lift my heart to the Holy Spirit in prayer. "What a difference *you* have made in my life." This is certainly true in my experience. I came to Christ as a boy and I am so grateful for what God the Holy Spirit has done in my life as a Christian. Only the Holy Spirit can bring about the kind of differences we need in our daily lives.

The Holy Spirit's work in the life of a person can be described in a threefold manner. First, there is the work the Holy Spirit does *for* you. We call this salvation. We are born of the Spirit into God's family. By the Holy Spirit, we are baptized into Christ's body. At salvation the Holy Spirit comes to live in us. We have the seal and the anointing of the Holy Spirit. All this and more is involved in the work of salvation that the Holy Spirit does in us.

Then, there is the work the Holy Spirit does *through* us. Let's call this "service." You might teach a Sunday school class, or sing in the choir, or lead a youth group as service to the Lord. This is a result of the work of the Holy Spirit through us. We serve by the power and with the blessing of the Holy Spirit.

The Holy Spirit also does a work *in* us. The Bible describes this as *sanctification*. Holiness is another word with the same meaning. Sanctification! Holiness! I am a Baptist preacher. To mention these two words to Baptists causes most of us to break out in hives! I wonder sometimes if Baptists are interested in being sanctified or holy. It is strong terminology for too many Baptists.

The word *sanctification* is a good Bible word. It is the Greek word *hagiasmos*. It means simply "to set apart." To be sanctified is to be set apart for God. The Bible often calls Christians "saints." This word is built upon the same word used for sanctification. Saints are holy ones—set apart ones.

Let's connect sanctification with the person of the Spirit of God. Jesus referred to our Friend, the Spirit, as the Holy Spirit (John 14:26). Romans 1:4 speaks of the "spirit of holiness." Sanctification is also specifically mentioned as a work of the Holy Spirit. This is seen in 2 Thessalonians 2:13 and 1 Peter 1:2.

Sanctification involves the work of the Holy Spirit as he makes a difference in our lives. In the Old Testament, 1 Samuel 10:6, 9–10 indicates that the presence of the Holy Spirit, coming upon Saul, turned him "into a different person." Verse 9 indicates that this presence of the Holy Spirit "changed Saul's heart." My purpose at this point is not to discuss the puzzling and enigmatic life of Saul, but to indicate that the presence of the Holy Spirit in the life of a person makes a profound difference in his or her life.

One can often see a kind of tension in Bible truth. There is a sense in which Christians are sanctified. This is certainly seen in passages such as 2 Thessalonians 2:13; Hebrews 10:10; 1 Corinthians 1:1–2, 30; 6:11. This is known as *positional* sanctification. But there is another more practical sanctification which we can grow toward each day. Hebrews 12:14 says, "Make every effort to live in peace with all men and to be holy; without holiness no one will see the Lord." In this sense, sanctification might be defined as a progressive growth in righteousness by which believers yield themselves to the control of the Spirit. Like a budding flower, each Christian needs water and sunlight for nourishment. He cleanses us, taking out the weeds of our lives, and he changes us, putting into our lives those characteristics which should be there.

How can the Holy Spirit make a difference in our lives? Misconceptions are abundant. Christians are certainly not perfect. If you should run across someone who claims to have reached perfection—talk to his or her mate! That will settle the issue! The difference the Holy Spirit brings to a Christian's life doesn't put an end to a good time. When the Holy Spirit makes a difference in one's life, that person is set free to really enjoy life. Second Corinthians 3:17 is certainly true: "Where the Spirit of the Lord is, there is freedom."

Several aspects are involved as the Holy Spirit makes a difference in our lives and brings us to sanctification.

The Holy Spirit Cleanses Us

Second Corinthians 7:1 sets before us the cleansing aspect of the Holy Spirit's sanctification. It says, "Since we have these promises, dear friends, let us purify ourselves from everything that contaminates body and spirit, perfecting holiness out of reverence for God." As we have seen, when we receive the Lord Jesus as our Savior, the Holy Spirit comes to live in our lives. Obviously, for the Holy Spirit to make his home in you, some cleaning must occur. But those annoying tendencies and bad habits of the old life are not eliminated.

When Lazarus was raised from the dead, Jesus said, "Take off the grave clothes and let him go" (John 11:44). The grave clothes which bound him from head to foot had to go. In like manner, the "grave clothes" of the old life need to be removed and the "grace clothes" of the new life need to be put on. This takes a while.

One way to put on the "grace clothes" involves changing our attitude toward sin. When I was a teenager, I was going one evening to a school party. I was all dressed up as I walked to school. I had no car or driver's license. A car came near the sidewalk where I was walking and hit a mud hole. A few drops of mud landed on me, but I wasn't worried about it. Remember, though, it was nighttime.

As I got closer to my school, I got closer to the lights of the building. As I came nearer to the light, I realized how much mud was on me. Finally, when I walked into the building, in the full light, I saw that the mud was all over me. This is exactly what happens when the Holy Spirit comes into your life. Things are seen in a light they have never been seen in before. The closer a person gets to Jesus, the more aware he or she is of sin in one's life.

There is another way to illustrate this. A boy has been a bachelor for a number of years. He is messy. (Girls, be patient with these boys. Most of them are bums by nature!) This young man marries a sweet, beautiful, neat, clean young woman. After the marriage, she moves into his apartment. The first day she comes into the apartment, she takes one look and says, "What a mess!"

He is astounded to hear her say that. He thought things looked pretty good. It didn't matter to him there was a month-old pizza in the refrigerator. He didn't care that six months of *Sports Illustrated* were scattered around the floor. The fact that the sheets hadn't been changed in nine months didn't bother him! Everything looked fine to him.

But when she moves in, a cleanup has to take place. She starts cleaning and washing and scrubbing and fixing up. It's painful for the boy. He gets a little uneasy and unsettled. But once she gets the apartment looking good and clean, the boy begins to enjoy the cleanness. It was unsettling at first, but now that he sees the difference, he likes it. There had to be an adjustment period as the cleaning process started and continued.

This is exactly the way it is when the Holy Spirit comes to live in a person's life. The Holy Spirit looks around in your heart's home and says, "Oh, my! What a mess! There are some things I have to get out of here." There are some drinks in the refrigerator that don't fit your lifestyle anymore. There are some magazines lying around that don't belong anymore. You used to go places that don't seem appropriate anymore. Some of your language is out of place now. What a difference the Holy Spirit makes when he comes to live in your life.

Look at 2 Corinthians 7:1 again. A startling word is used to describe sin. It is the word *filthiness*. This is how God describes sin. Sin is filthiness. It is to the soul what dirt is to the body. Sin is moral and spiritual filthiness. How very different God's definition of sin is from the human definition. Some years ago, I read this interesting contrast:

Man calls sin an accident; God calls it an abomination.
Man calls sin a blunder; God calls it a blindness.
Man calls sin a chance; God calls it a choice.
Man calls sin a defect; God calls it a disease.
Man says it is an error; God calls it enmity.
Man says sin is frivolity; God says it is a fatality.
Man calls sin a trifle; God calls sin a tragedy.
Man says sin is weakness; God says sin is wickedness.

God hates sin just as a doctor hates cancer in a human body. He hates sin like a sharpshooter hates a mad dog in the children's playground.

The Bible presents a devastating picture of our fallen nature as humans. Romans 1:29–32 gives a full-blown x ray of the human heart. It is like a visit to the sewer. Sin is filthiness. The Holy Spirit comes into a life to get rid of the filth. Note also that 2 Corinthians 7:1 refers to contamination of the flesh. There is uncleanness of the flesh which the Holy Spirit has to clean out of your life. Is there any dirt that needs to be removed? What about your eyes? Are you looking at anything with your eyes which the Bible would call filth? Any videos that need to be destroyed? Any television programs that might be called filthy? What about images on your computer? Job 31:1 says, "I made a covenant with my eyes."

What about your ears? Are you listening to any music that would be displeasing to the Holy Spirit? Too much of contemporary music dwells upon such themes as sexual perversion, profanity, racism, bigotry, and hatred. A Marilyn Manson Band rants about sexual themes and hatred for Christ. A Snoop Doggy Dog raps of murder of police. Perhaps there is some music your ears are hearing which could be described as filthiness.

What about your lips? Once the Holy Spirit enters your life, some words are not appropriate. Profanity is certainly out of place. The Holy Spirit dwells in you; you are set apart; you belong to the Lord. Our lips are to be holy before the Lord. Do you remember the little song we used to sing in Sunday school?

Be careful little ears what you hear.
Be careful little eyes what you see.
Be careful little lips what you say.
For the Father up above
Looks down with tender love.
So be careful little lips what you say.

The Holy Spirit wants to get rid of all the filthiness of the flesh.

Looking even more carefully at 2 Corinthians 7:1, we see it talks about "filthiness of the spirit" (KJV). This reference to spirit is to our human spirit. Sometimes Christians feel smug and arrogant when filthiness of the flesh is discussed. They do not seem to have great problems with sins of the flesh. But the Bible also discusses sins of the spirit or sins of the disposition. These kinds of sins are more respectable. They are also harder to see. And they are harder to eliminate. And yes, they do more harm. Who does the most harm to the testimony of a church? The young Christian struggling with alcohol or the older Christian who has a gossiping tongue? Which do you think hinders the cause of Christ more?

Perhaps you heard about the church member, known to be a gossip, who came forward one Sunday and said to the pastor, "I feel I need to lay my tongue on the altar." The pastor said, "Our altar is only fourteen feet long, but do the best you can!" Is there any gossip you need to get out of your life? Have you heard anything about anyone that you need to keep to yourself?

What about malice? Do you have ill will toward other people? Have you had a serious conflict with someone which is causing growing animosity?

Perhaps a judgmental spirit resides in your heart. Too many Christians have appointed themselves as spiritual detectives. They are constantly snooping around the lives of other Christians and passing judgment on their activities. My observation is that most of us have enough problems of our own to deal with. We really don't have a lot of time to pry into the lives of other Christians.

There is a cleanup job the Holy Spirit has to do when he comes to live in our lives. He's the "Mr. Clean" of the human spirit. How is this dirt revealed in our lives? Second Corinthians 7:1 continues to help us. The verse begins, "Since we have these promises." The reference is to the promises in the Bible. The Bible is the "detergent" which the Holy Spirit uses to wash away the dirt in our lives. John 17:17 says, "Sanctify them by the truth: your word is truth." John 15:3 adds, "You are already clean because of the word I have spoken to you." Ephesians 5:26 says, "To make her holy, cleansing her by the washing with water through the word."

This is why a daily time to read the Bible and pray is so vital to every Christian. I like to have my daily quiet time (or whatever you would like to call it) in the morning. Reading the Bible and praying in the morning allows a person's mind to be focused on God. It also provides a way for the Holy Spirit to take control again for that day.

Colossians 3:5 says, "Put to death, therefore, whatever belongs to your earthly nature: sexual immorality, impurity, lust, evil desires and greed, which is idolatry." As you read your Bible, you see some things in your life that ought not to be there, and the Bible says, "Put them to death." Then you make a shocking discovery! You can't put them to death. There may be profanity in your life. You decide, *I'm not going to use profanity anymore.* But just as soon as you get under pressure, you slip up and use a profane word. You struggle with a temper. You decide, *I'm not going to lose my temper anymore.* But just as soon as your mate crosses you, you blow your top. You can't put your temper to death. What do you do?

You go to Romans 8:13: "For if you live according to the sinful nature, you will die; but if by the Spirit you put to death the misdeeds of the body, you will live." None of us is strong enough to kill the deeds of the flesh. The Holy Spirit must be the divine Executioner, putting all of our worldly deeds on the electric chair. In that morning quiet time, you will often be led to pray, "Holy Spirit, take charge. You must put to death these dirty, filthy things in my life."

Here's how it works. First John 1:9 says, "If we confess our sins, he is faithful and just and will forgive us our sins and purify us from all unrighteousness." We confess; the Holy Spirit cleanses. Confessing means we agree with God about our sin. Then the Holy Spirit begins to cleanse our hearts.

Let's go back to the girl who married the messy boy. When she came in washing and scrubbing, it was uncomfortable and uneasy for him. But he did enjoy the cleanness after a while. Let's look at the picture again. One good, thorough cleaning job and she exclaims, "There! I have this place clean."

"Wonderful," he says, "that's the end of that!"

The next day the wife comes in again. "Charles," she exclaims, whining a bit, "this place is dirty again! I've got to get out the soap and cleansers and mop and do it all again."

"Again?" he says. "You just did it yesterday."

"I know," she sighs, "but I've got to clean it again. You've let it get dirty again." And that's not all. She says, "And you, sweet husband, are going to help me get it clean."

That's how the Holy Spirit works. He says, "I'm going to clean up your life and you're going to help me. I'm going to be the divine Executioner. I will provide the power to put all this to death, but you are going to help" (see 1 John 1:9). We confess (that's our part). He cleanses (that's the Holy Spirit's part).

The Holy Spirit makes a difference in our lives and this is the negative part of that difference. He cleanses us.

The Holy Spirit Changes Us

As we saw in 1 Samuel when the Spirit came upon Saul, he became another man. Even so, when the Holy Spirit begins to do his sanctifying work in our lives, his intention is to make a positive difference in our lives. He wants to put the right kinds of things into our lives. Sanctification, as we have seen, means to set apart. In a negative way, it means set apart from sin. But if that's all you have, you become a legalist. A legalist is someone who tries to live the Christian life by obeying a set of rules. You are a prime candidate to become a Pharisee (the religious group in Jesus' day which turned religion into rules). There must also be the positive side of being set apart to God.

Have you ever wondered what God's purpose was in saving you? Why does he want to sanctify you? Philippians 2:13 explains it, "For it is God who works in you to will and to act according to his good purpose." God's purpose and goal in salvation's plan is to make you like his Son, the Lord Jesus Christ. The Holy Spirit helps you not only to be what you ought not to be, but to become what you ought to become—more and more like the Lord Jesus.

Second Corinthians 3:18 is a marvelous statement of the Holy Spirit's positive purpose to change our lives and make us like the Lord Jesus. It says, "And we who with unveiled faces all reflect the Lord's glory, are being transformed into his likeness with ever-increasing glory, which comes from the Lord, who is the Spirit." Actually, this is a beautiful picture of that daily devotion time. As we read the Bible and pray, the Holy Spirit not only does the negative work; he also does the positive work. Sanctification is the negative process. We look into God's Word every day and see things that ought not to be present in our lives. This verse compares the Word of God to a mirror.

Perhaps the first thing you do in the morning when you get up is look into the mirror. I know that's what I do. When I take the first shocking look, I am made aware of all the repairs that need to be made! I see myself just as I am. I certainly can't be seen in public like that. I have to wash my face. I need a shave. I need to make myself look as presentable as possible. This is what happens when we see ourselves in the Bible through sanctification.

There is also a positive side. The verse says, "Beholding as in a glass the glory of the Lord" (KJV). When you read the Bible, not only do you see yourself from a negative perspective, but you also see the positive picture of Jesus. This is why the Bible is such an exciting book. As you read the Bible, look for the Lord Jesus. When you come to a place in the Bible that you don't understand, ask yourself, "What does this passage teach me about Jesus?" Many times this question will clear up a verse for you.

Also, as you see Jesus in the Bible, you will notice how kind Jesus was in his dealings with people. You will read a verse that says, "Be kind and compassionate to one another" (Eph. 4:32). The Holy Spirit will lead you to pray, "Dear Lord, help me to be like Jesus. Help me to be kind to others." Then you will read in the Bible about the wonderful forgiving spirit that Jesus displayed. You will hear him as he says to a sinful woman, "Neither do I condemn you. Go now and leave your life of sin" (John 8:11).

You will then read this statement in the Bible, "Forgiving each other" (Eph. 4:32). The Holy Spirit will lead you to pray, "Lord, help me to be like Jesus. Help me to forgive others." As you read your Bible, you will see the beautiful love that Jesus displayed to others. You will see him in his loving relationships with his disciples. Then you will read, "By this all men will know that you are my disciples, if you love one another" (John 13:35). The Holy Spirit will lead you to pray, "Please Lord, help me to be loving like Jesus." Indeed, "with open face beholding as in a glass the glory of the Lord" (2 Cor. 3:18 KJV).

But the verse continues, "we are changed." The word for "changed" is a beautiful term. We get our English word *metamorphosis* from it. Metamorphosis is the process by which an insect becomes a beautiful butterfly. The insect wraps a cocoon around itself, goes through a phase known as chrysalis, and emerges from the cocoon as a beautiful butterfly. The same word is used in Romans 12:2: "Do not conform any longer to the pattern of this world, but be *transformed* by the renewing of your mind." Transformed. Metamorphosis. This is what the Holy Spirit does. He changes us and makes us more like the Lord Jesus.

So how does this change come about? Second Corinthians 3:18 helps us again: "Even as by the Spirit of the Lord" (KJV). Christlikeness is not produced by us, but in us by the Holy Spirit. Every day, as we study the Bible and pray, the Holy Spirit will help us become more like the Lord Jesus.

The verse also tells us something else. It says we are changed "from glory to glory." A process is indicated. We do not become like the Lord Jesus all at once. There is a process involved. It takes time.

We are so interested in instant remedies. I read about a new pill which will help people lose weight and get in shape. If it's true—watch out for the stampede! Who wants to go through grueling physical exercise if all we need to do is take a little pill? Unfortunately, it probably won't work! There is still very little chance of instant fitness. Nor is there instant spirituality. One does not become like the Lord Jesus overnight. It is a process. We go "from glory to glory" (KJV). Day by day, step by step, the Holy Spirit makes us more like the Lord Jesus.

But here's the good news. As the Holy Spirit is allowed to change your life, you will be pleased by the change. Others will notice you are not as ill-tempered or grumpy as you used to be. They will observe that you are a sweeter person. Your language will be cleaner than it once was. People around you will start noticing and they will like the person you are becoming. Your associates at the office will see a difference in your life. Your schoolmates will observe the difference. Around church, people will notice that something good is happening to you. At home, your kids and your wife will say, "Daddy's a better man than he used to be."

When people start saying you're a better person or that you're a different person than you used to be, find a place somewhere alone with the Holy Spirit and tell him, "What a difference you've made in my life."

Some more good news: You will also start liking the new you. You will feel better about yourself. Some more good news: One day, you will be like the Lord Jesus. First John 3:2 says, "Dear friends, now we are children of God, and what we will be has not yet been made known. But we know that when he appears, we shall be like him, for we shall see him as he is." As we go from glory to glory and become more and more like the Lord Jesus by the Holy Spirit, one day we shall be like the Lord Jesus. Think of it! Walking on the streets of gold, you will come up to me and say, "Vines, is that you?"

"Yes, it's me all right."

And you'll say, "My goodness, Vines, you look just like the Lord Jesus."

And I will say, "Hallelujah! What a difference he's made in my life!"

There is another aspect of the difference the Holy Spirit makes in our lives.

The Holy Spirit Controls Us

We ask the Holy Spirit to cleanse us, to take the dirt out, to get rid of the filth. We ask the Holy Spirit to change us and to help us be less of what we are and more like the Lord Jesus. How does this come about? This brings us back to the

81

subject of our previous chapter, being filled with the Holy Spirit. Remember that the main idea is to be under the control of the Holy Spirit.

As you yield to the control of the Holy Spirit, you will be—in the best sense of the term—a spiritual Christian. He is cleansing and changing. But if we do not yield to his control, we will remain a carnal Christian, which means we will be controlled by our old self instead of our new self. If this happens, the Holy Spirit will be grieved. But who wouldn't want to yield to the Holy Spirit's control? Left to ourselves, we humans make quite a mess of things.

A little child is trying to tie her shoestring. She gets things all tangled up. Crying, she comes to mama and asks her to untangle the strings and tie them correctly. We get our lives tangled up. We get life's knots tied so hard we can't untie them. The Holy Spirit can take control, untie the knots, and tie things together correctly.

Imagine that you own a restaurant which is not doing well. The building is in need of repairs. On the inside, the furniture is shabby and worn. The service is slow. The food is poor. The restaurant is on the verge of going under. Then one day an expert in the restaurant business comes and says, "How about letting me take over, run this place for you, and make you a successful restaurant owner?" You agree.

The new manager comes in, cleans up the outside, paints a new sign, and makes things look great. The old furnishings are taken out and replaced with beautiful new ones. New tablecloths are placed on the tables. Competent, energetic waiters and waitresses are employed. Things are moving briskly. In the kitchen, a new, award-winning chef is preparing award-winning food. A new sign goes up on the outside saying, "Under new management." People are coming from everywhere to eat in the restaurant. It is wonderful when your restaurant is yielded to the control of someone who knows how to run it. You get great results this way! You find success!

This is exactly the way it is in our new lives as Christians. To yield to the control of the Holy Spirit is to allow him to get on with the process of cleansing and changing our lives. Remember, this is not a once-for-all experience. It is a continual process. The Bible says, "Be continually being filled." The process must be a continual one.

Romans 12:1 says, "Therefore, I urge you, brothers, in view of God's mercy, to offer your bodies as living sacrifices, holy and pleasing to God—this is your spiritual act of worship." The same word translated "present" in Romans 12:1 is translated "offer" in Romans 6:19. To present yourself to the Holy Spirit is the same thing as offering or yielding yourself to him. When you yield yourself to the Holy Spirit, you allow him to take control of your life. He is now in charge. He is running your life. In effect, he's the president in your life.

It's like an interior decorator who says, "I'm in the business of coming to homes that are run down and cleaning them up and decorating them and making them beautiful." Two people down the street decide they want the services of this decorator. She comes to the first house and the owner says, "I want you to renovate and redecorate my house." She starts to work, cleaning up one room, cleaning up another, putting pictures on the wall, etc. The decorator then goes to the next room and tries to open the door, but she cannot. The decorator says to the owner, "I need to get in there and decorate it."

The owner says, "I'm sorry, but I can't let you in that one. It's a room I have reserved only for myself."

The decorator goes to another door and says, "This one is locked also."

"Sorry, but you can't get in that one either," says the owner. Parts of this house might get decorated, but several rooms will stay the same.

The same decorator goes down the street, walks into another house, and the owner says, "This house is in need of repairs. I want you to clean it up, decorate it, change it, and make a mansion out of it. Here are the keys. You take over every room of the house. Don't stop until it's brand new." This is exactly what it means to yield to the control of the Holy Spirit. Let him redecorate the house of your life.

Suggested Procedure for a Good Heart Renovation Project

1. Ask the Holy Spirit to take control of every room of your heart.

2. Trust the Holy Spirit to do his cleaning, changing work in every room of your heart.

3. Don't hide any of the keys! Let him have them all!

4. As you see the work in progress and the "heart home improvements" being made, be sure to thank him and say, "What a difference you've made in my life."

CHAPTER 7

WHO
BAKES
THE BREAD?

When I was a small boy, my father was a bread man. He delivered bread for the Merita Bread Company for ten years. The work was not easy. He distributed bread to our little county-seat town in Georgia and to all the stores in the entire county. Rising at 4:00 A.M., he would go to the warehouse where the bread truck was parked. There he would meet a larger truck coming from the bakery where the bread was actually baked. He would get his day's supply of bread, then begin his long route. My father didn't bake the bread. The bread was baked at the company bakery fifty miles away. He delivered the bread to the customers. That was his responsibility—to deliver the bread.

In the years since my father was a bread man, I have often thought about him and this time in his life. This is a very helpful way of understanding the key to Christian service. I presume most who are reading this book are Christian believers. Perhaps most of you are involved in some area of service for the Lord, through your church or in some other Christian organization. You sing in the choir, or you teach a Bible class. Maybe you are involved in visitation. The real question in Christian service is—who bakes the bread? Do we have to manufacture the power and strength and blessing to pass on to others in this life? Or is our role more in the area of delivering what is prepared by God and his Holy Spirit?

Remember the simple arrangements of statements summarizing the three-fold work of the Holy Spirit. There is the Spirit's work *for* us. We call this salvation. When a person repents of sin and receives Jesus Christ as Lord and Savior, the spiritual birth occurs. This is salvation.

There is also the Spirit's work *in* us. This is sanctification. The Holy Spirit comes to live in the heart of an individual. Working in the life of that person, the Holy Spirit seeks to bring about positive change. Bad habits and thought patterns are eliminated. A new life is begun. This is the Spirit's work of sanctification.

Then, there is the Spirit's work *through* us. This we call Christian service. The Holy Spirit wants to use us as vessels to carry blessings to others. He wants us to be a channel through which he can transmit his life-giving, life-changing work to others. This is what Christian service is all about.

Most of you who read this book are engaged in serving the Lord in some capacity. There may be Sunday school workers and teachers reading the chapter. Perhaps a church usher holds this book in his hand. Maybe a young mother is working in the children's choirs. Some man is working with young people. Every believer should be involved in some kind of Christian service because to do so is the natural result of a meaningful relationship with Christ.

Many Christians try to serve the Lord by using their own gifts and abilities. Most are very sincere. They really want to serve the Lord. They may generate much activity. Yet there seems to be little effectiveness and not much helpfulness in their service. The real secret in Christian service is learning that we do not produce fruit. By fruit I mean the beneficial results for others which Christian service produces. This "fruit" is the evidence of the Spirit's presence in a human life. Only the Holy Spirit can grow the fruit. We do not bake the bread. The Holy Spirit is the divine Baker.

So much of what people do today in the name of Christian service can be classified as mere activity. These people may be very busy doing all kinds of work! They are attending committee meetings, singing in the choir, folding church bulletins, preparing food for a church fellowship, playing on the church softball team, or visiting the hospital. Lots of activity and an abundance of energy are evident. But this activity is being done in the energy of the flesh, or with human power only. Natural gifts drive the activity. The result is very busy people staying very busy.

On the other hand, ministry is Christian service empowered by the Holy Spirit. Recognizing our own human limitations, we ask the Holy Spirit to be the "bread maker" in the bakery of our lives. Only then does our busy activity become fruitful ministry.

Ralph Herring's book *God Being My Helper* (Broadman) is one of the most helpful books I've read on the Holy Spirit. Dr. Herring was a Southern Baptist pastor, and his book is filled with simple and practical help for believers as they try to understand the role of the Holy Spirit. His book points out a fascinating phrase in Philippians 1:19. Paul was discussing his imprisonment and the obstacles in his ministry. He was hopeful that he would experience a release from prison to continue effective ministry. In this setting he declared, "For I know that through your prayers and the help given by the Spirit of Jesus Christ, what has happened to me will turn out for my deliverance."

The little phrase "the supply of the Spirit" (KJV) certainly hooks our interest. The use of the word *supply* is fascinating. The Greek word is *epichoragias*, which means to supply or to furnish. Look at the center of the word *chora*. Our words *chorus* and *choir* come from it.

The background of the word is informative. Greek cities often put on elaborate dramas and musicals. A great deal of expense was involved. Very often some wealthy citizen of the city would supply the necessary funds for the chorus. This is the word used here—"the supply of the Spirit." The phrase could be translated "the lavish supply of the Spirit." The point is that we don't have to depend on our meager human resources to serve the Lord. We may claim the generous resources of God the Holy Spirit. His supply is like a huge oil well on a Texas prairie. His resources are as helpful as a reference librarian who locates obscure but needed material.

In 1 Peter 4:11 the Bible says, "If anyone speaks, he should do it as one speaking the very words of God." You and I do not have to produce the necessary ingredients to serve Jesus Christ effectively. The Holy Spirit provides all we need. We do not bake the bread. We are God's delivery men—not his bakers. Our responsibility is to distribute the bread to the hungry. This has been a very helpful truth in my attempts to serve the Lord through my years of Christian life and ministry.

Whether you preach, sing, teach, pray, or witness, the Holy Spirit, our Friend, supplies all the necessary abilities. This is the only way we can be effective. True Christian service and ministry is produced inside an individual Christian by the Holy Spirit. Looking busy or paying attention to what is happening on the outside is not as important.

Several years ago the Lord gave me a very difficult assignment. I was sent by the Lord to serve in an area where an ocean of problems existed. I soon became keenly aware that I was totally unequipped to minister effectively. I sought the help of the Holy Spirit in this difficult ministry, and I was led to 2 Timothy 1:7: "For God did not give us a spirit of timidity, but a spirit of power, of love and of self-discipline." It was exactly what I needed—power for my difficult assignment. I needed love for people who were often unloving. I also needed a sound mind so I would have God's wisdom to make right decisions.

The verse became my daily prayer. Each morning after reading my Bible, I prayed and asked God for power, love, and wisdom. Actually, I prayed this verse in reverse order. Each day, I prayed for the Lord to give me a sound mind. (I'm sure a lot of folks feel like the Lord really needs to give me a sound mind!) I prayed every day that the Holy Spirit would show me what he wanted me to do. I asked for a supply of wisdom to know the will of God for my life and the lives of others in the sphere of my ministry.

I also prayed that the Holy Spirit would give me his love. I asked the Holy Spirit to show me what to do and to enable me to do it in the right spirit. Romans 5:5 helped me: "And hope does not disappoint us, because God has poured out his love into our hearts by the Holy Spirit, whom he has given us."

Only the Holy Spirit can produce this kind of love. A person can do the will of God, but doing it has little effectiveness if it is not done in a loving spirit.

Finally, I prayed every day for power—spiritual power. I wanted to know what to do (a sound mind). I wanted to do what God wanted me to do in the right way (love). I also needed the power to be able to do what God wanted me to do. So I prayed for power. I could claim this power on the basis of Acts 1:8. "But you will receive power when the Holy Spirit comes on you."

Keep in mind that I am not talking about the outward expressions of our Christian service, whether singing, teaching, visiting, or whatever. I'm talking about the inside motivation for everything we do. What drives us? All we do in Christian service must be motivated by a sound mind, love, and power. This threefold division explains the Holy Spirit's supply to us.

Spiritual Comprehension

The word translated as "sound mind" in the King James Version is not an easy one to translate into our English language. The King James renders it "a sound mind." Other translations use "wisdom" or "self-discipline." Literally, the word means a "wise head." The promise here is that the Holy Spirit will give you a "wise head" or sensible wisdom. It's that kind of sensible wisdom which helps you understand what God wants you to do.

What is God's will for my life? Perhaps no other question becomes as pressing and vital to young people as this one. Do you have a desire for God to show you what he wants you to do? Do you seek the wisdom to know the will of God for your life? With a "wise head" from the Holy Spirit, you can know the wisdom hundreds of times each week.

Hundreds of times each week I do not have the wisdom I need. My mental capacity is too limited. I always get in trouble when I try to run my life by using my own wisdom and understanding. Proverbs 3:5 has been a favorite verse of mine for many years: "Trust in the LORD with all thine heart; and lean not unto thine own understanding" (KJV). There it is! God's direction! We have a higher power, and we don't have to depend upon our own mental ability.

The Old Testament provides a beautiful illustration of the need for wisdom. Solomon was the young king of Israel. He succeeded his illustrious father David, Israel's greatest king. After Solomon's inauguration, the Lord appeared to him one night. The Lord offered him a breathtaking opportunity: " That night God appeared to Solomon and said to him, 'Ask for whatever you want

88

me to give you'" (2 Chron. 1:7). Wow! What if God asked you that now? What if God extended to you a blank check and simply told you to fill it in? What would you ask God for? What is your greatest desire from God?

Solomon's response to that question was magnificent. He did not ask God for great riches. There was no request for a long reign. He didn't even ask God to make him famous. Rather, in beautiful humility and sincerity, Solomon requested, "Give me wisdom and knowledge, that I may lead this people, for who is able to govern this great people of yours?" (2 Chron. 1:10). God's great heart was thrilled! What a request! Wisdom to be able to know how to lead God's special people.

God not only granted the request—God made Solomon the wisest man who ever lived. Even the Queen of Sheba came to listen to his wisdom. After she heard Solomon discuss every imaginable subject, she exclaimed, "Not even half the greatness of your wisdom was told me; you have far exceeded the report I heard" (2 Chron. 9:6).

"God said to Solomon, 'Since this is your heart's desire and you have not asked for wealth, riches or honor, nor for the death of your enemies, and since you have not asked for a long life but for wisdom and knowledge to govern my people over whom I have made you king, therefore wisdom and knowledge will be given you. And I will also give you wealth, riches and honor, such as no king who was before you ever had and none after you will have'" (2 Chron. 1:11–12). God not only gave him wisdom; he also gave him riches and wealth. The point is that Solomon needed wisdom to lead the people well. God supplied the wisdom Solomon needed.

This same God has promised us the spirit of a sound mind. We can request his wisdom. James 1:5 says, "If any of you lacks wisdom, he should ask God, who gives generously to all without finding fault, and it will be given to him." Each day, we can claim God's wisdom for our difficult decisions and dilemmas.

The book of Acts offers a fascinating survey of the work of the Holy Spirit through the lives of Christians. These early disciples had been given an assignment to be completed after Jesus returned to heaven. It was to make disciples (Matt. 28:19–20). The book of Acts shows us how the Holy Spirit provided them with the specifics of their assignment. Let me give you three examples.

In Acts 8 we read the exciting account of Philip, the evangelist. Philip was engaged in a great revival in Samaria. We all enjoy the big meetings, don't we? Don't you love those mountaintop experiences in public worship services or revival crusades when excitement is running high, big crowds are gathering, and miraculous experiences are transpiring? But right in the middle of this big meeting in Samaria, an angel of the Lord told Philip, "Go south to the road— the desert road—that goes down from Jerusalem to Gaza" (Acts 8:26).

Say what? Don't you know this must have puzzled Philip. *What in the world is the Lord telling me to do? Leave this big meeting and go to the desert?* But Philip obeyed the Lord. Verse 27 is simple but to the point: "So he started out." Once there, he encountered a man from Ethiopia, who was a notable official in the Ethiopian government. In addition, he was a soul who needed to know about Jesus.

Philip had received the general instructions. Now the Holy Spirit got very specific: "The Spirit told Philip, 'Go to that chariot and stay near it'" (Acts 8:29). I guess I have read that verse hundreds of times. Only recently did I notice that the Spirit said specifically, "Join thyself to *this* chariot" (KJV). I had never seen it before. There it is: *this* chariot. How specific! The Holy Spirit knew that in that desert, at that juncture of the road, riding in that chariot was a lost man ready to receive Christ. The Holy Spirit supplied wisdom so that a lost sinner and a seeking Savior could be brought together by a faithful Christian. The Spirit kept Philip's appointment book. Does he keep your Daytimer today?

The second example occurred in Acts 10. Simon Peter was at the home of Simon in Joppa (see Acts 9:43). It was about dinner time. He was on the roof of a house, and he was really hungry. A typical preacher! A big plate of fried chicken would be good! At that time, he received a vision from the Lord. God revealed to him that no person is common or unclean and that every individual deserves to hear the gospel. Acts 10:19–20 says, "While Peter was still thinking about the vision, the Spirit said to him, 'Simon, three men are looking for you. So get up and go downstairs. Do not hesitate to go with them, for I have sent them.'" Peter obeyed the Holy Spirit.

What was the Spirit doing? He was supplying Simon Peter with wisdom. He was given specific guidance to know what God wanted him to do. When he arrived at the house of Cornelius in Caesarea, where the Holy Spirit directed him to go, Cornelius, his family, and a large group of people had gathered. Simon Peter preached a gospel sermon. The hearts of the people had already been prepared. The result was exciting! While Peter was speaking, the Holy Spirit fell on those who heard God's message. The result was a marvelous salvation time. Again, the Holy Spirit provided specific wisdom to know where to go and what to do. The Spirit set those appointments.

Let's look now at a third example. In Acts 16, Paul was engaged in a missionary journey. He understood God's assignment in general terms. He knew he was to carry the gospel to all people. At this time, though, he needed specific wisdom and guidance from the Lord. He wanted to go where God led him.

Have you ever needed specific guidance concerning life decisions? "Where do you want me to go to school, Lord?" "What kind of work do you want me to do?" "Where do you want me to live?" "Is this the man you want me to marry?" Paul wanted to know where God would have him go on this particular missionary journey.

According to Acts 16:6, Paul had gone through Phrygia and Galatia. Evidently, he desired to preach the word in Asia. But he was "kept by the Holy Spirit from preaching the word in the province of Asia." Forbidden. This must have been puzzling to Paul. Verse 7 is even more enigmatic: "When they came to the border of Mysia, they tried to enter Bithynia; but the Spirit of Jesus would not allow them to." They tried to go to Bithynia but the Spirit wouldn't let them. In verse 8 he continued, passing by Mysia and arriving at Troas. Then, during the night, the vision came: "Come over to Macedonia and help us" (Acts 16:9). This was the guidance he needed. The next day he said to his team, "All right boys, load up. Macedonia by morning! God has called us to preach the gospel there."

Have you ever wondered how the Holy Spirit directed Paul? How did the Holy Spirit forbid Paul from going one direction and lead him in another direction? The Holy Spirit did it most likely the same way he does in our lives. Sometimes the Holy Spirit leads us by opening and closing doors. Very often he uses the circumstances of our lives.

There are also situations where the Lord impresses us deep within our hearts. After a time of Bible study and prayer, earnestly seeking the Lord's wisdom, there comes this deep impression within: *This is what I want you to do; there is where I want you to go.* Always be careful that these circumstances and impressions are brought to the authority of Scripture. The Holy Spirit will never lead us contrary to the Word of God.

Have you ever had a series of circumstances in your life that were totally beyond your control? At the time you didn't understand them. Later, as you looked back, you understood that the Lord was leading in every detail. I don't know about you, but I find it is much easier to see the will of God looking back than looking forward! I have not always felt that the Holy Spirit was leading me through my life circumstances. The Bible says, "If the LORD delights in a man's way, he makes his steps firm" (Ps. 37:23). Someone once said that not only are the steps of a good person ordered of the Lord; sometimes the stops are as well!

Cars are now equipped with computers which provide directions for a trip. Put in the necessary data and the computer tells you what roads to take, when to turn right or left, even where to find a good restaurant! Modern technology is impressive, but it is just catching up with the Holy Spirit. He offers us wisdom on the highway of our Christian lives and service.

By the way, the wisdom of the Holy Spirit takes the worry and the hurry out of serving the Lord. I think about the earthly ministry of Jesus. He accomplished so much in only three and one-half years. His days were always full, but not hectic. As you read the life of the Lord, there is a beautiful serenity and calmness about his work. His life wasn't as frantic as ours—with beepers, cell phones, and satellite imaging! Jesus said one time, "Are there not twelve hours of daylight?" (John 11:9). There was time enough to complete everything he wanted done.

Shhh! I'll tell you a secret! The great secret of effective Christian service is the wisdom and guidance of the Holy Spirit. How can we get this wisdom of the Holy Spirit? We need to be listening to the direction of the Holy Spirit. Isaiah 30:21 is helpful in this connection: "Whether you turn to the right or to the left, your ears will hear a voice behind you, saying, 'This is the way; walk in it.'" The promise here is that if we have an ear to hear, we will receive guidance from the Lord.

Romans 8:14 teaches us, "Those who are led by the Spirit of God are sons of God." Well, you need a trained ear. Isaiah 50:4 says, "The Sovereign LORD has given me an instructed tongue, to know the word that sustains the weary. He wakens me morning by morning, wakens my ear to listen like one being taught." Notice he talks about the learned first.

Did Jesus ever speak with the tongue of the learned? He certainly did. Where did he get that word, that wisdom? Obviously, he was God in human flesh. But he also had a listening ear to hear the will of the heavenly Father. The same is true of us. Jesus often said, "He that hath an ear, let him hear."

I love to listen to an orchestra. Our church has a magnificent orchestra. These musicians must have a trained ear. Their instruments must be in tune if the music is to be melodic and harmonious. If the tone of the instruments is a little flat, it must be adjusted. Their ears are trained to the music and to stay in tune. Our ears need to be trained to the music of the Holy Spirit so that we stay in tune with him.

Have you noticed that mothers are different from fathers? Fathers can sleep through almost anything. When we brought our first child home from the hospital, I proclaimed myself the "world's greatest dad." I was going to be there for her every need. My title lasted only until her first feeding time. I never heard her! At the first whimper, Janet was up and on the job. Mothers have a trained ear. Their little baby can make just a small whimper in the middle of the night and Mother is wide awake. Her ear is trained to hear the faintest cry of her baby. Likewise, our ears must be trained to the slightest prompting of the Holy Spirit.

So the question in Christian service is, Where do we get our wisdom? Do we manufacture it ourselves? No. We don't bake the bread. We just deliver it.

Spiritual Compassion

The great motivation for Christian service is love. It must motivate all we do. Why do you do what you do for Jesus? You are teaching a Sunday school class. Why? You sing in the choir. Why do you sing? Some people serve to stay busy. Others serve out of fear. What fear? Fear they will not be accepted by the church fellowship. Fear some bully around the church will punish them if they don't take a job. What a miserable way to serve Jesus. It certainly doesn't sound like a fun life!

Others serve because they desire praise. Many yearn to hear someone say to them, "Oh, that is wonderful. You are doing such a great job." We ought to praise people for their work, but we should not seek praise as our motive for serving Jesus.

Others serve out of selfish interests. The desire to accomplish some self-determined end is motivation for some. If you are serving Jesus Christ for any other reason than love for Jesus and others, then your Christian service may become a misery to you and a barren experience for others.

Love is the key, but where does it originate? Again, Romans 5:5 makes it clear: "And hope does not disappoint us, because God has poured out his love into our hearts by the Holy Spirit, whom he has given us." The Holy Spirit comes to dwell in your heart. God's love moves in as well. Your life can be a channel through which this love can flow. Jesus expressed it beautifully when he said, "'Whoever believes in me, as the Scripture has said, streams of living water will flow from within him.' By this he meant the Spirit, whom those who believed in him were later to receive. Up to that time the Spirit had not been given, since Jesus had not yet been glorified" (John 7:38–39). You have a divine fountain of love inside you. It is your choice. You can either allow this love of God to flow out from you to others or not. If there is no love flowing out of your life, then evidently something has happened to stop the flow of love. You've got a blockage.

We have much to learn about love. Personalities of the Old Testament teach many important truths. Have you thought much about Isaac? Caught between a famous father, Abraham, and a famous son, Jacob, he is not one of the better known Old Testament personalities. As you study his rather uneventful life, you find one feature that seems to be characteristic of him. He devoted a lot of his life to redigging some wells the Philistines had stopped up. By trade, he was a well digger.

If we are to have the supply of love necessary to serve Jesus Christ, perhaps we need to unstop the channels of the wells of love and concern that are choked in our hearts. Perhaps there is some dirt and debris of pride or jealousy stopping the flow of love out of your heart.

Often, as people get older, their hearts get harder. Life is so hard that the heart tends to harden. Perhaps your heart has grown bitter. Mistreatment by others has caused you to be filled with the trash of bitterness and animosity. The love of God is stifled inside you and cannot flow out. Maybe reading a page from Isaac's life would be helpful. Perhaps some wells in your life need to be cleaned out. People are not easy to love. Only God can help us love people as we should.

D. L. Moody was a remarkable man. Although never ordained, he was a great evangelist and pastor. One time a man named Henry Moorhead came to preach for Moody in his absence at the Moody Tabernacle in Chicago. Moorhead preached for one month. When Moody returned, he asked his wife, "How did things go?"

She said, "Oh, it's wonderful, we're having revival."

He said, "What's he preaching?"

"John 3:16," she replied.

"That's a great text, but what else is he preaching?"

"That's all he's preaching."

"Every service?"

"Yes, that's all he's preaching. John 3:16."

Moorhead took only one text for his whole ministry—John 3:16. The sermons were different, but the text was always the same.

D. L. Moody was fascinated by this, and he started studying about the love of God in the Bible. He read everything he could find in the Bible about the love of God, how much God loves us, and God's gift of love in his Son, the

Lord Jesus. The scope of God's love absorbed him. Moody told of one day when he was walking down the street. He received a mighty baptism of love from the Holy Spirit. So powerful and so overwhelming was the experience that he rushed to a nearby room, fell across the bed, and asked God to "hold by" some of his power. He could not stand the impact of what he referred to as "waves of liquid love."

I would encourage you to study about the love of God. Meditate on his love. Think about how much God loves you. What about the great songs of the love of God? Ask the Holy Spirit to fill your heart with the love of God. Ask the Holy Spirit to supply all the love you need in your relationships with others. He will! You will be amazed at the change that will take place in your life.

One day you will discover that you love everybody. Just seeing people will cause love to flood your heart and to flow toward them. You will speak with love. You will act with love. The love of God supplied by the Holy Spirit will change your life! There will be a difference in your tone of voice. Love will affect the glint in your eyes. Love will soften the expression on your face. Holy Spirit love will improve your behavior. The love of the Holy Spirit will be expressed in the words you say.

We need to know what God wants us to do. That's wisdom. But we also need to do his will in the right spirit. That's the love the Spirit supplies. That's spiritual compassion.

Spiritual Combustion

We are living in a day of power. Nuclear power has changed the way we view our world. The awesome power of nuclear weapons has created a world of frightening possibilities. We also live in a day when information is power. There is literally an explosion of information available to people today. We also have technological power. Think about the tremendous power exerted by lasers. Laser surgery enables trained doctors to perform routine procedures which used to be quite complicated and difficult. Amazing technological power!

Yet in the midst of a world with this kind of power, there are many areas where we are utterly powerless. Many parents lack the power to raise their children successfully. City governments do not have the power to solve horrendous crime problems. Nor can nations seem to generate the power to help different races live in peace and in love with one another. We have political power, intellectual power, scientific power, but we pitifully lack spiritual power.

Some Christians are shocked to find they are utterly powerless when it comes to serving the Lord effectively. We want to know what God would have us do and we want to do it in the right way. But often, we find we are not able to do what God wants us to do. We need empowering.

Jesus promised power. Shortly before he returned to heaven after his resurrection, he promised, "I am going to send you what my Father has promised; but stay in the city until you have been clothed with power from on high" (Luke 24:49). *Clothed with power.* The idea is to be immersed with power.

Jesus gave another promise: "But you will receive power when the Holy Spirit comes on you; and you will be my witnesses in Jerusalem, and in all Judea and Samaria, and to the ends of the earth" (Act 1:8). Jesus could not have been clearer. He promises to supply power. And we need it!

This is encouraging. God promises the needed power when we do his will. It's like a power supply on a big machine. To run the machine, turn on the power supply. Does he want you to pray? Then he speaks of praying in the Holy Spirit (see Jude 20). Does he want you to witness to others? He promises, "For it will not be you speaking, but the Spirit of your Father speaking through you" (Matt. 10:20). He provides the power to pray. He provides the power to witness. He is the power supply for us.

Ephesians 1:19–20 is a tremendous prayer promise: "And his incomparably great power for us who believe. That power is like the working of his mighty strength, which he exerted in Christ when he raised him from the dead and seated him at his right hand in the heavenly realms." This is part of one of the greatest prayers in the Bible. It is the third part of a prayer begun in verse 18. The promise here is about the power of God in our lives.

Five different Greek words for power are used in these two verses. The Holy Spirit seems to have exhausted the whole Greek vocabulary to come up with the best words for power. This reminds me of one of those old *Gunsmoke* shows on television. The entire program seemed to be filled with gunfire. Pow! Pow! Pow! This verse is Power! Power! Power! Paul said the Holy Spirit wants us to have power!

In the Old Testament, when God wanted to demonstrate the power he makes available to us, he pointed either to the creation or to the parting of the Red Sea. In the New Testament, when God wanted to show his power, he pointed to the resurrection of the Lord Jesus. Power in the Old Testament? The Red Sea! Power in the New Testament? The empty tomb! Ephesians 1:19–20 says that the same power which raised Jesus from the dead is available to us as we serve the Lord. Fantastic! Awesome! The very power that brought Jesus Christ out of the tomb is available for us as we serve him.

Philippians 4:13 gives us this empowerment idea very simply: "I can do everything through him who gives me strength." Literally, the author is saying, "I can do all things through Christ who puts the power inside me." It could be rendered, "I am a match for all things through him who keeps pouring his power into me."

I don't know what the Holy Spirit wants to do through you. I am unaware of the particular ministry or area of service the Lord has assigned to you. Yet I do know this. You don't have to bake the bread. You don't even have to stand in the kitchen. The Holy Spirit is the divine Baker. He bakes the bread. You simply deliver the goods. You want to know what God wants you to do? The Spirit supplies the wisdom. Do you want to do God's will in the right way? The Spirit supplies the love. Do you want the power to do God's will? The Spirit provides the power.

Mendelssohn was a great German hymn writer and organist. He had heard of a fine organ in a church nearby. He went to the church and asked the church janitor to let him come in and play the organ. The church janitor was reluctant to do so. The organ was so expensive and magnificent. Mendelssohn pressed the issue, urging the janitor to let him play for just a few minutes. "Okay," said the janitor, "I'll let you play it."

Mendelssohn sat down at the organ and in a few moments the church was filled with the most gorgeous music imaginable. He soon stopped playing and thanked the church janitor as he walked away. Tears flooded the janitor's eyes as he said, "Just to think, I almost refused to let him play."

The Holy Spirit wants to supply you with everything you need to be effective for the Lord Jesus Christ. Don't refuse to let him play on the instrument of your life. The bread is available from the bakery. Many need the bread. Don't refuse to deliver it.

Some Suggestions from the Bakery

1. The fresh bread of wisdom is available. Load it up and haul it out.

2. Sweet cakes of love are coming out of the stoves. People yearn for the sweetness. Carry it to them.

3. Bakery goods to nurture and give strength are coming off the assembly line. Load it up and take it out to a weak, undernourished world!

CHAPTER 8

THE GIVER OF THE GIFTS

"It's not the gift, but the giver," she said as she handed me a lovely wooden spice rack. I knew my wife would love it.

She then handed out marble letter holders, wooden breadboards, leather handbags, fans and tablecloths, attractive paintings and works of art. Mrs. Ira Porter, acting commissioner of prisons in Jamaica, was presenting gifts to a group of men from First Baptist Church, Jacksonville, Florida, during the summer of 1997. These men had traveled to Jamaica for a prison crusade. I had flown down for an evening rally, and I saw God bless this time in a tremendous way.

As Mrs. Porter spoke of the gift and the giver, I thought of other times when gifts are given. Christmas and birthdays went through my mind and then, the gift of my Friend, the Holy Spirit. The Holy Spirit gives gifts to us, God's children. These gifts are wonderful and vital to Christian ministry. Yet the Giver is more important than his gifts. The Holy Spirit gives us these supernatural gifts, and for that we must be truly thankful.

When I was a junior in high school, I was given an aptitude test. It was standard procedure. One's natural inclinations and abilities were expected to bubble up from the depths of teenage insecurity. Hopefully, the information would point us in the direction of an appropriate career.

My aptitude test produced interesting results. I should pursue something in the area of science or mathematics, according to this analysis. I should definitely avoid pursuing occupations requiring speaking or writing. (I guess those who hear me preach and those of you who are reading this book might say, Amen!) At that time, I was not at all interested in writing or speaking. I almost failed junior English because I was required to give a five-minute speech in front of the class. Impossible, I thought! I was so shy, timid, and fearful that about all I could do was stand up there and giggle nervously.

I was shy. I was nervous. And my dad had aspirations for me to become a surgeon. Think about that! Jerry using a scalpel day in and day out? I wouldn't know where to make the first cut! (Ask me about cuts on the pro football drafts, and we have a different story.)

In the middle of this atmosphere, the Lord called me to preach his Word. I was the most stunned, surprised person of all when the Lord did this. Other people were certainly shocked. I knew I couldn't speak. I was well aware I did not have the natural abilities expected in a preacher. So I concluded that if I had been called to preach, God would have to give me the necessary abilities and equipment to carry out this call.

During this time, the Lord led me to a verse of Scripture. First Timothy 1:12 says, "I thank Christ Jesus our Lord, who has given me strength, that he considered me faithful, appointing me to his service." The verse indicates that the same God who puts people into the ministry is also the God who enables them to perform his ministry. The point is clear. God gives a person the ability to perform the ministry he desires. When God places you in service, he is committed to giving you the abilities you need to accomplish the tasks he has in mind.

Remember our summary of the threefold work of the Holy Spirit in a Christian's life. The Holy Spirit does work *for* us. This is the work of *salvation*. When we are Spirit-born, we receive the wonderful gift of the Holy Spirit. In Acts 2:38 we read, "Peter replied, 'Repent and be baptized, every one of you, in the name of Jesus Christ for the forgiveness of your sins. And you will receive the gift of the Holy Spirit.'" The Holy Spirit comes to dwell in your heart and to live in your life. What an awesome and overwhelming thought. This is big, really big!

Alexander, the great Greek general, once gave a magnificent golden cup to one of his lowly servants. The servant was overwhelmed. "Your majesty," he said, "this is too much for me to take." Alexander looked at him with a smile and said, "But it is not too much for me to give."

Once the wonderful gift of the Holy Spirit is given to us, we understand just how unworthy we are and what truly sinful people we are. God's gift is overwhelming. This is the Holy Spirit's work for us.

Secondly, there is also the work of the Holy Spirit *in* us. This we have called *sanctification*. God the Holy Spirit produces certain graces in our lives. Galatians 5 tells us about these graces pictured as the fruit of the Spirit. The Holy Spirit produces fruit in our lives as we yield to his control. The Spirit's work of sanctification cleanses us and changes us so that we become more and more like our Savior, the Lord Jesus Christ.

Lastly, there is the work of the Holy Spirit which he accomplishes *through* us. This is the area of *Christian service*. Spirit-blessed service is faithfully serving the Lord by using the gifts the Holy Spirit has given us.

Remember Mrs. Porter's words, "It's not the gift, but the giver." Carefully distinguish between the gift of the Spirit, which is the Spirit himself indwelling us at salvation, and the gifts of the Spirit which he bestows on individual Christians so they may effectively serve the Lord Jesus.

Let's consider these spiritual gifts. Unfortunately, this topic is problematic and controversial for modern Christianity. Some Christians become a little uneasy and even afraid when this topic comes up. It's an area which lends itself to the dangers of abuse. Some people magnify spiritual gifts out of proportion. They become prideful on the subject. The gifts are looked upon as merit badges. Some Christians may even use them to feed their feelings of superiority over others.

There is also the tendency to exalt certain gifts. The gifts are placed in some kind of order of spiritual preference. Those who have the most preferred gifts tend to look down on those who may not have them. Another tendency involves using spiritual gifts as excuses to ignore the clear commands of Scripture. The Bible clearly teaches every Christian is to "make disciples." However, if a Christian feels he doesn't have the gift of evangelism, he may use this as an excuse not to witness. The Bible teaches that all Christians are to give. But some Christians, because they do not have the gift of giving, ignore the Bible teaching about faithful giving. In addition to all this, some people feel that to get involved in the gifts of the Holy Spirit is to go into extremes of fanaticism.

Not only is there the danger of abuse concerning spiritual gifts, there is also the danger of neglect. Many Christians have never studied the subject of spiritual gifts. Fortunately, the church has rediscovered this helpful area of Christian service in recent years. To understand and apply the truths of spiritual gifts can make a person a better Christian. A life can be absolutely transformed. In recent years, spiritual gifts inventories have enabled Christians to understand and apply their spiritual gifts.

This can be revolutionary in the life of a church. If a church understands the subject of spiritual gifts, and if its members are faithful in exercising those spiritual gifts, there can be a powerful and effective ministry. The proper use of spiritual gifts can cause a surge of evangelism and revival in a church.

The first part of 1 Corinthians 12 gives an introduction on the subject of spiritual gifts.

How Spiritual Gifts Are Described

The gifts of the Holy Spirit are spiritual in nature. They come from the Holy Spirit. These gifts are not necessarily emotional in nature. The emotional side is not the essential nature of spiritual gifts. Paul actually puts some distance between the subject of spiritual gifts and human emotions. He said to the believers in Corinth, "Ye know that ye were Gentiles, carried away unto these dumb idols" (1 Cor. 12:2 KJV). He was referring to the mystery religions which were prevalent at the time.

Just outside the ancient city of Corinth is a hill, the Acro-Corinthus, the hill of Corinth. On top of that hill was the pagan temple of Aphrodite. All kinds of pagan ceremonies were conducted on this hill. Hundreds of religious prostitutes participated. The ceremonies were filled with extreme emotional frenzies. The worship was filled with ecstasies, incomprehensible babblings, sexual orgies, and perversions.

Paul was reminding the Corinthian Christians of what they used to be. People are complex composites of many experiences in life. It is inevitable that our background will affect or tint our Christian experience. Psychologists call this background "baggage." Our MTV culture today is emotion-oriented. Naturally, people saved in this kind of culture bring the characteristics of their culture into their Christian experience. Often, this becomes a frame of reference for what they believe their religious experience should be. Paul indicated, though, that after people come to Christ, there is a new basis of experience. The emotions do not dominate. The Holy Spirit must take control of our religious experiences.

First Corinthians 12:3 guides us with this statement: "Therefore I tell you that no one who is speaking by the Spirit of God says, 'Jesus be cursed,' and no one can say, 'Jesus is Lord,' except by the Holy Spirit." Paul said that the most spiritual thing a Christian can do is to acknowledge the lordship of Jesus Christ. It means to yield one's life to the control of the Holy Spirit from the depths of one's being so he or she can say, "Jesus Christ is Lord of my life." To yield to the total control of the Holy Spirit and to acknowledge him as Lord of every area of life positions us on the high hills of spiritual life.

Spiritual gifts are also salvation gifts. First Corinthians 12:4 says there are "different kinds of gifts." It is time for us to look at the word *gifts*. The Greek word is *charismata*. Have you ever thought someone you know is charismatic? Sometimes this word is used in a religious way—a charismatic church. Other times it's used in a secular way—this television sportscaster is very charismatic. The root of the Greek word *charismata* is the word *charis*. The name *Karen* comes directly from this word. Also, our word *grace* comes from this word. The charismata, or the gifts, are a result of God's work of grace. They are salvation gifts. Every born-again believer receives one or more gifts at salvation. These are your birthday gifts. The Holy Spirit is the Gift, but you also receive one or more spiritual gifts.

When little babies are born, gifts are brought to them. When you are born spiritually, God the Father, God the Son, and God the Holy Spirit give you birthday gifts—charismata. They are salvation gifts.

These salvation gifts are not natural talents. Some people are naturally gifted to play the piano. Others have a marvelous gift to paint or write. We say these individuals are "gifted." Charismata are not natural talents. God may take certain natural talents and elevate them to the level of spiritual gifts. He can endow them with God's grace and the involvement of God's Holy Spirit.

Some people have a natural singing gift. Their singing thrills and excites people. Then, the singer comes to Christ. God may take that natural gift of singing, elevate it to a spiritual gift, and anoint it with the presence and blessing of the Holy Spirit. When the person sings after this anointing, people are not only thrilled, they are also blessed.

First Corinthians 12:7 says, "Now to each one the manifestation of the Spirit is given for the common good." Spiritual gifts are also service gifts. They are given to bless other people. Spiritual gifts are not intended solely for your personal enjoyment. Spiritual gifts are intended to bless other people. I have heard my friend Warren Wiersbe say on many occasions that spiritual gifts are not toys to play with, but tools to build with. Often, there is a sense of fulfillment and enjoyment as spiritual gifts are exercised. But remember that spiritual gifts are primarily for employment, not enjoyment.

Spiritual gifts are equipment to be used in the Christian life, not necessarily evidence that one is unusually spiritual. To have a spiritual gift does not prove anything about your spiritual level. In fact, spiritual gifts do not provide evidence that a person is spiritual at all. Some people are surprised to discover that Paul did not regard the Corinthian believers as very spiritual. In fact, he said in 1 Corinthians 3:1, "Brothers, I could not address you as spiritual but as worldly—mere infants in Christ." This is an amazing statement in light of what he said in 1 Corinthians 1:7: "Therefore you do not lack any spiritual gift as you eagerly wait for our Lord Jesus Christ to be revealed." These believers were in a church fellowship where all the spiritual gifts were present, but Paul said to them in essence, "You are carnal, not spiritual, babes in Christ."

How Spiritual Gifts Are Designed

How do spiritual gifts function in the overall plan and purpose set before us in God's grand design? If they are intended for Christian service, how do spiritual gifts function? Function is very important. Design is essential to proper function. A car designed with wheels on its roof and an engine on the bottom might look modernistic, but it won't function very well. A building is constructed according to blueprint specifications. Exact dimensions, select materials, and particular design are all part of the building's function. First Corinthians 12:4–6 sets before us the design and function of spiritual gifts in a beautiful way: gifts, verse 4; administrations, verse 5; and operations, verse 6.

This process of spiritual gifts functioning according to design is a beautiful picture. In 1 Corinthians 12:13 we read, "For we were all baptized by one Spirit into one body." Then, verse 14 uses the illustration of the human body to explain spiritual gifts. The body has a foot, a hand, an eye, and an ear. The point is that each part of the body has a role. Each has a proper and vital function in the body.

Think of a hand. It functions according to design. A little baby grasps a pacifier. A boy reaches for an apple. A baseball pitcher uses his hand to throw a 95-mile-per-hour fast ball. The hand has a specific function. As a born-again believer, you have certain gifts which plug you into the body of Christ, the church, at a critical point. These are our spiritual abilities. Like a hand, they help the church function better.

For every gift there is a place of service in the church. In this sense, every Christian is a minister and has a ministry. Ephesians 4:12 makes it clear that our places of ministry are the realm where we serve others. Read 1 Peter 4:10: "Each one should use whatever gift he has received to serve others, faithfully administering God's grace in its various forms."

As members of a church fellowship, every Christian has a ministry. Their spiritual gifts are to be used in their places of ministry. Many churches miss this. Too many have the idea that there is to be a one-person ministry. I have served my entire ministry in Southern Baptist churches. The last figures I read indicated that the average Southern Baptist church has a Sunday school attendance of about 110. Why are most Southern Baptist churches this size? Sometimes it's location. In some places, an attendance of 110 is well above average, especially if there are just a few people in the surrounding area. Thank God for these faithful churches in sparsely populated areas.

Some churches are small, however, because they have the idea that the church is to be a one-person ministry. One person is to do it all. Just who is that person? You get it. The pastor. The church is the arena and the pastor is the performing superstar. Sometimes pastors have the same perception. Some pastors are so insecure that they are not able to allow other people to do ministry in the church, so they try to do it all. They preach, administer, visit, and everything else! If a pastor decides he's going to be a one-person show, he limits the potential of the church.

Many churches want their pastors to be one-person shows. They want him to do it all. He is to do all the visiting. He is to do all the ministering. Then, if the church doesn't grow, guess who gets the blame? That's right. The pastor.

For a church to mature spiritually, its members must have an understanding of spiritual gifts. A spiritually mature church understands that no one person can do everything that needs to be done in the ministry. I am fortunate enough to be pastor of a people who are unusually mature spiritually. They understand that no one person (or even group of people) can do everything that needs to be done in our church. They are willing to accept the ministry of others. Too few are doing too much in the average church. It's like a football game. Someone has described a football game as twenty-two players in need of rest being watched by fifty thousand people in need of exercise!

In the early years of my ministry, I served rural churches. These were joyful, happy, blessed days. But I had to do almost everything. I did all the visiting. If the song leader didn't show up, I led the singing. This isn't the best way to do it. Our church has a church staff. Each member of the staff is an extension of the pastor. We have youth directors, music directors, hospital pastors, and a number of other ministers with various specialties. In addition to this, we have tremendous involvement by our laypeople. Our church could not function apart from faithful laypeople who serve by using the spiritual gifts which God has given them.

As a Christian, you have one or more spiritual gifts. You have a ministry, a place where you can serve and exercise those gifts. Perhaps it is in Sunday school. Possibly it's visiting others. Maybe it's working in prisons. Or you may use your gift in the music ministry. Whatever it is, just as certainly as God has given you a spiritual capacity, he has also given you a spiritual ministry.

So, you may ask, what if a ministry is not getting done in a church? One of two reasons most likely explains it. It may be that the church is attempting a ministry which God does not intend for it. I believe that God places into the fellowship of every church enough Christians with the proper spiritual gifts to do everything God wants for that church. Keep in mind, however, that God does not produce churches in "cookie-cutter" fashion any more than he clones Christians. Although there are certain basics which are to be true of every church (Bible preaching, prayer, evangelism, etc.), each church has its own special ministry.

Secondly, believers in the church may be neglecting their spiritual gifts. Are you fulfilling the ministry God has given you? Are you using the gifts God has bestowed on you? One of the most encouraging words Paul ever gave was to a Christian believer named Tychicus. In Colossians 4:7 Paul said to him, "Tychicus will tell you all the news about me. He is a dear brother, a faithful minister and fellow servant in the Lord."

Follow the pattern laid out in these verses. There are spiritual capacities— these are our gifts. There are spiritual ministries—these are the places of service where the gifts are to be used. Then, note the word *operations*. Literally, the word here is *energies*. What is the source for these energies? The Holy Spirit enables spiritual gifts to function in places of ministry.

A Christian can seek to serve the Lord and use spiritual gifts in one of two ways. One way is by working in the energy of the flesh. Many Christians try to serve the Lord in this way. When ministry is driven by human energy, self is glorified and problems develop. The result is spiritual death. On the other hand, ministry can be performed and gifts can be exercised in the power of the Holy Spirit. In the previous chapter "Who Bakes the Bread?" the point was made that all the necessary ingredients to serve the Lord effectively are provided by the "supply of the Spirit" (see Phil. 1:19 KJV).

The typical modern home has many appliances. The coffeemaker brews the morning coffee. The toaster browns our bread just right. A can opener allows us to eat fruit cocktail for lunch. Each of these appliances has a different capacity and a different function. But they are all plugged into the same power source. Likewise, in the spiritual realm, whatever the gifts are and wherever they function, the power source is the same. The Holy Spirit provides the necessary power. Household appliances require electricity. Likewise, serving the Lord requires power from the Holy Spirit.

Gifts—ministries—energies! This reminds me of firing a cannon. Your gift is the cannonball. Your ministry is the place of service. The power of the Holy Spirit is the gunpowder. When the cannonball is in the proper cannon and the gunpowder goes off—BOOM! There is a dynamic explosion. Likewise, when spiritual gifts are exercised in the power of the Holy Spirit, there will be a spiritual explosion of blessing and effectiveness in a local church.

How Spiritual Gifts Are Distributed

Paul said these gifts are distributed individually: "Now to each one the manifestation of the Spirit is given for the common good" (1 Cor. 12:7). This means that every believer is given gifts individually. Each believer is given one or more. I don't know how such a thought affects you, but it ought to do wonders for your self-esteem. Here's a cure for an inferiority complex. God has given you spiritual gifts because you are important to him. You have God-given capacities. God does not waste his gifts on unimportant people. You are special to him!

People often ask how to discover their gifts. As I have already indicated, there are a number of spiritual gift profiles available which help Christians understand what their spiritual gifts may be. But I would not be too worried about this. As I have studied the Bible, I have concluded that there is not much said about discovering our spiritual gifts. There is no definite pattern given. You will discover your gifts. Don't worry too much about it.

I do believe, however, that 1 Corinthians 12:1–2 gives some indication about how a person might discover his or her spiritual gifts. Romans 12 lists several spiritual gifts. It is interesting that the opening two verses begin, "Now about spiritual gifts, brothers, I do not want you to be ignorant. You know that when you were pagans, somehow or other you were influenced and led astray to mute idols" (1 Cor. 12:1–2). This is fascinating to me. As you present yourself to the Lord (yield your life to the control of the Holy Spirit), the Lord will lead you in the direction of your spiritual gifts. The Holy Spirit will move in your life and indicate to you what your spiritual gifts and capacities are.

These questions may help us find out what God has given us to do for his glory and for the good of others: What do you enjoy? Do you feel comfortable with what you are trying to do for the Lord? Some Christians seem to do work in the church with a great deal of difficulty. They seem stressed. They are not at ease. They are uncomfortable. Their ministries seem to be burdensome. On the other hand, some people serve in the church in a relaxed, joyful mood. They seem to be greatly fulfilled. Does the Holy Spirit want you to enjoy doing what he wants you to do? I think so!

As I mentioned earlier in the chapter, as a young man I could hardly stand before people and speak. I must admit that I still stand before people with fear and trembling. I agree with another preacher who said that every time he stands to preach, he feels like "a lamb led to the slaughter!" But I believe God has called me to preach and he has given me the necessary gifts to fulfill my ministry. Now, I must say to you that preaching and teaching the Word of God is the most enjoyable thing I do. There is a deep sense of joy and fulfillment. Although I often feel inadequate, I know deep in my heart that I am doing exactly what God wants me to do.

The Holy Spirit of God loved us enough to dwell in us. The Lord Jesus loved us enough to die on the cross for us. The heavenly Father loved us enough to send his Son to die on the cross and to send the Holy Spirit. Don't you think they want you to have joy and fulfillment in your life? Doesn't it make sense that the Holy Spirit of God would give you a gift, then make you comfortable in it, and then give you a sense of joy in completing your ministry?

Here's another helpful question to ask about your gifts: Do other people encourage you in your chosen ministry? How do others respond? Proverbs 18:16 says, "A gift opens the way for the giver and ushers him into the presence of the great." This is a constant problem in the music ministry of many churches. All through my ministry I have seen people who felt they had the gift to sing. But the problem was that no one seemed to have the gift to listen to them! There's nothing sadder or more frustrating than a person who wants to sing but can't. Too many churches have Bawl-Bearing Quartets. They bawl and everybody bears it!

Do others encourage you in your gift and ministry? George Truett was one of America's great pastors. For more than forty years he served as pastor of the First Baptist Church of Dallas, Texas. As a young man, he prepared himself to be a lawyer. People around his church began to say, "George, don't you think maybe you ought to preach?" He said, "No, I'm preparing to be a lawyer." Finally, the church just announced to him, "George, God has called you to preach. We're going to set you aside for the ministry." This got his attention, and he spent several days in prayer. God confirmed in his heart what the people were trying to tell him.

Truett surrendered to the gospel ministry and served more than forty years as pastor of this great church. Sometimes, what other people encourage you to do is an indication of the Holy Spirit's purpose and plan for your life.

Here's another question you might ask yourself: What has the Holy Spirit said down deep in your heart? What impression has the Holy Spirit given you? What desire has the Holy Spirit given you? But be sure the Holy Spirit is leading you.

I heard about a boy plowing in the field one day. He stopped for a rest, wiped the perspiration from his brow, and looked up into the sky. The clouds had formed two letters—PC. "That's it," he exclaimed. "Preach Christ." He went to several churches and tried to speak. He just couldn't do it. Finally, an old deacon set him down and said, "Son, what makes you think you've been called to preach"? He said, "I saw it written in the clouds—PC—*preach Christ.*" The deacon said, "Son, I think you missed it. I believe it meant *plow corn.*" Be sure it's the Holy Spirit who has spoken to your heart.

Remember Mrs. Porter in Jamaica and her statement, "It's not the gift, but the giver?" The Holy Spirit is the one who gives the gifts. First Corinthians 12:11 says, "All these are the work of one and the same Spirit, and he gives them to each one, just as he determines." Then verse 18 says, "But in fact God has arranged the parts in the body, every one of them, just as he wanted them to be." We do not decide which gifts we want and then take them. The Holy Spirit sovereignly bestows these gifts. This is why there is no room for any person to brag about anything he or she does in the Lord's work. First Corinthians 4:7 says, "For who makes you different from anyone else? What do you have that you did not receive? And if you did receive it, why do you boast as though you did not?" If you can sing and be a blessing to people, there's no need to be prideful or arrogant about it. God gave you the gift to sing. If you can teach with effectiveness and people are blessed by your teaching, there's no reason to get puffed up about it. God gave you the ability to teach.

An organist was playing one of those old organs which required bellows to supply the air. A young boy pushed the bellows as the organist performed. After the first hymn was finished, the little fellow working the bellows looked up at the player and said, "We did a good job on that one, didn't we?" The organist said, "What did *you* have to do with it?" On the next hymn, the organ player put her hands to the keys, but nothing happened. In desperation she looked over at the young boy. The young boy said, "Shall it be *we*?"

To attempt to use spiritual gifts in spiritual ministries without the power of the Holy Spirit is like trying to play an organ without any power. Although you are certainly part of the process, you don't supply the power.

I must go back to Mrs. Porter's statement again: "It's not the gift, but the giver." The Holy Spirit gives the magnificent gifts. How wonderful this is. The Gift, the Holy Spirit, is also the Giver of the gifts. God saves us and gives us himself in the person of the Holy Spirit. Then he gives us one or more spiritual capacities. In addition to that, he gives us a place of ministry to use our gifts. He then supplies the power of the Holy Spirit to make sure we use these gifts effectively in the ministry. Then he rewards us for using the gift he has given us with the power of the Holy Spirit he has provided! What a deal!

The Adventure of Gift Discovery

1. Accept what the Bible says about spiritual gifts. The Holy Spirit has given each believer one or more gifts.

2. Be thankful that God has provided a church ministry. In that church's ministry, God has given you a place to serve.

3. What kinds of spiritual activities do you enjoy? Will the Holy Spirit ask you to do something that is a constant frustration and misery to you?

4. What activities or areas of service do we perform that people seem to enjoy and request us to do?

5. Have you thanked the Holy Spirit today for being not only your Friend, but your giving Friend?

CHAPTER 9

LOOK WHO'S TALKING!

Have you ever noticed how many words we hear or speak each day? Our television sets, our radios, and our telephones all produce constant communication. I often find myself seeking peace and quiet, a place to get away from all the noise. It's hard!

Throughout history, there have been skilled communicators. Some speakers have been able to motivate entire nations to fight wars or to support difficult causes. Others can influence young people to dodge the draft or to stay in school.

Adolph Hitler understood this. Few speakers have equaled his power and persuasiveness. This German leader was a volcano, spewing speeches as deadly as white-hot lava. Through his ability to speak the language, he was able to capture the minds and hearts of his people and to lead them in some of history's worst chapters.

At the 1935 Olympic Games in Berlin, Germany, Hitler was at his fiendish best. He took the podium and ranted and raved into the microphone. Sixty thousand Germans leaped to their feet, charmed by a madman bent on exterminating a large part of their population. The Germans enthusiastically supported their leader, although he was responsible for the atrocities of the Holocaust.

It was his speaking gift which enabled Hitler to manipulate thousands. The people listened to him and followed him blindly. They were unaware of his power over them. Subsequent events indicate that demonic forces were speaking through him. Today we must pay attention to our communicators and their communications. We must realize how powerful gifted communicators can be. We must always remember to examine who's talking!

Another gifted speaker, Billy Graham, has spoken to more people than any other communicator in the history of the world through the use of modern technology. His longest crusade was held in Manhattan in 1957. After the first six weeks, Graham was out of sermons and was having to prepare a new one each day. He recounted that he would sit on the platform in the evenings and pray like this: "Oh, God, you have to do it. I can't do it. I just can't do it." When he would stand up, he explained, "All of a sudden the words would begin to come—God giving strength and spiritual power in a way that could not be explained in human terms." At the final session at Yankee Stadium, one hundred thousand people jammed the stadium. Another twenty thousand were on the outside trying to get in. When Graham spoke the simple terms of the gospel, thousands came forward to receive Christ. [1]

Obviously someone else was speaking through Billy Graham. The "spirit" speaking through Graham was quite different from the one speaking through Hitler. As we continue our adventure in Spirit living, it is vital to examine who's talking.

"The tongue has the power of life and death" (Prov. 18:21). This verse is vividly illustrated in the contrast between the speaking of Hitler and that of Graham. What a remarkable gift is the ability to speak. How very devastating is the gift when it is Satan-driven. How very wonderful and blessed is the gift when it is Spirit-directed.

Every Christian has one or more spiritual gifts. The Holy Spirit gives these gifts to individual believers according to his own sovereign will and purpose. These spiritual gifts are not given primarily for our own enjoyment or pleasure but to make us a blessing to other people. Through the power of the Holy Spirit, we are enabled to be effective as we minister in churches, on our jobs, and in our schools.

Spiritual gifts are listed in four chapters in the Bible: Romans 12; 1 Corinthians 12; Ephesians 4; and 1 Peter 4. None of the lists is the same. Some spiritual gifts are not on any lists. Celibacy is mentioned in 1 Corinthians 7:7 as a spiritual gift. Martyrdom seems to be a spiritual gift in 1 Corinthians 13:3. I don't know anyone who is seeking this gift!

Why are these lists different? They are not intended to be exhaustive but suggestive. The body of Christ, the church, is constantly growing and changing. In every age and in every stage, the Holy Spirit gives the necessary gifts so that Christians may use them to bring glory to God and be a blessing to people.

Also notice that each of the lists of spiritual gifts gets smaller. In the King James Version, 1 Corinthians 12 mentions nine in one place and eight in the other. Romans 12 mentions seven. Ephesians 4 gives four of the gifts. First Peter 4 seems to summarize these various gifts into categories. As we survey the different lists of gifts, we see that they fit into certain categories. There are speaking gifts, serving gifts, and sign gifts.

Our purpose in this chapter is to consider the speaking gifts. Speaking gifts are Spirit-given abilities to speak for the Lord—to say a helpful, healing word for the Lord Jesus.

I am not thinking primarily about the matter of witnessing as I discuss the speaking gifts in this chapter. Every believer is to be a witness for the Lord. I have found Matthew 10:20 especially helpful in the matter of witnessing: "For it will not be you speaking, but the Spirit of your Father speaking through you." The Holy Spirit speaking in us provides the boldness, the courage, and the ability to be a witness for the Lord. If you want to be a witness, you can be a witness. Ask the Lord to help you. He can use your voice, your words, your speech to tell others about the Lord Jesus.

I do believe there are some believers who have an unusual gift of evangelism. Ephesians 4 indicates there are some who are uniquely called to serve as evangelists (see Eph. 4:11). God has given to the church gifted people who serve as evangelists. They preach in great citywide crusades. They also have itinerant ministries which take them from church to church.

Second Timothy 4:5 says, "Do the work of an evangelist, discharge all the duties of your ministry." An evangelist is one who tells the evangel, which is the good news. All of us as believers are evangelists in the sense that the Holy Spirit will enable us to tell others about Jesus and to share the good news (the gospel) with the unsaved.

First Peter 4:10 gives an interesting presentation of the subject of spiritual gifts: "Each one should use whatever gift he has received to serve others, faithfully administering God's grace in its various forms." This verse indicates we are to use spiritual gifts to be blessings to other people, "as good stewards of the manifold grace of God" (NKJV). Then it says, "If anyone speaks, he should do it as one speaking the very words of God" (v. 11). As the believer is controlled by the Holy Spirit, he allows the Spirit to work through him to bless others. Such speech is like God's dialogue with someone. It is as if God is speaking through believers. The speaking gifts are those gifts which allow God to speak in and through believers.

Sometimes I watch the show *Inside Edition* in the evening. I love to listen to the newscasters pronounce and enunciate their words. They speak so clearly with little trace of any regional accent. Often, as the newscaster ends one story and sets up the next one, she will say, "But first . . . " and start telling her audience about something else. With this in mind, we will consider several of the speaking gifts in detail, "but first" let me share how the Holy Spirit's power can be utilized in our daily speech.

You may recall 2 Timothy 1:7: "For God did not give us a spirit of timidity, but a spirit of power, of love and of self-discipline." Perhaps you have a problem in a relationship. You are trying to deal with a specific matter in that relationship and you do not know whether to say anything about it. As you yield yourself to the control of the Holy Spirit, yield your lips and your speech to the Holy Spirit as well. Most of us do not have a problem saying too little. We say too much! I would love to erase some of the words I have spoken.

Yield your speech to the Holy Spirit every day. Say to him, "Holy Spirit, if you don't want me to say anything about this particular matter, then help me keep my mouth shut. I'm turning my speech over to you." Most married partners would do well to pray that prayer every day! We should also pray, "Holy Spirit, if you want me to say something, help my speech to be effective, courageous, and loving. Give me a sound mind so I might have the wisdom to say what needs to be said." This surrender to the indwelling Holy Spirit would enhance our communication in important relationships.

Our speech must be controlled by the Holy Spirit. First Peter 4:11 might be loosely translated: "So that our very words would be like God speaking." If you speak the very words of God, you aren't as likely to hurt people with your words. Your words will have an uplifting effect.

Now, let's shine our spotlight of examination on some of the speaking gifts. At least two gifts in the speaking category are foundational in nature. First Corinthians 12:8 talks about "the message of wisdom" and "the message of knowledge." They are also "feeder" gifts. They feed the specific gifts of speaking for the Lord.

Consider for a moment the gift of the word of knowledge. What is knowledge? Knowledge is the acquisition of information. Think of how much information we store on computers. The Holy Spirit is the heavenly computer programmer, giving certain people the abilities to gain and to arrange spiritual information.

This is clearly illustrated in the work of the apostles. The Spirit of God inspired several apostles to write the books of the Bible. For example, Simon Peter was used of the Spirit to compose 1 and 2 Peter. By trade he was a fisherman. The religious establishment of the day considered him an unlettered and ignorant man. He had not been officially trained in academic schools. He was not ignorant, of course. But he was a fisherman—not a scholar. Yet he was inspired by the Holy Spirit.

This truth is exemplified in his second letter, chapter 3, where he gave an astounding account about the future destruction of the world. The world is on fire and the elements of the universe are melting. Scientists today have examined the words of Peter and found them accurate regarding modern nuclear fission. Where did a fisherman get knowledge that could be understood in the twentieth century and be declared accurate by scientists? It did not come out of Simon Peter's own knowledge. The Spirit of God gave him a word of knowledge. The Holy Spirit programmed Simon Peter's mental computer. The Holy Spirit also does this today by giving words of knowledge to people.

The second foundational gift is the word of wisdom. What is the difference between wisdom and knowledge? Knowledge is the acquisition of information, while wisdom is the application of this information. Once again, the parallel with computers is interesting. Knowledge is acquiring data; wisdom is manipulating that data through programs (which are applications). It is possible to know many facts without knowing how to apply them with wisdom. The Holy Spirit enables people to apply God's truth in a practical way to the circumstances and situations of life.

The word-of-knowledge gift can be seen in several New Testament settings. Stephen, one of the original deacons, was giving his testimony for the Lord. What he said was tremendously effective. Acts 6:10 says, "But they could not stand up against his wisdom or the Spirit by whom he spoke." God empowered Stephen with that kind of wisdom. The Lord Jesus promises just such wisdom: "For I will give you words and wisdom that none of your adversaries will be able to resist or contradict" (Luke 21:15).

God also promises supernatural wisdom to his people today. James 1:5 promises, "If any of you lacks wisdom, he should ask God, who gives generously to all without finding fault, and it will be given to him." All believers have access to the knowledge of God as given in Scriptures and the wisdom of God to apply this knowledge to the daily circumstances of life.

In 1997, America Online had access problems. The volume of their business increased so rapidly that they were unable to accommodate their customers. The difficulty of access to their on-line service became so great that many people left the service out of frustration. Having access is critical. Believers have heavenly E-mail capability! Just send your request to Holy Spirit @heaven.com.

Another New Testament illustration helps us see the importance of the word of wisdom. The early church was faced with a major problem. The whole question of salvation was at risk. Some were saying Gentiles had to become Jews before coming to Christ. Others correctly said that salvation was not becoming a Jew but receiving Jesus Christ by personal faith. In Acts 15, the church gathered to consider this problem. James stood and spoke a word of wisdom. Acts 15:22 indicates the decision pleased the church. This shows that when God gives a word of wisdom, there is an amazing understanding on the part of the people that they are hearing the wisdom of God.

The word of knowledge and the word of wisdom can be illustrated like this. A chemist finds a combination of chemicals which, compounded together, provide a cure for insomnia. This combination compares to the word of knowledge. Then, a doctor prescribes the medicine for a patient who is having difficulty sleeping. The doctor's prescribing skill compares to the word of wisdom. These two gifts serve as foundations so those believers who are given the gifts to speak a word for the Lord may do so with knowledge and wisdom.

Several of the spiritual gifts fit into the category of speaking gifts. Romans 12 mentions three speaking gifts. Verse 6 says, "If a man's gift is prophesying, let him use it in proportion to his faith." Verse 7 says, "If it is serving, let him serve; if it is teaching, let him teach." Then verse 8 says, "If it is encouraging, let him encourage." All three of these spiritual gifts are given by the Holy Spirit to believers in the church. They provide preaching, teaching, and encouraging so that the body of Christ is encouraged, edified, and built up.

Let's examine these three speaking gifts.

Preaching

Prophecy. The modern equivalent of prophecy is preaching. That's what I do. I normally preach standing behind a pulpit.

The word *prophecy* carries an element of prediction. This was especially true in the Old Testament. These preachers were prophets. They predicted the future. One of the remarkable proofs for the inspiration and accuracy of the Bible is fulfilled prophecy. Think of the miraculous fulfillment of the Old Testament prophecies about the first coming of Christ. It has been estimated that 330 individual prophecies foretell his coming. All were fulfilled in the person of Jesus Christ. The mathematical probabilities of this taking place are astronomical. In one sense, the Old Testament prophet was a foreteller. But he was also a *forthteller*. He also spoke a powerful, pertinent word to the people of his day.

In the New Testament, there is the role of the prophet. Ephesians 4 discusses some of the gifted people whom the resurrected, ascended Lord gave to the church. What were these gifts? Verse 11 explains: "It was he who gave some to be apostles, some to be prophets, some to be evangelists, and some to be pastors and teachers."

Clearly defined requirements are given for the role of an apostle. An apostle had to be an eyewitness of the resurrection of Jesus (see Acts 1:22). In this sense, no office of apostle exists today.

But the word has a larger meaning. The word *apostle* literally means "to send forth." In this larger meaning, an apostle is one who blazes new trails for the Lord. He is sent forth on a mission.

Look at the next gift. He gave "some to be prophets." The role of prophet is very specific. In New Testament times, there was no Bible like we use today. They had only the Old Testament. The New Testament books were in the process of being written. While these were being composed and completed, there were gifted men who were able to speak the word of God. Evidently, they spoke the word immediately from God.

When I preach, I am not speaking the word of God directly from heaven. Rather, I am speaking the word of God as I expound it from the Bible. How do the people who listen to me determine whether what I say is correct? They must be like the Bereans of Acts 17:11: "Now the Bereans were of more noble character than the Thessalonians, for they received the message with great eagerness and examined the Scriptures every day to see if what Paul said was true." Check everything a preacher says by the Word of God to see if his words are consistent with Scripture.

The New Testament Christians didn't have a New Testament like we do, so there were Spirit-gifted people who were prophets. Ephesians 2:20 indicates that the church was "built on the foundation of the apostles and prophets, with Christ Jesus himself as the chief cornerstone." Foundations are laid only one time. The foundation of the church was laid on the Lord Jesus Christ. When this foundational work, completed by the apostles and prophets, was over, there were no more apostles and prophets in the New Testament sense. So, the role of prophet has passed away.

Today God gives certain people the gift of preaching. Preaching is the Spirit-given ability to proclaim the word of God. This gift may be exercised in public, such as in the worship services of your local church. Preachers may exercise this gift in areawide crusades. Others use the gift of preaching on radio and television, and even on the Internet.

The church where I preach has a pulpit standing at the focal point of the building. Why? There is an architectural and a biblical reason for this design. The preaching of the word of God is to be central to all that goes on in the church building. Everything is built around the public preaching of God's word.

I am thankful for music. Music is a blessing. Spirit-directed and Spirit-inspired music can prepare the hearts of preacher and people for the preaching of the word. But the music is not the main business. Preaching the word is. Thank God for the testimonies of the people. Yet testimonies are not the main thing. The preaching of the word of God is.

God calls people to preach, and I know God called me to preach. Under no circumstances would I dare to stand before others and speak for God unless I knew beyond a doubt that he had called me to do so.

God calls preachers. The terminology may seem old-fashioned, but I still believe in a God-called ministry. We think about Billy Graham and thank God for calling him to preach. But any pastor in the smallest rural church, if he has been called of God, is just as much a preacher as the most notable preacher on earth.

About every five or ten years I hear the same refrain: "The day of preaching is over. Preaching is dead." I don't believe it. There may be some dead preaching, but preaching is not dead! Perhaps you heard of the preacher who used a lot of notes. One day as he was preaching, a gust of wind blew through the window and scattered his notes out the other window. A cow came along, ate the preacher's notes, and dried up! There may be some dry, dead preaching out there, but the preaching of the word of God should not be a dry experience.

It's exciting to be in a preaching service where a person who has been called of God preaches under the power of the Holy Spirit. Amazing things happen. Anything can happen when a man of God stands before the people of God and speaks the word of God in the power of the Spirit of God!

To whom do preachers preach? First Corinthians 14:22, 24 tells us that "prophecy . . . is for believers, not for unbelievers . . . but if an unbeliever or someone who does not understand comes in while everybody is prophesying, he will be convinced by all that he is a sinner and will be judged by all." The Holy Spirit, using a preacher as his instrument, can make Bible truth relevant to people of any culture or background.

What happens when preachers preach? First Corinthians 14:3 is a remarkably complete statement of what takes place: "But everyone who prophesies speaks to men for their strengthening, encouragement and comfort." Notice these three words—edification, exhortation, and comfort. When preachers preach, people are built up, cheered up, and strengthened! I am amazed at what God does through the preaching of the Bible. Often a preacher says something in a message that meets a need in the life of a person. It's astounding and astonishing. It's supernatural! Preachers constantly have people tell them that something they said helped meet a need in their lives.

There is a great deal of discussion these days about preaching to "felt needs." Some say that Bible exposition is no longer able to speak to the needs of people. They say it's outdated. Aside from the fact that this reveals an alarming lack of confidence in the relevancy of the Bible, it just isn't so. I have been preaching more than forty years. I stand in awe at the power of the preaching of the word of God. People of all ages, races, and backgrounds are encouraged, challenged, and comforted when the spiritual gift of preaching is used.

First Corinthians 14 also indicates that the preaching of the word of God is effective in reaching the non-Christian. Verse 24 says, "But if an unbeliever or someone who does not understand comes in while everybody is prophesying, he will be convinced by all that he is a sinner and will be judged by all." What happens when preachers preach? Lost people are convicted of their condition and their desperate need for Jesus Christ. Many people have left rejoicing after a service where Bible preaching has occurred. They go away saying, "I met God here today."

The spiritual gift of preaching may also be used in more private ways. As those so gifted go about daily activities, they may speak a word for God. Some may not be as gifted in the public forum as others. They may be more gifted in sharing the word of God with those whom they meet on a daily basis.

Whether publicly or privately, the gift of Spirit-empowered preaching is wonderful!

Teaching

The second speaking gift to consider is teaching. Romans 12:7 says, "If it is teaching, let him teach." I thank God for the teaching gift. The distinction between preaching and teaching is not clear-cut. Someone said, "The difference between teaching and preaching is that you 'holler' louder when you're preaching!" I have done my share of shouting. Perhaps this distinction will be helpful. Preaching is the Spirit-given ability to proclaim the word of God. Teaching is the Spirit-given ability to explain God's word. There is certainly an element of teaching in all good preaching. Most effective teachers I know also do a little preaching along the way!

Jesus was called "the Teacher." "He came to Jesus at night and said, 'Rabbi, we know you are a teacher who has come from God'" (John 3:2). To be like Jesus, the church is to have a teaching ministry. In the commands the Lord Jesus gave to his church, he said, "Therefore go and make disciples of all nations, baptizing them in the name of the Father and of the Son and of the Holy Spirit, and teaching them to obey everything I have commanded you" (Matt. 28:19–20). When people are won to the Lord, the job is only partially completed. They are to be baptized into the fellowship of the local church. Then they are to be taught.

A church needs many teachers. Adults, teenagers, and children need people who are willing to teach them about the Lord.

I read a book once which said that anybody can teach Sunday school. I do not believe this is true. There is a definite *spiritual* gift of teaching. The natural ability to teach is not this gift of teaching. A certified teacher may not be spiritually equipped to teach the word of God. Through the years, I have known many people trained in the secular field of teaching who also seemed gifted of God to teach the Bible. But I also have known some who had the ability to teach academics but not the Scriptures. Some people accumulate a great deal of Bible information and knowledge. They are able skillfully to arrange the facts of the Bible. They are Bible-whizzes! But there is something missing in their teaching. No blessing. No substance.

This is much like those nondairy whipped toppings. It tastes good and it looks good, but it has little substance. The Holy Spirit must give the gift of teaching the word of God. Then the blessings come out and the fruit blooms.

Thank God for wonderful, Spirit-filled teachers. What blessings these gifted individuals are. They explain the word of God in a powerful way to those who listen and hear.

Some people have the gift to teach, but they don't use it. Do you think you might have this gift? There are two characteristics which might indicate your teaching potential. A keen interest in personal study of the Bible might mean God wants to give you the gift of teaching. Also, the ability to communicate the Bible in a practical and helpful way may be another indication. Pray about it and listen to what others say about the things which you share with them.

One of the most effective teachers I ever knew was a man named Ed Shellhorse. He was limited in his formal education. He worked all his life in a tire factory. Ed and I lived across the street from one another, just behind the church I served as pastor. Often on Sundays we would walk home together after the services. He was always so positive and complimentary of my messages. Often he would say, "Pastor, I was thinking about the verse you used today. I had never noticed before . . . " Then Ed would give an explanation and interpretation of the verse that had never occurred to me. My congregation probably wondered why I didn't talk to Ed before I preached the message instead of afterward! Ed's teaching in our Sunday school was a constant source of encouragement and blessing to his class members. Thank God for the great host of Bible teachers in our churches.

Let me state a word of caution here. James 3:1 says, "Not many of you should presume to be teachers, my brothers, because you know that we who teach will be judged more strictly." To be a teacher is a great responsibility. Those of us who preach and teach the written and spoken word are held to a higher degree of accountability. Matthew 12:36 says, "But I tell you that men will have to give account on the day of judgment for every careless word they have spoken." While this verse may apply to speech in general, it certainly has application to those of us who use words in public preaching or teaching.

Encouraging

One more speaking gift is mentioned in Romans 12:8: "If it is encouraging, let him encourage." The word here is the same word used of the Holy Spirit in John 14:16. To encourage is to come alongside to help. The Holy Spirit is the Comforter and Friend. He is our Encourager. Encouraging is the Spirit-given ability of speaking a word to counsel or to encourage others. It is the ability to speak a word that lifts another heart. It's speaking the healing word. As result of the gift of encouraging, people are helped.

This gift can be exercised in many ways. New Christians need to be encouraged and helped. The sick should be comforted. People grappling with perplexing problems and choices need a word of counsel. Those who are away from the Lord's fellowship who need to be brought back can be urged on by the encouraging word. A college student who is wandering away through a swamp of confusing ideas can be called back by the word of encouragement. Confused people who are seeking guidance can receive it from an encourager who is inspired by the Holy Spirit.

Sometimes the gift of encouragement is used publicly. At one time, churches had public exhorters. These gifted people, in just two or three minutes, would speak words to encourage the entire congregation. (Some seem to have the gift of discouragement. In just a few words they can put everybody in the depths of despair!) These public encouragers were like fire pokers. Do you know what that is? You younger readers probably don't! A fire poker is used to stir up the fire and make it burn better. Exhorters are like this today as well.

Public exhorting or "fire-poking" is illustrated through preaching. In another sense, it is public counseling. Exhorting, encouraging, and counseling are triplet children from the same parents. Much of my preaching falls into the category of preventive counseling. To heed the truths of God preached in the pastor's sermon is to avoid many problems. I try to explain what the Bible says and to apply its truths to our daily problems. Many tragedies would be prevented if this counsel by Spirit-filled preachers were heeded.

Preaching addresses a group, such as a congregation. But there is also a more personal kind of encouragement. In every church there are people who have been given the ability to soothe aching hearts and to refresh tired souls. The local church needs these gifted individuals.

The church also benefits from established levels of encouraging or counseling. Most Sunday school classes have group leaders. (I think a better term is *care leaders*.) These individuals listen to people, hear their problems, and come to their side to help them. There are so many hurting people in our churches. What better place to get help and who better to give it than care leaders in our Sunday school classes? Christians are missing out on an important ministry if they are not involved in a small group in the church where someone can exercise his or her ministry of encouragement.

Some churches are large enough to have one or more staff members. Churches often provide some kind of counseling ministry. Biblically done, this is a ministry of encouragement. There are also people in the professional fields of counseling who are gifted of God to help people untangle the problems of their lives. I have two daughters. When they were small, their long hair used to get tangled after a day of play. My wife would take a brush and slowly smooth out the matted hair. The girls cried at first, but once the tangles began to come out, they felt much better. Christian psychologists and psychiatrists can serve as these "spiritual brushes" to people. These gifted people have such an opportunity to help people under the authority of Scripture. No person should attempt the role of psychologist or psychiatrist without being a Christian committed to the authority of Scripture.

There is also the ministry of encouraging people along the way. Some grumps never have an encouraging word. They are critical and ornery. A hundred things can go right around the church, but if one thing goes wrong, they gripe about it.

But don't you love those people who always have a positive word? They are always excited about what God is doing. They have a happy, cheerful, uplifting word for everyone. Bud Whittaker does this. For many years Bud has been a faithful deacon and head of the Sunday service counselors who deal with people who come forward at First Baptist Church, Jacksonville. Hardly a week passes without this wonderful Christian speaking a special word of encouragement to me. People like this have the spiritual gift of encouragement. If God has given you this gift, let me encourage you to use it often. You will be a blessing!

If God has given you the gift of preaching—preach! If God has given you the gift of teaching—teach! If God has given you the gift of encouraging—encourage!

One person in the Bible came to be known as the son of encouragement. His name was Barnabas. "Joseph, a Levite from Cyprus, whom the apostles called Barnabas (which means Son of Encouragement)" (Acts 4:36). Everytime he appears on the pages of the New Testament, he is encouraging someone.

When Paul came to Christ, the church didn't trust him. Barnabas took Paul under his wing and introduced him to the members of the church. "When he [Saul] came to Jerusalem, he tried to join the disciples, but they were all afraid of him, not believing that he really was a disciple. But Barnabas took him and brought him to the apostles. He told them how Saul on his journey had seen the Lord and that the Lord had spoken to him, and how in Damascus he had preached fearlessly in the name of Jesus" (Acts 9:26–27). What an encouragement Barnabas was to this young Christian with such a bright future.

Barnabas then went to Antioch, where large numbers of people were being saved. "News of this reached the ears of the church at Jerusalem, and they sent Barnabas to Antioch. When he arrived and saw the evidence of the grace of God, he was glad and encouraged them all to remain true to the Lord with all their hearts. He was a good man, full of the Holy Spirit and faith, and a great number of people were brought to the Lord" (Acts 11:22–24).

Barnabas was spiritually alert to what God was doing. He saw the grace of God at work. He encouraged the entire church. And what an example he set for us.

There was also a man named John Mark. John, like us, made some mistakes. He turned back on one of Paul's missionary journeys. Paul was ready to give up on him. But Barnabas saw potential in this young man. Barnabas determined to take Mark with him: "They had such a sharp disagreement that they parted company. Barnabas took Mark and sailed for Cyprus" (Acts 15:39).

Barnabas was able to encourage a faltering young man. His encouragement was not in vain. John Mark made it! Later on, Paul said, "Take Mark, and bring him with thee: for he is profitable to me for the ministry" (2 Tim. 4:10 KJV). How many of us have benefited from such encouragers?

What if Barnabas had not been willing to be an encouragement to a John Mark? But he did, and a young man who had a shaky start had a strong conclusion. I would like to be a Barnabas, wouldn't you?

Let's look again at 1 Peter 4:11: "speaking the very words of God." As we exercise the Spirit-given speaking gifts, believers will be blessed and encouraged. Unsaved people will be brought to the Lord Jesus Christ. Proverbs 18:21 is indeed true: "The tongue has the power of life and death, and those who love it will eat its fruit." Let's just be sure that every time we speak, we are speaking as the Holy Spirit would have us to speak. Look who's talking!

Talking Points

People who speak publicly often organize several "talking points." These are points which guide them in what they say. How about a few "talking points" for believers?

1. It's better not to say anything than just to say something.

2. Preaching is not dead. Dead preaching is not preaching.

3. When do teachers teach? When they teach with the gift of teaching, the Holy Spirit provides.

4. More people are teachers in the church than are teaching in the church.

5. Words can encourage or words can discourage. Are you an encourager or a discourager?

6. If God has given you the ability to speak, then what are you waiting for? Let it out!

CHAPTER 10

IT'S SUPPER TIME. WHERE'S MARTHA?

It's supper time and I'm getting hungry! I need a servant like Martha. Her story appears in Luke 10:38–42. She was the proactive member of the delightful Bethany household. Her brother Lazarus and her sister Mary were also friends of Jesus. He often visited this delightful and happy home.

The account in Luke tells of Jesus visiting in their home for a meal. Of course, Martha was the one who welcomed him at the door. Mary, the quiet one of the two sisters, sat at Jesus' feet listening to his words. Martha stayed busy in the kitchen. She didn't have a modern kitchen with microwaves, electric stoves, automatic appliances, etc. Rather, her cooking fire was probably fueled by a dry thorn bush and some camel dung. No air conditioning! It gets hot in Bethany. She was "distracted by all the preparations that had to be made" (Luke 10:40).

In a rather impatient and irritable state, she came to the door and instructed Jesus to send Mary to the kitchen to help her. In response to this, Jesus said, "Martha, Martha . . . you are worried and upset about many things, but only one thing is needed. Mary has chosen what is better, and it will not be taken away from her" (Luke 10:41–42).

Jesus made a good point. All effective work must be preceded by worship. We will serve more effectively if we spend time first at the feet of Jesus, in his teachings.

I have really been hard on Martha through the years. But when supper time arrives, where is she? Just watch Martha in the kitchen. She's one of those Type A personalities. She's always active. She's getting the table in order. The servants move quickly at her instructions. She is baking and cooking and roasting. We all know Marthas. They are the Christians who attend a continual round of meetings. They serve on committees. They are involved in projects. Thank God for the Marthas. What would the church do without them?

First Peter 4:10–11 gives two categories of gifts. The speaking gifts were discussed in the previous chapter. Now let's examine the serving gifts. These are mentioned in 1 Peter 4:11: "If anyone serves, he should do it with the strength God provides." The ability to serve is one of these spiritual gifts. In verse 10, it's clear that we are considering the spiritual grace gifts which the Holy Spirit gives to believers. If you have experienced the grace of God, the Bible says God has gifted you. His gifts are manifestations of his grace in your life.

Verse 11 mentions "the strength which God provides." As we have seen, a spiritual gift is a God-given ability to be a blessing to the Lord's people and to bring honor and glory to the Lord. The word *provides* is similar to the word *supply* in Philippians 1:19. It means "to furnish or supply." So these gifts are

God-given abilities of strength which supply the necessary power to serve the Lord effectively.

Again, verse 10 of 1 Peter 4 says we are to "minister" these gifts to one another "as good stewards of the manifold grace of God" (KJV). The word *minister* is the action form of the noun *deacon*. The reference is to practical service. We are to use our spiritual gifts, not for selfish purposes, but to serve.

Verse 11 also says these gifts are to be exercised "so that in all things God may be praised." Spiritual gifts are for the good of other believers. They are also for the glory of God. We are to do what God gifts us to do so the church might be built up and in order that God might get the glory.

We must, however, be very careful never to use our God-given abilities to excuse us from being faithful to our responsibilities. For instance, all Christians are to give tithes and offerings to the Lord. Some Christians have a special gift in this area. Also, all Christians are to show mercy in dealing with others. Some people are especially gifted with mercy. All Christians are to help. Some Christians have a special gift of helping.

Now let's consider again the serving gifts—the Martha gifts. These are the gifts God gives Christians so they might bless others. First Corinthians 12 lists several of the serving gifts. As they are surveyed, the Lord may set off his heavenly alarm clock in your heart. A light bulb may blink on in your mind. The Holy Spirit may help you see an area where you have the spiritual capacity to serve the Lord Jesus.

Church members who have these serving gifts are the active part of the church family. These are the go-getters in the church. They are like the plasma in the lifeblood of the church. They are the Marthas. The purpose of these serving gifts is practical ministry to others. They enable believers to perform the practical tasks and responsibilities of the church. Let's look at these serving gifts.

Believing

Verse 9 of 1 Corinthians 12 mentions the gift of faith. Let's call this the gift of believing. It means having an extraordinary kind of faith. Some believers have a definite spiritual gift to believe God in extraordinary ways.

This faith is different from saving faith. Each of us has the ability to exercise saving faith. Romans 12:3 teaches that God has dealt to every person the measure of faith. Anyone who is lost can, by faith, receive Jesus Christ as Lord and

Savior. Ephesians 2:8 puts it very simply, "For it is by grace you have been saved, through faith—and this not from yourselves, it is the gift of God." This kind of faith is not a spiritual gift. It is a faith God gives every human being—the ability to trust Jesus Christ as personal Savior.

The gift of faith is also different from the faith every believer is to exercise in a relationship to God. Jesus said on one occasion, "Have faith in God" (Mark 11:22). Galatians 5:22 indicates that faith is a part of the fruit of the Holy Spirit. Every saved person can grow and mature in faith. All of us can grow in our confidence and trust in the Lord. But this faith evidenced as fruit is not the gift of faith.

In Paul's first letter to his young converts in Thessalonica, he was concerned about their faith and its development. In 1 Thessalonians 3 he mentioned several times "your faith." In his second letter, he rejoiced in the good report of their faith. He was thrilled and he said, "Your faith is growing more and more" (2 Thess. 1:3).

Would you like to have more faith? Would you like to trust God more? Romans 10:17 tells us how: "Consequently, faith comes from hearing the message, and the message is heard through the word of Christ." If you want your faith to grow, give yourself to a diligent study of the Scriptures. As you study your Bible, see what God has done for you and read the wonderful promises he gives you. Your faith will begin to expand and grow.

But there is a special gift of faith or believing. It is the Spirit-given ability to believe God for extraordinary things. Simply put, it's extraordinary faith in God—mountain-moving faith! People who have this kind of faith can see things that need to be done. It may look impossible, but they have the faith to believe that God can do it! The insurmountable can be accomplished. Although a river and a mountain looms ahead, no river is too deep and no mountain is too high for God. Those who have the gift of believing laugh at impossibilities and shout, "It shall be done!"

These are the dreamers, the visionaries. They are willing to attempt the impossible for God. A church needs many of these people. The church has plenty of skeptics and pessimists. They figure out how it can't be done! They constantly repeat the seven last words of the church: "We've never done it that way before." Churches need a lot of people who have the Spirit-given ability to believe God for big things. Not all Christians have this kind of faith.

I heard about a young pastor who was averaging about fifty people in Sunday school attendance at the church where he served. He got all fired up at a church growth conference. He hurried back to his church and set a goal of five thousand in attendance for a big Sunday. Do you think he made it? Obviously he didn't. That's not faith; it's folly!

But there are some Christians who do believe God for big things. These Christians build new buildings, devise new ministries, and plan future programs. Once I heard about a young pastor who was doing great things in his church. Someone asked a deacon in his church, "How is your young pastor doing?"

"Great!" replied the deacon. "He's asking God for things we didn't even know he had!"

In the Bible we read about people who had this kind of faith in God. It's almost like the drive-through at a fast-food restaurant. You order a combo meal with burger, fries, and soft drink. But as you wait in line, you get hungrier. Once at the window, you "upsize" your order from small to large fries. Some believers trust God to "upsize" their ministries. They expect more from God than most people. Hebrews 11 is devoted to these people. It contains a list of people who had extraordinary faith in God. Hebrews 11 could be called the "hall of fame of the faithful." We read about Abel, Enoch, and Noah. We are thrilled at the exceptional faith of Abraham, Isaac, and Jacob. The faith of a Joseph or a Moses amazes us.

The author summarizes these remarkable people of faith by saying, "who through faith conquered kingdoms, administered justice, and gained what was promised; who shut the mouths of lions, quenched the fury of the flames, and escaped the edge of the sword; whose weakness was turned to strength; and who became powerful in battle and routed foreign armies" (Heb. 11:33–34). That is extraordinary faith in God.

It's the kind of faith David had. David took a meal to his big brothers who were in the Israelite army. When he got there, the whole crowd was shaking in their boots, including King Saul himself. David said, "What's up?"

"Haven't you heard?" they said. "There's a big giant out there and he wants to fight us. We're afraid of him."

David said, "Who does he think he is?" The Israelites were looking at Goliath and saying, "He's too big to hit." David looked at Goliath and said, "He's too big to miss!" David took a slingshot, five stones, and declared, "The battle is the LORD's" (1 Sam. 17:47). He hit Goliath in the forehead, and the giant fell to the ground dead.

David's faith was about believing God for miracles, devising new methods for reaching people for the Lord, and believing God can do big things. This is extraordinary faith in God.

I serve as pastor of First Baptist Church, Jacksonville, Florida. Through the years, God has given us many people with this unusual kind of faith. We have been able to build buildings, create programs to reach people, and have a truly miraculous ministry in Jacksonville because we have a lot of people with this supernatural gift of faith. It is a serving gift, and it sets the atmosphere in a church for God's miracle-working power.

Has God given you the gift of believing God for big things? Use it! But don't allow your enthusiasm and excitement to carry you away with projects that may not be wise. Inform your faith by Scripture and the leading of the Spirit. The Holy Spirit will never lead you to believe God for anything contrary to the teachings of the Bible.

Discerning

First Corinthians 12:10 mentions another serving gift, "distinguishing between spirits." The word *distinguishing* means literally "to judge through" or "to tell the difference between things." It's the ability to know the difference between things or to discriminate between them. The spiritual gift of discernment is the Spirit-given ability to distinguish between truth and error, between the divine and the demonic. What an important gift this is to the church, especially today.

Why is discernment needed? The Bible tells us that Satan is a deceiver. He is a counterfeiter. He wants to copy the things of God and to confuse believers. His desire is to turn Christians around to take off after something that is false. It happens all the time.

Second Corinthians 11:14–15 says, "And no wonder, for Satan himself masquerades as an angel of light. It is not surprising, then, if his servants masquerade as servants of righteousness. Their end will be what their actions deserve." Satan will see to it that there are always false prophets and false preachers and teachers.

Much in the religious community today is obviously not from God. Some teaching heard on television and radio, in pulpits, and in books is contrary to the teachings of the Bible. Christians have to be very careful. A person in a pulpit with a Bible in his or her hand is not necessarily a true servant of God.

He may be teaching false doctrine. Further, his life may be phony. Gathering a crowd does not guarantee God's blessing. It's really not too hard to draw a crowd these days. In most any coliseum or stadium in the country, "Herman and the Dirty Noses" can bring in thousands. Monster trucks draw large numbers. Wrestling is a huge draw. Country singers perform to mega audiences. Just because it's big and some Scripture is sprinkled on it does not mean it is of God. We desperately need discernment in the modern church.

Some believers have been given the spiritual gift of discernment. They have the ability to do supernatural analysis. They run radar on spiritual matters just like our F-18 fighter jets run radar on military matters. They sense when something is not of God. They can listen to a speaker and catch subtle errors which others miss. They can read a book and spot problem areas immediately.

There are several levels of discernment. There is a natural discernment which many people have. One might call this good judgment or common sense. We in the South refer to it as "horse sense." Even unsaved people may have natural discernment. They can spot a faulty advertisement. They catch on to a con artist quickly. This is natural discernment.

Then there is a level of spiritual discernment which every believer possesses. First John 2:20 points to this spiritual discernment available for all believers: "But you have an anointing from the Holy One, and all of you know the truth." This reference is to the Holy Spirit. Every believer has the anointing, according to this verse. The Holy Spirit within our hearts is our spiritual alarm system on the doors and windows of our spiritual house.

Have you ever listened to someone speak, and it just didn't sound right to you? Have you ever heard someone preaching on television or on radio, and it was like a loud buzzer went off in your heart? That's discernment—and it's available to every believer. Listen to the quiet caution of the Holy Spirit in your heart. It will immunize you from the various "isms" floating around. It's your spiritual flu shot. First John 4:1 says, "Dear friends, do not believe every spirit, but test the spirits to see whether they are from God, because many false prophets have gone out into the world." A good rule for Christians concerning any message they hear or read is, "Before you trust it, test it."

There is also another level of spiritual discernment. It is special. These Christians are very important to the fellowship of the church. Dr. Paige Patterson, president of Southeastern Baptist Theological Seminary, Wake Forest, North Carolina, is a longtime friend of mine. He is an unusually gifted expositor and a brilliant theologian. I believe he has the gift of discernment. Dr. Patterson can read a book or listen to a person and immediately pick up on error. Southern Baptists have benefited from his gift of discernment.

Another person who has an unusual gift of discernment is Dr. John MacArthur. A worldwide radio speaker and prolific author, Dr. MacArthur can often catch errors which many people miss. One does not have to agree with Dr. MacArthur on every point to be helped greatly by his gift of discernment.

Simon Peter apparently had the spiritual gift of discernment. There are few accounts in the Bible as startling and sobering as Peter's encounter with Ananias and Sapphira. In Acts 5, the Holy Spirit revealed to Peter the lying and hypocrisy of this New Testament couple. How did he know such details about their hearts? Peter said, "Ananias, how is it that Satan has so filled your heart that you have lied to the Holy Spirit and have kept for yourself some of the money you received for the land?" (Acts 5:3). It could only have been through the Spirit's gift of discernment.

There are times when those who have the gift of discernment are irritating. If they point out a problem you have missed, this is especially annoying! Also, those gifted in this way must be careful. A prideful arrogance could develop. In addition, these gifted individuals can be harsh in their criticisms. Discerning Christians must be careful that they not engage in character assassination or make mountains out of molehills. The gift of discernment must be exercised very carefully.

God called me to preach at age sixteen. I went to college at eighteen. The school I attended was very liberal. I had a four-year indoctrination in liberal theology. During my freshman year, I became somewhat enamored by certain aspects of liberal teaching. I was fed a constant stream of liberal books. One particular theologian I read was an extremely good writer. His material was fascinating. It intrigued my intellect to read it. If you could show in class that you understood what he was saying, your professors would brag on you. That made me feel good!

I remember coming home with that book and telling a woman in my home church about it. She was the mother of a friend of mine and a sweet, godly Christian. She expressed that she would like to read the book because she had heard about the author. I loaned it to her and she read it. When she returned the book, she included a letter which I have kept in the book now for more than forty years. You'll understand why I've kept it after you read what she wrote.

Jerry, thank you for letting me read your book. I had heard much about the author. On page 47, he says this—"We should not worry so much about certain narrow-minded, literalistic interpretations of the so-called second coming of Christ." What a contrast to John 14, Acts 1, and others. There are approximately 325 references to the second coming in the New Testament. No wonder our dear brother (that's me) was so confused reading after such a modernist. God has called on us to study and to rightly divide the Word of God. Certainly there are many voices in the world today, and it is not always easy to distinguish the true from the false. But God's Holy Spirit, our Teacher, will make known the truth to us (John 16:13). We cannot receive part of the Word and reject other portions and be pleasing to God. Jerry, we thank God for you and the other young men who are preaching the unsearchable riches of Christ's grace to a lost world. May God bless you richly in all you do. Yours in Christ, Mrs. Smith.

You will never know what that letter meant to me. God had a sweet Christian woman with the gift of discernment who could read that book and pick up things I had missed. She was able to point them out to me. Thank God for those who have the serving gift of discernment. They serve the church in a vital role.

Helping

Jump down in 1 Corinthians 12 to verse 28. In the middle of that verse there is a little gift you may have missed. I don't want you to miss it because there's a blessing here. In the middle of the verse there is the little word *help*. The word is the Greek word *antilamphseis* which means to take hold of, to take a burden to one's self. It refers to helpful deeds or assistance—the gift of helping.

What is this gift? Helping is the Spirit-given ability to serve Jesus in any supporting role. Christians who have this gift are the kind of people who are willing to serve cheerfully, joyfully, unselfishly wherever and whenever God needs them. It is a beautiful thing to see people in the fellowship who have the gift of helping. They work behind the scenes. They often take the unspectacular, undesirable jobs around the church. The church runs smoothly because of these people.

As you read the Bible, you will encounter many people who seemed to have this gift. I think young Timothy had the gift of helps. He was willing to serve as an assistant to the apostle Paul. John Mark is another one. He was willing to take a supporting role and, by the end of his ministry, was very helpful to Paul. At the end of some of Paul's letters, he gives lists of believers who have been a help and a blessing to him (see Rom. 16). These people had gifts of helps.

Of course, Martha fits into this category. We read of her in Luke 10, where the Lord had to correct her service somewhat. We also read of her in John 12. Jesus, his disciples, and several others had come for a supper. John 12:2 says, "Martha served." Thank God for the John Marks and Marthas of the church. I don't know what we would do without them (especially when I'm hungry, Martha).

The church today is utterly dependent upon these faithful Christians who exercise their gift of helps. The need for the helping gifts in the fellowship of a church is massive. Think of some of the supporting functions that go on around a church.

We have a large congregation in Jacksonville. There is much to be done. We must have many helpers. Occasionally, when I'm out visiting, people will say, "We've been thinking about coming to your church, but we aren't sure you could use us there. We aren't sure you need anybody else to work." I always reply, "The bigger the church is, the more people are needed to help." Our church needs a vast host of people to exercise their gift of helps.

I can't list all of the places where the gift of helps might be exercised, so I'll name just a few. If I leave yours out, please don't feel neglected or be offended. We need ushers. Have you ever thought what chaos would exist in the church if there were no ushers? These people provide order in the seating of the worshipers. They also welcome people into the presence of God and bid them Godspeed as they go out to live for God. Ushers are often the workers who leave a lasting impression of the church with visitors.

What about those who work the parking lots? These people park the cars. They are often the first contact which people have with a church. What a place for happy, smiling, cheerful Christians!

Think about Sunday school secretaries and group leaders. These people take the roll, keep up with the attendance, contact absentees, and find out about the spiritual needs of individuals. What about those who work in the nurseries. Only heaven will reveal how many people who worked in nurseries have enabled young couples to sit in the service, hear the gospel, and be saved. Think how few babies you heard crying in the sanctuary last Sunday and then go thank a nursery worker! I am so thankful for people who are willing to take their turn in the nursery.

Then there are those wonderful people who work in the choirs. Our church has a large children's choir ministry. Many of our people are willing to serve in supporting roles in these children's choirs. They help so much.

Think of those who operate sound systems and lights. If you can't hear or see in a church building, you're in trouble! The people in media and communications often perform a thankless task. If everything goes smoothly, few people seem to notice. If anything goes wrong, everybody speaks up!

I could go on and on. Hats off to the silent host of Christians who work behind the scenes in our churches. Obviously, the gift of helps is very important.

We might also consider the gift of intercession. In 2 Corinthians 1:11 Paul said, "as you help us by your prayers." I believe that God gives some people a special gift to help the work of the Lord through intercessory prayer. Some Christians have come to a time of declining health. They are not able to attend the services as regularly as before. At that point, God may give them the spiritual gift of helping by intercessory prayer.

I have known a number of homebound people through the years who have had a tremendous helping ministry through intercessory prayer. I believe it is one of the most important ministries in the church. Most people never even know about it. These Christians pray, and their prayers for the church ascend to heaven like sweet incense which fills the heart of God with pleasure.

You probably won't be asked to speak on any television program if you have the gift of helps. You probably won't be asked to share your testimony at a prayer meeting. I doubt that people will ask you to lay hands on them so the Holy Spirit can give them this gift through you. In fact, I've never heard of a "helps cult." Have you? I've never seen a "helps movement" getting started. It's simply not a glamorous or expressive gift. But the church must have the gift of helps. Don't worry if the gifts of helps are little seen.

First Corinthians 12:22 talks about members of the body—though they "seem to be weaker are indispensable." They "are necessary." Your big toe may not be the prettiest part of your body. Most of the time it may be covered by a smelly sock or chipped nail polish! But if yours ever gets hurt, it makes walking more difficult. Thank God for Christians who exercise their gift of helps in faithful service.

Leading

There is another word in 1 Corinthians 12:28 which indicates a spiritual serving gift. It is the word *administration*. This is the gift of leading. The word literally means "to steer a ship." It refers to someone who guides a ship through treacherous waters. This person is skilled to avoid the rocks and shoals of the seas. Some people are gifted to help administer the church and keep it from getting into dangerous waters where the rocks of difficulty and disaster exist.

There is another gift that ties in to the gift of leading. Romans 12:8 says, "If it is leadership, let him govern diligently." The word *ruleth* means "to preside over." It means to stand in front of others. I remember the football games at my Georgia high school. Our fans always enjoyed halftime because our marching band would perform. I loved to watch the drum major lead the band. It was impressive to hear such a big sound on the drum major's downbeat. Picture someone leading. What is this gift? It is the Spirit-given ability to lead the church. The same word is used in 1 Timothy 5:17: "The elders who direct the affairs of the church well are worthy of double honor." It is also used in 1 Timothy 3:4: "He must manage his own family well." Again, it is used in 1 Thessalonians 5:12: "Now we ask you, brothers, to respect those who work hard among you, who are over you in the Lord and who admonish you."

This is why a church has pastors and deacons. There are also committee chairmen, youth leaders, and children's leaders in churches. We must have leaders.

Obviously, some people rise to the top in leadership. God has gifted them with leadership ability. Unfortunately, there are some who desire to be church leaders out of impure motives. Their leadership is not a spiritual gift but a carnal desire—the spirit of Diotrephes all over again. Third John 9 says, "but Diotrephes, who loves to be first." He was fond of being first. He was interested only in what suited him. He didn't care what was best for the church. Nor did he care what was best for the Lord's work. He was his own first priority.

Sometimes churches have a "church boss." Like a political boss, he runs things. He pushes for his own desires and purposes. The smaller the church, the worse the church boss is. They seek to rule in a dictatorial and bullying spirit. This can create great difficulty in a church. For some, it is human nature to want to dominate and to rule others. These individuals are power seekers. If unsaved or carnal people lead in the church, they can cause great problems.

This is one of the reasons why church schools get into trouble. A person is placed on a board of trustees because of his ability to give substantial gifts to the church. Fortunately, many wealthy people are also very godly. But if a wealthy trustee is carnal or even lost, the decisions made can be devastating to the institution. Many churches have "church bosses." They are the power behind the scenes. The pastor dare not cross them. This is not good leadership. It is a form of spiritual intimidation.

In contrast, Spirit-gifted believers lead in an altogether different manner. Wisdom, tact, and humility are characteristic of them. The qualifications for leaders in a church are different from the secular setting. The qualifications for leadership in the church are to be spiritual in nature. Therefore, spiritual leaders must be spiritual people. They must have a close and evident walk with the Lord.

Thank God for gifted leaders who lead with a humble, prayerful spirit. These leaders walk closely with the Lord. They love Jesus and they love God's people. They want to help their church win people to faith in the Lord Jesus Christ.

Obviously, pastors need the gift of leadership. A pastor can lead effectively only with the gift of leading provided by the Holy Spirit. Churches should allow their leaders to lead. To call a pastor to be their leader and then to confine him so he cannot exercise his leadership ability is wrong. This does not mean that the pastor should be a dictator. He is a leader. He is the person whom God has placed in the congregation to seek God's will and plan for the church and to lead the people to pursue it.

Giving

Romans 12:8 mentions another of the serving gifts: "If it is contributing to the needs of others, let him give generously." This is the simple gift of giving. Some people have an unusual gift of giving. You may feel that you do not have the gift of giving, but this is not an excuse. All of us are supposed to give. The Bible teaches that we should give to the Lord one tenth of our income (the tithe) and give offerings on top of that.

Now this is a touchy subject with a lot of Christians. I've heard for a long time that the most sensitive nerve in the body is the one attached to the wallet! But all Christians are to be faithful in the matter of giving. One of the most helpful things I can do for a young Christian is to share the blessing of giving in obedience to the Lord's commands.

The spiritual gift of giving helps define the idea of stewardship. Paul says we are to exercise this gift "with simplicity" (Rom. 12:8 KJV). The word is an interesting one. It means literally "without folds." This refers to unfolded cloth. It means to give purely with no ulterior motives. It also means not to ruffle the mind by making folds in it. We are to give with openness of heart, without self-seeking and without expecting anything in return. Some people want to give their money to carry the favor of the pastor. Others give to be placed on a certain committee. That's not what the gift of giving is about.

God has gifted some people to make money. God knew better than to give some of us this gift! How foolish most of us would be! If God gave some Christians the gift of giving, they would be riding in a Rolls Royce with a ten-gallon hat on their heads and a cigar in their mouths! But God does give some people the ability to make money. He also gives them the ability and willingness to give that money to the work of the Lord. Thank God for those who have the gift of giving. In the New Testament, Barnabas had the gift of giving. He actually gave everything he had. He sold it all and brought the proceeds to the church (see Acts 4:36–37).

I have known some "Barnabas Christians" along the way. These are individuals who use their gift of giving to help the work of the Lord in times of great need. I think about the DeMoss family from the Philadelphia area. This family has given millions of dollars to the work of the Lord. I am reminded of a wonderful deacon who was a multimillionaire. He gave large gifts to enable the church to build buildings, to purchase property, to pave parking lots, etc. He never gave with any desire for attention or prestige. He never made any attempt to use his gifts to obtain personal power. He always gave with a sweet, unselfish spirit.

Perhaps God has given you the ability to make money. Use that gift to be a blessing to the Lord's work. Give consistently, liberally, sacrificially. You can do indescribable good for the work of the Lord.

Yet hear this word of caution. Some people with this gift of making money are a soft touch. Just about anybody who comes along asking for money can get it. To those of you who have the gift of giving, let me say that just because someone asks you for money doesn't mean that God wants you to give it to them. Be very prayerful and careful as you exercise this gift.

Caring

There is one other serving gift. Romans 12:8 talks about caring: "If it is showing mercy, let him do it cheerfully." The word *cheerfulness* means "gladness" or "graciousness." This is the Spirit-given ability to love and care for hurting people. It means to show practical, cheerful, compassionate love to those who are suffering.

We need people with the gift of caring. God's sunlight shines on these faces. How thankful I am for those people who have the gift of caring for others. What they feel and express for others is not pity. It is a genuine concern for hurting people.

I heard about a little boy who came home from school one day and said, "Sally came to school today after missing yesterday. She told us her mother had died. Mom, Sally cried and cried and cried."

The mother said, "Son, what did you do?"

He said, "Mom, I just sat down at my desk and cried with her."

All Christians should show this kind of mercy. To be merciful and care for others is a Godlike attribute.

God has given some people a tender heart. They are especially gifted in this area. Dorcas was this way. She had this gift of caring. She "was always doing good and helping the poor" (Acts 9:36). She evidently had a gift of sewing. When she died, those who had been blessed by her ministry, widows in the church, "stood around him, crying and showing him the robes and other clothing that Dorcas had made while she was still with them" (Acts 9:39). She exercised the gift of caring with a dedicated sewing needle.

I often think about those who care for others. Or I think about wonderful Christians in the medical profession who care for the sick and dying. Research shows that patients need more than just medical treatment. There must also be emotional care and compassion. This helps the healing process.

There are so many hurting and diseased people. Christians with the gift of caring can be a blessing by visiting hospitals and rest homes. They can work with the handicapped. Christians gifted in caring can work in jail ministries, with alcoholics, or with cancer or AIDS patients. Do you look out for people who need encouragement and blessing? God may have given you the gift of caring.

There are more serving gifts than we could ever number or name. As the body of Christ grows and develops, many serving gifts may be given by the

Holy Spirit to the church. This evolution is exciting. Just remember that these serving gifts must be used to benefit the body as a whole.

When all the cells of the human body function in cooperation with one another, health is the result. There are times when some body cells get selfish. They live in the body and take in all the benefits without sharing the work-load. These kinds of cells are cancerous. They destroy the body through cancer. Likewise, when Christians share the benefits of their Spirit-gifts, the result is a healthy church. If you have one or more spiritual serving gifts, put them to work for the good of others and the glory of God!

Final Word to Martha

1. Martha, I hope you realize now how very important you are to all of us.

2. Martha, I want to remind you again that you will serve more effectively and with less frustration when you spend a little time each day at the feet of Jesus.

3. Martha, you make the best apple pie. No one can fry chicken like you. And, oh, that cornbread . . . !

CHAPTER 11

ANOTHER UGLY DUCKLING MIRACLE

Hans Christian Andersen is a favorite author of many. His fairy tales, such as "The Princess and the Pea," "The Emperor's New Clothes," and "The Little Mermaid," have entertained children for generations. One story, though, seems to be more popular than any of the others—"The Ugly Duckling."

In this appealing story, a young duckling finds that he looks different from the beautiful swans in his neighborhood. He is very sad. He feels rejected by the other, prettier ducklings. Then a miracle occurs. He realizes that he has become one of the beautiful swans he has admired for so long. Young people enjoy this story because it illustrates some of the difficulties encountered in adolescence, before the "swan" transformation into young adulthood takes place.

Some say another "ugly duckling miracle" happened in December 1996 in Florida. A customer of the Seminole Finance Corporation noticed an image on the window of the office building which was owned by none other than Ugly Duckling Car Sales. The image resembled the virgin Mary. News of this "sighting" spread quickly. During the holidays, nearly sixty thousand people produced a traffic gridlock trying to view what appeared to be a miracle. A Clearwater, Florida, policeman, Sergeant Pat Anderson (another Anderson— Is this a miracle?) said, "People come in, pray, and then leave."

Many people brought flowers to place below the window. Others were sure the image was a miracle sign from God. Digna Feldman brought her twenty-month-old grandson to see the image. "This is a miracle," she said. "I pray for her to protect him." Tammy Parke, another visitor, said, "She's beautiful. It's just unbelievable." Tammy brought her daughter to see the window, hoping for a miracle cure for her disability.

Later the image was vandalized. Someone threw an unknown liquid on the shape, marring it. After two days of heavy thunderstorms, the blemishes were no longer visible. Pauline McClain said, "We heard she was healing herself. It looks like it."

A number of explanations have been given for the image. Some say it was caused by a bronze reflective agent applied to the outside of the glass before it was cut into panels. This agent evidently changes as it ages, affected by heat, moisture, and sunlight. Others explained the image as stains left from the sprinkler system. Some accept the explanations. Others continue to insist it is a miracle.

A religion professor at the University of Kansas said about the phenomenon, "They want some reassurance that, in fact, God is in charge of things."[1]

It seems all religions claim miracles as part of their belief systems. According to a newspaper article, the words *Allah* and *Mohammed* appeared miraculously on a sliced potato, reported Momina Ahmed of Ganhati, India. As she was fixing lunch, she found the word inside a potato. She and her husband took the potato to the local mosque, where the man confirmed the "potato miracle." Since then, more than ten thousand pilgrims have flocked to Momina's home to see the miracle.

Many people long for evidence of the miraculous and supernatural. All around us there are claims being made that the miracles of the New Testament are being restored to the modern church. This may indeed be a response to the death and defeat of so many churches.

Miracle crusades are advertised across the land. Others are declaring confidently, "A miracle a day keeps the devil away!" "Signs, wonders, and miracles are being witnessed in our revival," claim many church advertisements. Others feel that if miracles can be restored, many people will be saved.

There is a third category of gifts of the Holy Spirit mentioned in the New Testament. We have already considered the speaking gifts and the serving gifts. Now we consider sign gifts. Although the categories are somewhat arbitrary, it is possible to arrange the gifts mentioned in the New Testament as either speaking, serving, or sign gifts.

In the New Testament, there were signs and wonders and miracles. These occurred over and over again. They also occurred in Old Testament times. These included the miracles at the creation, the plagues in Egypt, and the miraculous parting of the Red Sea. People witnessed a number of miracles throughout Bible days.

Signs and wonders and miracles are also mentioned in the life of Jesus. Acts 2:22 says, "Men of Israel, listen to this: Jesus of Nazareth was a man accredited by God to you by miracles, wonders and signs, which God did among you through him, as you yourselves know." The apostles also performed miracles and wonders: "Everyone was filled with awe, and many wonders and miraculous signs were done by the apostles" (Acts 2:43). "The apostles performed many miraculous signs and wonders among the people" (Acts 5:12).

We know that signs, wonders, and miracles happened in Bible times, but is what we are seeing today the same thing we read about in God's Word?

Let me clarify that I am not attacking groups or individuals who may differ with me on this matter of signs and wonders. Many Christians love the Lord Jesus, believe the Bible, and take a different view. There is no intention on my part to be unkind or to belittle any church, denomination, or individual Christian.

Secondly, we must always be guided by what the Bible has to say. A personal account or testimonial is never to take precedence over Scripture. Our experiences must always be brought to the Word of God for confirmation. Experiences must never be placed above Scripture. Do not take the attitude of the person who declared, "I don't care what the Bible says. I've had an experience!" If the Bible does not validate our experience, then it is not valid. Let's delve into what the Bible has to say about the sign gifts. Then we will consider some of the modern claims of signs, wonders, and miracles.

First Corinthians 12 mentions four of these sign gifts. The first of these sign gifts is found in verses 10, 28, and 29. The second sign gift, healing, is found in 1 Corinthians 12:30. The third and fourth gifts are mentioned in verses 10, 28, and 30. These are speaking with tongues and interpretations of tongues, respectively. These will be considered in a later chapter.

At this point, let's discuss the gift of miracles mentioned in 1 Corinthians 12:10, 28, and 29 where the "workers of miracles" is referred to. The gift of miracles is the Spirit-given ability to do the supernatural.

It may be helpful to define a miracle. Various definitions are given. Here is the one which has been the most helpful to me. A miracle is a supernatural intervention of God into the natural course of things. When a miracle occurs, it is God doing what he chooses to do with his own creation. Belief in a supernatural God who is involved in his creation is fundamental to any discussion of miracles.

Jesus and Miracles

A study of the life of the Lord Jesus in the four Gospels indicates that Jesus performed miracles. The Bible makes this apparent. Jesus did the things Adam would have done if he had not sinned. Perhaps it is what believers will also be able to do in the new creation.

The New Testament records approximately thirty-five miracles performed by Jesus. Sometimes Jesus performed natural miracles or miracles in the realm of nature. At times a storm would strike the Sea of Galilee. Jesus would speak a word and the storm would cease (see Mark 4:39). On another occasion, thousands of people came to hear Jesus. He took a few loaves and some fish, broke them, blessed them, multiplied them, and fed thousands of people

(Luke 9:13–17 and Matt. 15:34–38). Jesus once suspended the laws of nature and walked on the water to go to the disciples on the Sea of Galilee (Matt. 14:25). These were all supernatural miracles.

Jesus also performed miracles relating to human beings. Some were physical miracles of healing. Jesus saw the crippled and made them walk. He made blind people see. Leprous people were made clean. On at least three occasions, Jesus even raised the dead. He brought a twelve-year-old girl back to life (Mark 5:35–43). He raised the son of the widow of Nain from the dead (Luke 7:11–15). He also raised his friend Lazarus from the dead. Lazarus had been buried for four days, but Jesus called him forth from the realm of the dead (John 11:43–44).

Why did Jesus perform miracles? One reason is apparent: He often did it to help people in need. Jesus loved people and he still does. His heart went out in compassion to suffering people. When Jesus saw hurting or diseased people, he often performed miracles to alleviate their suffering and pain.

The Scriptures also make it clear that Jesus performed miracles to provide validation for his ministry. Acts 2:22 says, "Jesus of Nazareth was a man accredited by God to you by miracles, wonders and signs." John 20:30–31 says, "Jesus did many other miraculous signs in the presence of his disciples, which are not recorded in this book. But these are written that you may believe that Jesus is the Christ, the Son of God, and that by believing you may have life in his name." John 3:2 declares, "He [Nicodemus] came to Jesus at night and said, 'Rabbi, we know you are a teacher who has come from God. For no one could perform the miraculous signs you are doing if God were not with him.'"

Also notice that Jesus never did spectacular miracles just to draw a crowd. For example, he refused to jump off the temple as Satan tempted him to do (Matt. 4:8–10). People were not necessarily converted by our Lord's miracles. In John 6:26, after the miracle of feeding the multitudes, he said, "I tell you the truth, you are looking for me, not because you saw miraculous signs but because you ate the loaves and had your fill." When Jesus performed miracles, he was demonstrating that he was indeed the Messiah predicted in the Old Testament.

The Apostles and Miracles

The New Testament reveals that the apostles of the Lord also performed miracles. Several specific miracles are mentioned in the book of Acts. Simon

Peter raised Dorcas from the dead (see Acts 9:36–41). After a lengthy sermon, the apostle Paul evidently raised the young man Eutychus from the dead. He had gone to sleep and had fallen out a window (see Acts 20:9–12). (I tell our people at church that if they go to sleep while I'm preaching, fall out of a pew, and kill themselves, I won't be able to help them. I've not yet been able to raise pew-sleeping Christians from the dead!)

Why did the apostles perform miracles? What was their purpose? Of course, they also loved people and had compassion toward hurting people. But the clearly stated reason for their miracles is given in Scripture. In 2 Corinthians 12:12, the apostle Paul makes an interesting statement: "The things that mark an apostle—signs, wonders and miracles—were done among you with great perseverance." Hebrews 2:4 makes a similar statement that the apostles' ministries and messages were confirmed by the miracles they did: "God also testified to it by signs, wonders and various miracles, and gifts of the Holy Spirit distributed according to his will."

In the days of the apostles, the New Testament was not yet complete. It was in process. Oral testimony was being committed to writing. Once the New Testament canon was completed, there was no longer any need for our ministry as believers to be validated by miracles.

Miracles Today

But what about the miracles of today? What about the perceived image of the virgin Mary at the Ugly Duckling Car Sales building or the miracle potato in India? What about the miracles that are being claimed in crusades and church services around the country? What about the reports of miracles being wrought on many mission fields? Are the miracles we see today a restoration of the miracles which occurred in New Testament times? Does God still perform miracles?

Yes, absolutely! God does perform miracles. He is a miracle-working God. Care must be taken that we never put ourselves in the position of denying or disbelieving the supernatural. Too often we try to explain the incomprehensible as coincidence. Christians must never become deistic in their view of God. A deist believes that God created the universe, set it in motion, and then abandoned it. God is Creator. He cannot be kicked out of his own creation! Remember my simple definition of a miracle? A miracle is God doing what he chooses to do with his own creation.

Let me add a warning here. The presence of signs, wonders, and miracles is not positive proof of God's work. The New Testament teaches that the last outbreak of signs, wonders, and miracles will not be of God—but of Satan. In 2 Thessalonians 2:9 Paul warned of the coming Antichrist and accompanying manifestations: "The coming of the lawless one will be in accordance with the work of Satan displayed in all kinds of counterfeit miracles, signs and wonders." Revelation tells about the appearance of the Antichrist and the kinds of miracles that will occur (see Rev. 11:6, 13–14).

Let me add another caution. Hebrews 13:8 is often used to teach that Jesus is still performing the same kind of miracles he did in New Testament times. The reference to Jesus Christ being the same yesterday, today, and forever is applied to miracles. But this verse does not describe his methods; it discusses his person and character. God, although he is the same God, has used various methods and modes in his dealings with humankind.

For this reason, miracles in the Bible seem to come in clusters. W. A. Criswell, in his classic book on the Holy Spirit, has pointed out this cluster arrangement of miracles.[2] The miracles of the creation; the miracles which occurred around the exodus of Israel from Egypt; the miracles which attended the birth and the death of Christ—all these illustrate these clusters. The miracles which appeared at the birth of the church and the miracles mentioned in relation to the return of Christ also appear in groups.

So you may ask, Are today's miracles the same? There is no indication that we are seeing the kinds of miracles today which occurred in New Testament times.

If a person should walk on water today, it would be big news. I live in Jacksonville, Florida. The beautiful St. Johns River flows through our city. If someone stepped out on the St. Johns River and walked across it, all the major TV news broadcasts would have live satellite linkups to Jacksonville! There is no documentation to support occasional reports of people being raised from the dead. The so-called miracle workers of our day don't spend a great deal of time at funeral homes. If someone were resurrected, television news reporters would let the world know!

Those who claim the gift of miracles as it was manifested in the New Testament need to go to places like Somalia and Rwanda, where hungry children are dying. Let them break the loaves and fishes as Jesus did and feed the multitudes of hungry children. If they have the same gift, then they should go to cemeteries where brokenhearted families grieve for departed loved ones, open up the graves, and raise those dead bodies. Simply put, we are not seeing the kinds of miracles which people in New Testament times witnessed.

You may ask if the ability to do miracles is proof that a person is a Christian. No. Jesus said, "Many will say to me on that day, 'Lord, Lord, did we not prophesy in your name, and in your name drive out demons and perform many miracles?' Then I will tell them plainly, 'I never knew you. Away from me, you evildoers!'"(Matt. 7:22–23). This is an interesting statement. Jesus said they could do miracles. But his statement "I never knew you" indicates they were not born-again believers.

Miracles do not necessarily produce converts. A new methodology, power evangelism, is attracting attention today. This method assumes that if the power of God can be manifested in the supernatural—by signs and wonders and miracles for all to see—then great masses of people will believe. This is not supported by the Bible. Psalm 78 gives an account of many miracles which occurred among the Israelites. Verse 11 specifically says, "They forgot what he had done, the wonders he had shown them." Verse 32 further states, "Inspite of all this, they kept on sinning; in spite of his wonders they did not believe." In spite of the miracles, people did not believe.

Jesus fed five thousand people. Were the people converted by the miracle? No. Jesus said, "I tell you the truth, you are looking for me, not because you saw miraculous signs but because you ate the loaves and had your fill" (John 6:26). Actually, people were drawn more by the supper than by the signs!

I heard a signs-and-wonders preacher say, "I believe the day is coming when we will raise people from the dead. When that happens, thousands will be converted." Scratch that! This is not what Jesus said.

In the account of the rich man and Lazarus, Jesus recounted a conversation between them. From hell, the rich man pleaded for Lazarus to be sent to his five brothers on earth. If someone from the dead came to witness to them, he logically concluded, they would believe. But the word came from heaven, "If they do not listen to Moses and the Prophets, they will not be convinced even if someone rises from the dead" (Luke 16:31). Even the miracle of raising a person from the dead isn't enough to convert some people.

To insist on miracles as an aid to evangelism is actually an assault on the power of the Scriptures. It is really a kind of "enriched bread" gospel with all the modern ingredients—"all you ever wanted in the gospel and more." Paul stated, "I am not ashamed of the gospel, because it is the power of God for the salvation of everyone who believes" (Rom. 1:16). Our gospel is a powerful, miracle gospel. It is contained in a miracle Bible. It is about a miracle Savior. Once believed, it brings about a miracle salvation.

Just before Jesus went back to heaven, he made an interesting statement: "I tell you the truth, anyone who has faith in me will do what I have been doing. He will do even greater things than these, because I am going to the Father" (John 14:12). Just what are these greater works Jesus intended for us to do? Perhaps the account of Jesus healing the man with palsy from Mark 2 is helpful. Four men brought a sick man to Jesus. When Jesus saw their faith, he said to the man, "Son, your sins are forgiven" (v. 5). The scribes who were there began to ask, "Why does this fellow talk like that? He's blaspheming! Who can forgive sins but God alone?" (v. 7).

Jesus knew what they were thinking. So he posed a question for them: Which was better for him to do? To forgive the man's sins or to heal him of palsy? (v. 9). Jesus told them he was going to perform a miracle of healing in the physical realm to show his power to forgive sin in the spiritual realm. Then Jesus healed the man and sent him home. Jesus declared that the spiritual miracle was far greater and more important than the physical miracle. The greater work is the work of salvation.

This narrative serves as a guide for us. Miracles do occur today because our God is a God of miracles. But it is a greater work for a person to be saved from sin than for a miracle to occur in the realm of nature. Salvation is the greatest miracle. Have you received Christ as your Savior? Has your life been changed? Then you are a miracle of God's grace. God's salvation can provide yet another "ugly duckling miracle" as a sinner becomes a beautiful swan:

> It took a miracle to hang the stars in place,
> It took a miracle to hang the world in space,
> But when He saved my soul, cleansed and made me whole,
> It took a miracle of love and grace.[3]

First Corinthians 12:29 asks, "Do all work miracles?" The answer is no. Even in the New Testament, only a few people performed miracles. Jesus gave his cousin, John the Baptist, the greatest compliment ever given to a person. Jesus said of him, "Among those born of women there has not risen anyone greater than John the Baptist" (Matt. 11:11).

John 10:41 gives a surprising statement about John: "Though John never performed a miraculous sign, all that John said about this man was true." Then verse 42 says, "And in that place many believed in Jesus." John didn't perform any miracles. Yet he pointed many people to the Lord Jesus Christ. What about you? Would you rather perform miracles that would shock people or lead them to know Jesus Christ as personal Savior and experience a changed life? Let's pray for more "ugly duckling miracles"—from sin to salvation!

How Many More Miracles Do We Need?

1. God has already done the big miracles—creation; the birth, death, and resurrection of Christ; the salvation experience. That's miracle enough for me.

2. Be very careful about miracles. The ability to perform a miracle is something Satan can also do. In the end times, this will be one of the ways Satan will confuse and deceive people.

3. Which had you rather have happen—a miraculous appearance of some kind of image on a building, a preacher walking across the water, or an alcoholic meeting Christ and being instantly changed and transformed?

4. What about your pastor? He may not be a miracle person; but if he is a gospel person, pray that God will use him in the lives of many people to bring about the miracle of salvation.

CHAPTER 12

HEALING IN THE NFL

"To be quite honest with you, I believe God is going to heal my knee. That's where my faith is right now. That's what I'm believing. I believe it can happen."

You've just read the words of Jacksonville Jaguars quarterback Mark Brunell. After signing a six-million-dollar per year contract, he was injured in the August 1997 preseason game against the New York Giants. Once he was tackled, silence fell upon the packed stadium as it became apparent that he was badly hurt.

Brunell's teammate, Bryan Schwartz, shared Mark's confidence and agreed with his claim. "I firmly believe it, "Schwartz said. "Mark is an obedient man of God and he firmly believes God will heal his knee. And [we], as his close friends and brothers do also . . . when they go in, I believe he's going to be fine."

The next Tuesday, Mark startled his teammates by walking onto the practice field. The surgeon examined him on Friday and found that the injury was not as severe as first thought. Surgery wasn't necessary. With rehabilitation he should return to the field of play within six to eight weeks. After consulting with his medical team, Mark said, "I want to say thank you to everyone for your prayers. This is great news and it is truly a blessing."

Schwartz rejoiced with his teammate, "Yeah, you can consider it a miracle. It's not raising someone from the dead or anything like that. But God has done those things, so why can't he heal a knee?"[1] On Monday night football, a month after he was injured, Mark trotted onto the field to thunderous applause. The knee held up under game pressure.

About this same time a young policeman and father in our church was battling cancer. A group of Christians in one of the local churches encouraged him and his wife to come to their healing services. The young policeman and his wife were told that his cancer was healed. There was great rejoicing. Shortly thereafter, the young policeman died.

These two different experiences bring many questions to mind. Does God heal today? Just who does God heal? Is an NFL quarterback's knee more important than a young policeman's life? Why do some people seem to receive healing while others do not? Did Brunell just have more faith than the policeman?

The subject of healing is of great interest to Christians, especially at those times when sickness or affliction occur. All of us, at one time or another, have probably asked God to heal us of some sickness. Most likely, on some occasions, we thought we were healed. On others we were not. Let's consider this intriguing subject.

Healing is a gift of the Holy Spirit. It is mentioned specifically in 1 Corinthians 12. Verse 9 talks about "gifts of healings." Verse 28 also mentions "gifts of healings." Verse 30 asks, "Do all have gifts of healing?" According to the Greek text, both words *gift* and *healing* are plural. The words literally rendered are "gifts of healings." This indicates a sign gift. Gifts of healings make it possible for healing to occur at every level of human experience, including healings in the physical, emotional, and spiritual realms. Diseases, both internal and external, can be healed by Jesus. The hymn "Rescue the Perishing" says it best: "Down in the human heart, crushed by the tempter, feelings lie buried that grace can restore."

In his excellent book, *Will God Heal Me?*, Ron Dunn points out several categories of healing. One is assisted healing. This healing occurs through the use of medical means, prescriptions, and diet. He refers to the fact that the mention of Luke, the beloved physician, in Scripture is an indication that assisted healing was recognized and endorsed in the New Testament.[2]

Another category is natural healing. The body has a marvelous ability to heal itself through its remarkable recuperative powers. Many people who have corrected their lifestyles and eliminated harmful habits have seen their physical condition improve dramatically.

Dr. Dunn also mentions faith healing. By this he does not mean biblical healing or the kind of healing claimed by the faith healers today. He means the positive attitude which helps the body recuperate from stress-related problems. A positive attitude increases the body's ability to repair itself. In this regard, Dr. Herbert Benson of the Harvard Medical School said, "Anywhere from sixty to ninety percent of visits to doctors are in the mind-body, stress-related realms."[3] Patients who have spiritual support also benefit. Surveys show that patients with spiritual support systems get better faster and go home earlier.[4]

Finally, Dr. Dunn mentions divine healing. In a sovereign act, God intervenes to heal a person without human means. The spiritual gifts of healings refer to this category. So the gifts of healings include the Spirit-given ability to heal people with God's direct intervention.

Jesus Healed People

A quick study of the four Gospels indicates that Jesus performed healing miracles. He healed people of many physical diseases. Healing was a vital part of his ministry. Matthew 4:23 summarizes the ministry of our Lord in three words: "teaching, preaching, and healing." What types of people did Jesus heal? He healed people with organic diseases, crippled legs, and withered hands. Blind eyes were able to see the sky again. The deaf could hear birds singing. Jesus even made dead people live again. Jesus definitely healed people.

Several distinct truths are evident in the healings of Jesus. Jesus never healed people in order to call attention to himself or to be spectacular. Rather, many times Jesus would say, "Don't tell anybody about this." Almost without exception, they would tell people! It was like gossip. Jesus said, "Don't tell it," and they told everybody! Today, he commands us to tell everybody, and we don't tell nearly as many as we should. We humans are backward, aren't we?

When Jesus healed, there were no failures. He never said, "I cannot heal you because you do not have enough faith." Jesus healed people who had faith, and at other times the people whom he healed didn't seem to have faith. But those who brought these people to him had faith. Luke 5:20 says that Jesus healed the crippled man "when [he] saw their faith." Others, showing no apparent faith, were healed, even when they didn't expect healing. When Jesus did not do mighty works in his hometown of Nazareth because of their unbelief (see Matt. 13:58), it was not because they didn't believe in his ability to do miracles. It was because they didn't believe he was the promised Messiah.

Our society is accustomed to instant everything—fast food, disposable cameras, ATMs! When Jesus healed, it was instant and it was complete. Symptoms disappeared immediately.

When Jesus died on the cross, he provided healing from all sickness and disease. Some people think the statement in 1 Peter 2:24—"by his wounds you have been healed"—is an indication that healing is in the atonement. A careful study of the context of this Scripture helps answer this. First Peter 2:24 refers to those who are healed from sin. The verse talks about being dead "to sins." It begins by saying specifically that "he himself bore *our sins* in his own body on the tree."

155

In addition, this verse is a quotation from Isaiah 53:4–5. The Old Testament reference makes it even clearer that physical healing is not intended, but a healing from sin. Verse 5 indicates that our transgressions, or iniquities, are what is intended. Matthew 8:17 builds on the same Isaiah 53:5 passage—Jesus casting out devils and healing the sick. Verse 17 says he did those things "to fulfill what was spoken through the prophet Isaiah. 'He took up our infirmities and carried our diseases.'"

Matthew indicates that this passage from Isaiah was fulfilled in Jesus' earthly ministry. It is closer to the teaching of Scripture to say that healing is provided in the incarnation, not the atonement. This means that ultimately all problems related to human sickness, like AIDS and cancer, will be resolved in the final stage of God's great salvation work—the resurrection of our body.

The idea that the death of Christ on the cross allows healing rests upon certain assumptions. First, since sickness is a result of the fall of man in the Garden of Eden, all sickness is a result of sin. Secondly, since Christ died for sin, the results of our sin-sickness are taken care of. Thirdly, every believer can claim healing for the physical body as well as salvation for the soul. This sounds good, but it fails to recognize that we do not reap all the benefits of Christ's incarnation and atonement in this present life.

Salvation is like a triangle with three sides. To say that I have been saved; I am being saved; and I am going to be saved is correct, according to the Bible. There are past, present, and future aspects to salvation. First Peter 1:5 talks about the future aspect of salvation when it speaks of "salvation that is ready to be revealed in the last time." Included in this future side of the salvation triangle is the redemption of the body. Romans 8:23 says, "We ourselves, who have the firstfruits of the Spirit, groan inwardly as we wait eagerly for our adoption as sons, the redemption of our bodies."

The Apostles Healed People

Healing was one of the assignments Jesus gave his apostles. He directed, "Heal the sick, raise the dead, cleanse those who have leprosy, drive out demons. Freely you have received, freely give" (Matt. 10:8). Acts shows us that the apostles did heal people. Simon Peter had the gift of healing. In Acts 9 he found a man named Aeneas, who had been bedridden for eight years with palsy. Palsy was a disease that affected the central nervous system, causing paralysis. "'Aeneas,' Peter said to him, 'Jesus Christ heals you. Get up and take care of your mat.' Immediately Aeneas got up" (Acts 9:34). Aeneas immediately got up, completely healed!

Paul also healed people. In Acts 14, he encountered a man who had been crippled from birth. Paul perceived faith in the man. With a loud voice, Paul declared, "Stand up on your feet!" The man jumped up and started walking for the first time in his life (Acts 14:8–10).

These healings helped real people who had real needs. As indicated in the previous chapter, healings were a part of the specific signs of apostles which authenticated their ministry (see 2 Cor. 12:12 and Heb. 2:4).

Does God Heal People Today?

Does God heal people? Absolutely! The Bible says, "I am the LORD, who heals you" (Exod. 15:26). God does heal people of their sicknesses. But what about these healings we hear of today? Our radios and televisions are flooded with healing claims and services. Are these genuine? Are people really being healed?

We do know that some people today who claim to heal are fakes. One spectacular healer seemed to have an uncanny knowledge of the physical ailments of people in his services. His services were remarkable. The bubble burst, however, when it was discovered that he was receiving information about certain people through a remote hookup with his wife. His "healing crusades" were discredited.

The lifestyles of some of the leaders in the healing movement leave a great deal to be desired. One female faith healer was married several times. She suffered from a variety of diseases for which no cures were available. She died.

Not all people involved in the healing movement are phonies. I mention the fakes only to make you aware that there is a healing racket today. Some of what we see is a con game. The hottest place in hell is reserved for such phonies. They have created much heartache and sorrow for hurting people who genuinely need help.

Many of the teachings which these "healers" profess are wrong. For example, some say all sickness is due to sin. Some is—but not all! Paul mentioned some people in the Corinthian church who were sick because of their personal sin. They participated in the Lord's Supper in an unworthy manner. He cautioned that they were eating and drinking damnation unto themselves. As a result, Paul declared, "That is why many among you are weak and sick, and a number of you have fallen asleep" (1 Cor. 11:30).

I do believe some people are sick because they are not right with God. As we have already mentioned, spiritual and emotional turmoil can contribute to physical problems. The classic example is an ulcer. Not every ulcer is caused by sin. But some people who worry excessively and carry a heavy load of unresolved guilt because of past sin do get ulcers. I guess I am old-fashioned enough to believe that a "mourner's bench experience" would help a lot of people—a down-on-your-knees with tear-filled eyes and getting-right-with-God kind of experience! I do believe some people could get well physically if they would get well spiritually.

Every time a person gets sick, though, this sickness is not caused by personal sin. The account of the man born blind in John 9 makes this clear. This man had been blind from his birth. The disciples wondered why. Some believed that the man might have sinned in some kind of prenatal existence. Others explained that he was blind as a punishment for his parents' sins (see v. 2). The answer Jesus gave is helpful: "'Neither this man nor his parents sinned,' said Jesus, 'but this happened so that the work of God might be displayed in his life'" (v. 3). Sick people may or may not be sick because of personal sin. There may be other reasons for the sickness.

In addition, it is not always God's will for everyone to be healed. Paul prayed for healing, but it did not occur. In 2 Corinthians 12, Paul talked about a physical problem that was a great burden to him. He asked the Lord three times (v. 8) to take the problem from him. The Lord's response to him is helpful to all of us: "My grace is sufficient for you, for my power is made perfect in weakness" (v. 9). The Lord did not heal Paul on this occasion. So Paul declared, "Therefore I will boast all the more gladly about my weaknesses, so that Christ's power may rest on me" (v. 9). Paul recognized God had some larger, greater purposes in mind. So it is with some Christians who are afflicted with cancer or other debilitating diseases.

Paul did not heal everyone who needed to be healed. In 2 Timothy 4:20, Paul mentioned a man named Trophimus whom he had left sick at Miletus. What was wrong? Did the man not have enough faith? Did he not believe God for his healing? Nothing like this is indicated. If it were always God's will for everyone to be healed, then no one would ever die. Every person Jesus healed eventually died.

Another mistake of some modern healing teaching is that the healing is conditional on the faith of the person. This is not taught in Scripture. At times, the Bible indicates that the faith of the person was a factor. But at other times, the faith of others came into play. On other occasions, no particular faith was involved in a person's healing.

Our faith is not the variable. The will of God is. God's will is the crucial point. Generally speaking, it is God's will to heal people. How do I know? Well, let's take a little test. Have you ever been sick? Yes. Did you get well? Yes. So you have experienced healing yourself! The good news is that ultimately all sickness will be healed!

I received an interesting letter from a fine doctor at Jacksonville's Mayo Clinic. One of our church members is his patient. She has a very debilitating terminal disease. Writing about healing, the Christian doctor said, "Modern scientific advances are truly blessings from God. Humans can mend some bodies and human words can comfort some hearts, but all this falls far short of the restoration of wholeness and deliverance from sin and destruction each one of us desperately needs from our Redeemer." Then he closed the letter, "In His Waiting Room, but with prescription already in hand." What an appropriate statement for Christians.

Bad teaching on the subject of healing has produced several detrimental results. For example, people may shun doctors and medicines. The result is tragic, unnecessary death. How sad to see little children die because their parents refuse to take them to the hospital or to allow medicines to be administered.

In addition, many suffering people are subjected to a great deal of cruelty. I know a very fine Bible teacher at one of my previous churches. Since giving birth to her daughter, she has had a crippling form of arthritis. She moves on crutches with difficulty and pain. This woman is a wonderful Bible teacher, a marvelous soul-winner, and a sweet Christian. Once she was waiting in line at a fast-food restaurant. A person approached her car window and reached in and grabbed one of her crippled hands.

"Poor little you," this stranger said. "God didn't keep his promise to you, did he?" What cruelty! Misguided and extreme people on the subject of healing can cause so much suffering.

Sometimes Christians who are sick are made to feel they just don't have enough faith. This creates an enormous amount of guilt. What a terrible thing to tell people, "If you just had enough faith, then you could be healed."

To teach that it is God's will for people always to be healed is to hinder them from learning the lessons God may be trying to teach through sickness. I heard Warren Wiersbe say in a message once that a fine lady in his congregation was going through a time of suffering and sickness. His heart was encouraged and blessed when she asked him, "Pastor, pray for me that I won't miss what God is trying to tell me." Sometimes God has lessons for us which can only best be learned in times of sickness. An old poem says it well.

> I walked a mile with pleasure,
> She chattered all the way;
> But I was none the wiser
> For all she had to say.
> I walked a mile with sorrow,
> And nere a word said she.
> But oh, the things I learned from her,
> When sorrow walked with me.

Incorrect teaching about healing can cause damage to our relationship with God. Remember the young policeman mentioned earlier? He died of cancer. Another policeman is now attending our church. His first wife had cancer. The pastor of the church he attended previously told him she was healed. But she died. My policeman friend is having a real struggle in his relationship with God.

A young man came to Christ and was called to preach under my ministry. When I first met him, he was a disc jockey at a radio station in a small Georgia town. His young wife had cancer and she died. The people in the church which she attended told him God killed her because he wouldn't come to their church. He almost went crazy. It took a long time to bring him to Christ.

In addition to these serious results of incorrect teaching on healing, note something else. The methods used by modern faith healers do not coincide with those used in the New Testament. How did Jesus heal people? Did he book appearances on popular television shows? Did he appear with his subjects on a talk show? No, there was no publicity. He did not announce in advance any healing crusades. In fact, he said nothing about it. He just healed people as he went along. He never healed people to create an atmosphere of evangelism, hoping to sensationalize salvation. In fact, the healings he performed did not always cause people to believe in him.

For those who say they have the New Testament gift of healing, I have several requests. Let them go to the hospitals where people suffer with devastating, painful, terminal diseases like AIDS and leukemia. Let them go into the cancer wards and cure people of this terrible disease. Let them board airplanes and fly to Zaire and Rwanda. Let them heal the thousands of sick and hungry people in these places.

The question persists: Does God heal people today? The answer must be that he does. The only extensive, elaborate passage of Scripture which gives any indication of how we are to go about healing is found in James 5. This does not, of course, deal with every circumstance. In fact, it's a rather specific circumstance. As you think of this passage, place it in the context of the variety of human emotions and conditions which Christians experience. For each experience, there is a spiritual response.

In times of affliction, the Christian response is to pray. In times of joy, the response is to sing psalms (see v. 13). In that context, verse 14 raises the matter of sickness. The question is asked, "Is any one of you sick?" Then verses 14–16 give the considerations involved in responding to sickness. Let's discuss these considerations in detail.

A sick Christian is placed before us. "Is any sick among you?" The word *sick* means "without strength." This person is so sick that he cannot attend church. What now? What is the church supposed to do? James says, "He should call the elders of the church." Note that it is the responsibility of the sick person to call for help from the church. The term *elders* may refer to pastors or other ministers on the staff. Perhaps even deacons could be included. Church ministers do not have miraculous powers to know when a person is sick. If nobody calls, they probably won't know about an illness. Unfortunately, some sick Christians seem to take pleasure in being sick, not letting the church know about it, and then getting angry when no one visits them.

The "elders" of the church (I believe this means the pastors and leaders of the church) are to consider matters such as this. These spiritual leaders are to be people of prayer. They are to determine if this is a situation where the prayer of faith can be prayed and God will heal. Once the church leaders arrive, they are to follow a specific procedure. First, they should pray. Then anointing with oil in the name of the Lord is mentioned. Actually, the tense of the verb indicates that the anointing with oil occurs first. It could be rendered, "Having anointed with oil, let them pray."

There are actually two views about the meaning of "oil" in this verse. One is that the word *oil* is used as a symbol of the Holy Spirit. The other view is that the oil refers to medicine. Two primary words for anointing are used in the Greek language. One is *chrio*. It is the more sacred word. *Christ* is taken from this word. Christ means the "Anointed One." The other word is *aleipho*. This is the more secular word. It is found in Mark 6:13: "They drove out many demons and anointed many sick people with oil and healed them."

Oil was used as a medicine in New Testament times. Its value was well known in the Middle East. Some referred to oil as "the best of all medicines." It was the antibiotic of the ancient world. Jesus used this word when he referred to the care the Samaritan gave to the man who fell among thieves: "He went to him and bandaged his wounds, pouring on oil and wine" (Luke 10:34). This latter word *aleipho* is the one used in James 5. Personally, I think the reference is to the use of medicine.

When a person gets sick, he or she must ease the discomfort. If necessary, the person should see a doctor. If the physician so prescribes, the sick person should obtain a prescription and have it filled at a pharmacy.

James 5:16 also talks about confession of sins to one another. Place this in proper perspective. The passage must not be misused. I have seen harm done when people confess matters openly. Never confess a sin beyond its circle of influence. Don't wash dirty clothes in public. Private sin requires private confession. Public sin needs public confession. Apparently, this sick man's sin had hurt his church. In an atmosphere of humility and mutual love, he confessed his sin to the elders. It may have been like this: "I have sinned against my church. Please forgive me." The elders may have replied, "We sin by not trying harder to help you and restore you."

Verse 15 describes the prayer of faith. This means a prayer proceeding from faith. I do not believe this prayer can be prayed in every instance. I believe it can be prayed only if God's will to heal is confirmed by the Holy Spirit in the heart of those who pray. In answer to this prayer, the promise is, "The Lord will raise him up" (v. 15). And in addition to this, "If he has sins [it seems he has], he will be forgiven." Note that it is the prayer, in addition to the oil, which brings the desired results—the "one-two punch" applied to healing the sick!

Every circumstance is not covered in this passage on prayer for healing. But it does give us several clear guidelines. The use of medical means is certainly acceptable. Sometimes sin is a factor in the sickness of the individual. The church does have a responsibility and a ministry in the area of prayer. Many times it is God's will to heal in answer to prayer.

You may get sick and be healed. If so, be sure to give praise to the Lord. You may get sick and not be healed. In this circumstance, praise the Lord for whatever he is doing in your life through the sickness. Sometimes God uses our sicknesses and the lessons we learn through them to help others. In 2 Corinthians 1 we learn, "Praise be to the God and Father of our Lord Jesus Christ, the Father of compassion and the God of all comfort, who comforts us in all our troubles, so that we can comfort those in any trouble with the comfort we ourselves have received from God" (1:3–4).

How wonderful to know that one day there will be no more disease or sickness. The Bible promises, "And God shall wipe away all tears from their eyes; and there shall be no more death, neither sorrow, nor crying, neither shall there be any more pain: for the former things are passed away" (Rev. 21:4). There will be no need for healing in heaven! But while we're here on earth, the Holy Spirit has given these "gifts of healings."

What to Do When You Get Sick

1. Pray for God to heal you.
2. Check to see if there is any unconfessed sin in your life.
3. If the sickness is such that you require it, seek a good doctor.
4. If he so prescribes, get a good medicine.
5. Keep on praying about the matter.
6. If God heals you, by whatever means, give the means your appreciation and give God the glory.
7. If you are not healed, look for transcending purposes which may be involved in the matter.

Since Mark Brunell's knee is not as bad as was first thought, and since he is a Jacksonville Jaguar, does this mean that God is no longer a Dallas Cowboys fan? (To all my Texas readers: Juuusst kiddin'!)

CHAPTER 13

FIVE WORDS ARE BETTER

I had been around the tongues phenomenon for many years, but this was different. Mrs. Burt (the name is fictitious, but the account is true) was the teacher of our church's strongest women's class. As her pastor I was grateful for her faithfulness to her class. The women loved her, and she loved them. But the word got out that she was involved in a new church group on the edge of town. A pastor had moved in, set up a small work, and was teaching people how to speak in tongues. Mrs. Burt had become a part of the group.

Mrs. Burt scheduled a meeting with me and the prominent Bible teacher who was speaking at our annual Bible conference. In the meeting she told me and the godly Bible teacher that what we taught was fine as far as it went, but we were just not giving the people the full gospel. We were not filled with the Spirit because we had not spoken in tongues. She felt we were depriving the people of the evidence of God's Spirit in the life of believers.

This was not my first experience with the tongues movement. Brought up in a small county seat town in northwest Georgia, I knew about many Pentecostal groups that were involved in tongues. My father was a singer. I would go with him to different churches where he and his musical group sang. It was not uncommon to see people speaking in tongues in some of the churches in our county.

When I first became a pastor, I came in contact with the tongues phenomenon. Where I came from, if you are a preacher, you must have a radio program. This goes with the territory. My fifteen-minute program came right after Sister Cunningham's. In order to make a smooth transition, I would slip quietly into the radio studio just two or three minutes before her program ended. Invariably, upon my appearance, she would break into babbling. I never knew if this was for my benefit, her listeners' benefit, or for her own benefit.

Along my journey in the Spirit, I have met many fine Christians who believe speaking in tongues is intended for modern Christians. Some believe it is *the* definitive evidence of being filled with the Spirit.

Mrs. Burt was different. She challenged my understanding of Scripture and my faithfulness to declare to the people the whole counsel of God. Really, I am thankful to her for this because I had to search the Scriptures for myself. I could not take anyone else's word for it. I had been taught that the Bible is our basis of authority, our guide for faith and practice. After several weeks of intense study of the Scriptures, my mind and heart came to a quiet, peaceful confidence on the subject. I asked Mrs. Burt to resign her Sunday school class. Although this caused minor disruption, the end result was peace and harmony for the congregation.

Just a few years later, I encountered a similar experience in my church in south Alabama. Another local Baptist church was involved in the tongues phenomenon. I had never known a Baptist church to become involved in this. A very loving, sweet family from that church joined our congregation. I was told that they had come to the church specifically to introduce tongues into our congregation. I started a series of verse-by-verse messages through 1 Corinthians. Carefully and calmly, I taught what the verses of those chapters meant to me. Within a month after this, the family quietly left our church.

Now I'll share with you the result of my study on the subject of tongues. To begin, let's consider again the subject of spiritual gifts. I have pointed out that each list of gifts, when placed in chronological order, gets smaller. In 1 Corinthians 12 there are two lists. Verses 8–10 give nine of the gifts. Then, in verse 28, eight of the gifts are listed. Seven spiritual gifts are listed in Romans 12:6–8. Then, in 1 Peter 4:10–11, only two categories of gifts are mentioned—*serving gifts* and *speaking gifts*. Some other gifts are mentioned in other passages. The gift of celibacy and the gift of martyrdom are not mentioned here (see 1 Cor. 7:7; 13:3).

These lists seem to be suggestive rather than exhaustive. The body of Christ constantly grows and changes. What is needed at one particular time may not be needed later. In his sovereign power, the Holy Spirit gives the church gifts as they are needed for a particular time and place.

Let's consider one further detail about these lists. When they are placed in chronological order, they do get smaller. The category of "sign gifts" is not included here at all. They drop out of the picture. These gifts were not gifts which all believers had. Specifically in 1 Corinthians 12:29–30, Paul indicated that not all Christians are apostles, prophets, or teachers. Neither are they workers of miracles; neither do they have gifts of healing; neither do they speak with tongues and interpret. So the possession of or lack of any of these gifts has nothing to do with being filled with the Spirit, or even spirituality itself.

Two ground rules must be established in this study of tongues. First, as your author, let me state I have no intention of offending or discrediting any person in the charismatic movement. I don't intend to belittle my Pentecostal brethren in any way. Nothing here is intended to question the sincerity of any of God's people. My purpose is to discover what the Bible says.

Our second rule is always to be guided by Scripture, not by experience. You may be thinking, "I know Bill and it happened to him. Mrs. Simon is one of the sweetest people I know, and she had that experience. If it is genuine to them, it must be real."

Life teaches us that to base decisions on experience alone is unwise. What has happened to us is not to be a sole guide for life—not my experience, not your experience, not any person's experience. *Scripture* must be our guide! There is only one way to test the validity of any experience, regardless of my feelings or beliefs about the experience. I must bring this experience to the Bible and find what it says. Then, my experience is determined to be valid or invalid based on its harmony with the teachings of Scripture.

The tongues movement has affected every major denomination. The movement is not limited to the mainline or evangelical denominations. In addition, speaking in tongues has been a part of various cults. Some non-Christian religions, like Hinduism and Islam, have also reported the phenomenon. Christians cannot evade the subject. We should be knowledgeable. Let's turn to the New Testament to determine what God says on the subject.

Historical Books

The first five books of the New Testament are historical in nature. The subject of tongues is mentioned in only two of them—the Gospel of Mark and the book of Acts. First, look at the Mark 16 passage. Why don't you get your Bible and carefully examine each passage as we discuss it.

In Mark 16:15 we are given an abbreviated form of our Lord's assignment to his followers: "Go into all the world and preach the good news to all creation." Next there is a statement in verse 16 about belief and baptism. Notice this verse does not say that those who are not baptized are not saved. It says those who do not believe are not saved.

Then, verses 17 and 18 say, "And these signs will accompany those who believe: In my name they will drive out demons; they will speak in new tongues; they will pick up snakes with their hands; and when they drink deadly poison, it will not hurt them at all; they will place their hands on sick people, and they will get well."

The word for tongues in this passage is *glossa*. Sometimes this phenomenon is referred to as *glossolalia*. The Greek word for tongue, *glossa*, and the Greek word for speak, *laleo*, are combined to make this word. *Glossa* always means "tongue," as in a foreign language.

Verse 18 continues with other statements about these followers of Jesus. With the exception of one statement—"When they drink deadly poison, it will not hurt them"—everything mentioned here is recorded as happening in the book of Acts. "In my name they will drive out demons." This happened in the book of Acts. "They will pick up snakes." In Acts 28:1–5, Paul was bitten by a snake but was unharmed. "They will place their hands on sick people, and they will get well." This they also did.

This passage states a specific promise made to the followers of Jesus. If we apply part of the promise today, we must apply all of the promises. In certain parts of the Southeast, there are churches engaged in handling snakes and drinking poison. These people take this very seriously. I have never attended one of these services, but I have seen some on television. However strongly we may disagree with these people, they are consistent. Inconsistency occurs when only a portion of this passage is applied.

The second mention of tongues occurs in the book of Acts. Tongues are referred to several times. "When the day of Pentecost came, they were all together in one place. Suddenly a sound like the blowing of a violent wind came from heaven and filled the whole house where they were sitting. They saw what seemed to be tongues of fire that separated and came to rest on each of them. All of them were filled with the Holy Spirit and began to speak in other tongues as the Spirit enabled them" (Acts 2:1–4).

The word for tongues here again is *glossa*. It means "other languages" or "tongues." A careful examination of these verses indicates beyond question that what took place on the day of Pentecost was the gift of speaking foreign languages. Continue reading in verse 5, "Now there were staying in Jerusalem God-fearing Jews from every nation under heaven." The Greek word for language here is one from which we get our English word *dialect*. Those present heard the disciples speak in their own dialect—the language of their day. I speak English fairly well. But when I am speaking up north or out west, people often refer to my southern dialect. Could it be my "ya'lls" and "sho'nuffs!"

Verses 7 and 8 continue: "Utterly amazed, they asked: 'Are not all these men who are speaking Galileans? Then how is it that each of us hears them in his own native language?'" The reference here is to dialect again. In verse 9 and following, the different nationalities present on the day of Pentecost are named. Then they said, "We hear them declaring the wonders of God in our own tongues!" (v. 11). The reference now is *glossa* or "foreign language."

What took place on the day of Pentecost? The Holy Spirit gave these believers the ability to speak other languages. People from many nationalities were in Jerusalem on that day and they heard these disciples speaking in their languages and particular dialects. How many responded? Three thousand people! That's speaking the language!

Turn to Acts 10. Simon Peter, led by the Holy Spirit, went to the house of Cornelius, a Gentile. In verse 44, Peter is preaching. He didn't finish his message: "While Peter was still speaking these words, the Holy Spirit came on all who heard the message." Acts 11:17 gives the interpretation of what took place in the house of Cornelius. Peter indicated, "God gave them the same gift as he gave us." The same thing occurred in the house of the Gentile Cornelius that had happened to Peter and the other disciples on the day of Pentecost. Acts 2 could be described as the Jewish Pentecost and Acts 10 as the Gentile Pentecost. This is one way to think of it.

Acts 19 reports another occurrence of tongues. Here was a group of people who were in transition, chronicled in Acts, which is a transitional book. One transition in Acts is from the Old Testament dispensation to the New Testament dispensation. This is why angels are mentioned in the first part of the book but are not described later in the book. Things were in transition. In Ephesus, we find a group of people who were "in between," much like you might be when you have to move from one computer software program to another. They had been baptized with John's baptism, but they didn't understand baptism in the name of the Lord Jesus.

In verse 2, Paul asked, "Did you receive?" They replied that they didn't know there was a Holy Spirit. Then, in verse 6 Paul laid his hands on these Ephesian disciples of John. As he did, the Holy Spirit came on them and they spoke with tongues (*glossolalia*, "foreign languages") and they prophesied. Remember, those people were in transition, and they had received the gift of the Holy Spirit. Beyond question, when the subject of tongues is mentioned in Acts, the reference is to a gift of foreign languages. The gift of speaking in foreign languages allowed people to hear the gospel and to be saved.

Here are three final observations before we leave Acts: (1) In each of these occurrences, Jews were present; (2) one or more of the apostles were present; and (3) Acts is a transition book. John Phillips is a wonderful friend of mine and a marvelous Bible teacher. I have heard him say on a number of occasions that we are never to build doctrine based solely on the book of Acts.

The Doctrinal Books

The next twenty-one New Testament books are doctrinal in nature. The subject of tongues is mentioned only in 1 Corinthians. The subject is not discussed in any of the other eight letters to the churches. Neither is the topic mentioned in the twelve general letters.

Paul dealt extensively with the subject of tongues in 1 Corinthians. First Corinthians 12–14 is the most extensive treatment of the subject anywhere in the Bible. This passage shows that something very different was happening in the Corinthian church. For instance, notice 1 Corinthians 14:2. If you have a King James Bible it reads, "for he that speaketh in an *unknown* tongue." Notice there is an italicized font used for "unknown." This means that the word is not in the original text. It was added in translation to make better sense of the passage. Perhaps the King James translators recognized that something different was going on in the Corinthian church.

The word for tongues in verse 2 is again *glossa*. But the word *unknown* is added. Does this indicate that the King James translators felt something was taking place in Corinth which was different from what took place in the book of Acts? I believe this is the case. Something fishy was going on in the Corinthian church! In Acts, tongues were foreign languages. In Corinth, tongues were ecstatic babbling.

A little background on the Corinthian church will help us here. The Corinthian Christians had been saved out of a very sinful lifestyle (see 1 Cor. 6:9–10). These believers had come from all kinds of immorality. They were involved in homosexuality, drunkenness, and other destructive behaviors. I have noticed that people who are saved out of deep sin generally experience a very emotional conversion.

A little boy, about nine, comes to know the Lord. He has been brought up in a Christian home. His mom and dad love Jesus and teach him about the

Lord. His salvation is a sweet, wonderful experience. But it may not be overly emotional. Actually, it may be quite matter-of-fact. On the other hand, consider a man who has been an alcoholic for twenty years and who has lived a rough life. He knows the depths of sin. At salvation, Jesus Christ rescues him from sin, and the power of God releases him from his shackles. He will probably be emotional about this. The change is dramatic.

The Corinthians were also emotional about their salvation! They were emotional to the point of being carried away, and they should have been. In too many places, there is too little emotion. The thought of what God has done for us in Jesus Christ should be overwhelming to our emotions. But each action has a reaction, as Newton said, and these Corinthians reacted in the extreme! They allowed their emotions to become dominant in their Christian life.

Several preachers came to preach at Corinth. Paul came and preached. They were saved and the church was founded. Apollos, the great orator, preached there, as well as Simon Peter. What was the biggest day Peter had experienced in his ministry? What was the most spectacular service he had witnessed? The day of Pentecost, of course.

Do you know any preacher in the world who would have three thousand people saved in one service and never tell anyone about it? What do you think Simon Peter told them when he came to Corinth? I can almost hear him now: "Folks, let me tell you what happened on the day of Pentecost." I can almost hear him describing it: "There was a sound of a rushing, mighty wind. Divided tongues came down upon us. We all spoke in tongues and three thousand people got saved. It was glorious!" I can almost hear the Corinthians saying, "We want that too." They got so carried away with the symbols *of* the power that they misunderstood the symbols *for* the power.

Let me explain. When the Lord called me to preach at age sixteen, I thought our pastor was the greatest preacher ever. He was a great preacher. Being a young preacher boy, I would sit in awe and listen to him preach. The word for his sermons was *dynomite!* I wanted to preach with power too.

As my pastor preached, he would wipe his mouth with a handkerchief. I must say I was intrigued by that. When I started preaching, I used my white handkerchief. Unfortunately, I didn't have my pastor's finesse and you could hardly hear me speak through my handkerchief! Several years later, I discovered that my pastor used notes as he preached. When he wanted to read his

171

notes, he would take his handkerchief and wipe his mouth. I mistook the symbol for the power!

I believe something similar to this happened at Corinth. The Corinthian Christians wanted everything God had for them. They heard about the experience of Pentecost. What took place at Corinth could be considered a Pentecostal imitation. At this point, Paul had a problem. How was he going to deal with this emotional excess among baby Christians? He certainly didn't want to stifle their enthusiasm or hinder their growth in the Christian life. So he established a series of guidelines in an attempt to help these young Christians. He knew if these guidelines were followed that the problems would be eliminated.

We face a similar problem today. We don't want to throw cold water on the enthusiasm of young converts. More churches today are like Thessalonica. They don't have the problem which the Corinthians had. They need Paul's exhortation to the church of Thessalonica: "Do not put out the Spirit's fire; do not treat prophecies with contempt" (1 Thess. 5:19–20).

Keep in mind several facts about the Corinthian church which indicate its spiritual condition: (1) the church was made up of carnal and childish believers; (2) tongues was a problem, not a blessing to the church; (3) Paul didn't write to encourage tongues, but to discourage them; and (4) after 1 Corinthians, tongues never appeared again in the New Testament.

Favorable Statements

I want to survey all the favorable statements Paul makes about tongues in 1 Corinthians 14. The first one is in verse 5. He says specifically, "I would like every one of you to speak in tongues." The word here again is *glossa*—"languages." Notice he makes the statement in contrast, saying, "But I would rather . . . " He is not praising the gifts of tongues as much as he is comparing it unfavorably to the gift of prophecy. His point is that the person who prophesies or preaches is greater in terms of gifts than the person who speaks with tongues.

A second favorable statement occurs in verse 18. "I thank God that I speak in tongues more than all of you." This statement qualifies Paul in the mind of some to speak on the subject of tongues. Some people say if you have not had the experience, you're not qualified to speak on it. Of course, this is nonsense. This is just like saying to an obstetrician, "You've never had a baby.

How can you deliver someone else's?" But Paul had known this experience. He had spoken with tongues more than they had. Paul indicated he did have the gift of speaking in languages he did not know in order to spread the gospel.

A third favorable statement occurs in verse 39. Paul said, "Therefore, my brothers, be eager to prophesy, and do not forbid speaking in tongues." This statement occurred after Paul concluded all the guidelines on the matter of tongues. In other words, if the guidelines were met, tongues were not to be forbidden.

Negative Statements

Notice that the gift of tongues is listed last. Why? There are three reasons found in the negative statements Paul made concerning tongues.

Verse 4 says, "He who speaks in a tongue edifies himself, but he who prophesies edifies the church." Paul is saying that tongue-speaking is basically a self-centered affair. The person who speaks in tongues builds up himself. He may have a sense of exhilaration or deep inner peace. No one else is helped or edified.

Secondly, in verse 14 Paul said, "For if I pray in a tongue, my spirit prays, but my mind is unfruitful." He is saying, if I pray in a language I don't know, I have no idea what I am saying. So is the prayer any good? Verse 15 says, "I will pray with my spirit, but I will also pray with my mind; I will sing with my spirit, but I will also sing with my mind." That is best. Paul is saying that it is much better to be able to pray and sing with understanding. When a person tries to bypass the intellect, understanding is not possible.

I was listening to a tape on the matter of tongues recently. The teacher said, "Now, don't expect to understand this. Your mind can't figure all this out." The Spirit of God does not bypass your mind! It is dangerous to be told that you must put aside your reason and intellect. If you ever hear someone suggest that you should put your mind in neutral and let your emotions go, you are on dangerous ground. True spirituality involves every aspect of the human personality. The mind is informed. The emotions are stirred. The will is activated.

The third negative statement occurs in verse 33: "For God is not a God of disorder but of peace. As in all the congregations of the saints. . . ." Paul is saying that we should pay attention to our surroundings. If there is confusion in the church and people are disturbed, know that God is not the cause. Someone else is.

Verse 40 summarizes the whole matter beautifully: "But everything should be done in a fitting and orderly way."

Guidelines

Let's examine the guidelines Paul gives the Corinthian church in the matter of speaking in tongues. As I indicated earlier in the chapter, I have been around the tongues movement all my life. The tongues movement is not new. It comes in waves. When I was a boy, there was a strong tongues movement. It waned. Now this phenomenon has reappeared. Many people speak in tongues on television programs. Almost without exception when tongues are used today, these guidelines set down by Paul are violated.

Paul's first guideline is in verse 27: "If anyone speaks in a tongue, two—or at the most three—should speak." What is the maximum number of people who can speak in tongues in a service? Three! I have seen this violated over and over again. Few people obey this clear command of Scripture.

The second guideline is also in verse 27: "One at a time." The speakers should talk in order, one at a time. This guideline is also routinely violated.

The third guideline, also in verse 27, says, "Someone must interpret." The word *interpret* means the ability to decipher a foreign language. Paul continues in verse 28, "If there is no interpreter, the speaker should keep quiet in the church and speak to himself and God." There must be interpretation of tongues. I have seen this principle violated over and over again.

This matter of interpretation is interesting. I have been in church services with people who claimed they had the gift of interpretation. I have heard a person speak in an "unknown tongue" for perhaps ten seconds. I have also heard a person "interpret" these short messages but take twenty minutes to do so! This is certainly amazing! The interpretation is often given in seventeenth-century English as if the Spirit of God must confine himself to 1611 jargon to deliver a message for today!

According to Paul, to validate whether a person is speaking a foreign language or a foreign tongue is to have three people with the gift of interpretation render its meaning independently of one another. Then their interpretations should be compared.

The fourth guideline occurs in verse 34: "Women should remain silent in the churches." Paul does not say that women can't pray or speak in the church services. This would certainly contradict what he taught in 1 Corinthians 11 about women praying and prophesying in the church. Obviously, this statement must be interpreted in context. He is saying that women can't speak in tongues in the church.

There is an interesting Corinthian background to this command. On the Acrocorinthus (the mountain at Corinth), there was a temple of Venus. A thousand temple prostitutes attended the worship of Venus. Frenzied, ecstatic babblings were part of their sensuous services. If Corinthian men should walk into the Christian church in Corinth and see women babbling, they would immediately identify it with the pagan, sexual worship of Venus. "What have we here? Let's go in and enjoy ourselves!" The point is that women speaking in tongues would give the wrong impression.

Tongues Shall Cease

"Where there are tongues, they will be stilled," Paul declared in 1 Corinthians 13:8. In fact, they do cease. They're finished! From here on out, no tongues. There is no reference to tongues in Romans or Galatians. The subject is not mentioned in Ephesians or Colossians. Nor do we find it in Jude or Revelation. Search the rest of the New Testament books. Tongues are not mentioned. What does this mean?

The main theme of 1 Corinthians 13 is love. In this chapter, Paul discussed the preeminence and permanence of love. Then, in verse 8 he referred to three spiritual gifts which were evidently temporary in nature. He mentioned prophecy, tongues, and knowledge. He said, "Love never fails. But where there are prophecies, they will cease." The verb he used is future passive in tense: "They shall be caused to cease." Something will cause this gift to cease. "Where there are tongues, they will be stilled." The verb here is future middle in tense: "They shall be stilled in and of themselves." Then, "Where there is knowledge, it will pass away." Again, the verb is future passive tense. Something will take place to cause the knowledge to pass away.

Verse 9 continues, "For we know in part and we prophesy in part." Paul seems to be saying that at the time of his writing, knowledge and prophecy were partial. Then, in verse 10 he continued, "But when perfection comes, the imperfect disappears." What does Paul mean by the phrase "that which is perfect"? (KJV). Some say the reference is to Jesus. But the word *perfection* is a neuter word. Scripture never refers to Jesus by a neuter word. Jesus is not a "that which is." Others say the phrase refers to the second coming of Jesus. With the possible exception of the phrase "face to face" in verse 12, there is no indication that the second coming of Jesus is intended here. To what does the phrase "when perfection comes" refer?

Verse 12 gives us a clue. The verse begins, "Now we see but a poor reflection as in a mirror." In those days polished metal was used for mirrors. It was an imperfect way to see—certainly not what we're accustomed to today. Can you imagine getting up tomorrow morning and not having a clear mirror in which to gaze at yourself? Verse 12 continues, "Then we shall see face to face. Now I know in part; then I shall know fully, even as I am fully known." Paul is saying that we don't have the full, entire revelation yet. We don't have full knowledge yet. But a time will come when a "perfect mirror" will be available.

James 1:23 makes the same point. James talks about a person beholding his or her natural face in a glass, and he uses the same word used in 1 Corinthians 13. Then, in James 1:25 he says, "But the man who looks intently into the perfect [same Greek word, *telion*] law that gives freedom." What is the perfect law of liberty? The Bible! The Word of God!

Another verse is helpful. Second Corinthians 3:18 also uses a mirror as an illustration of the Word of God. Let's give the entire quotation. "And we, who with unveiled faces all reflect the Lord's glory, are being transformed into his likeness with ever-increasing glory, which comes from the Lord, who is the Spirit." I have heard Warren Wiersbe summarize this verse like this: "The child of God looks into the Word of God, sees the Son of God, and is changed by the Spirit of God into the image of the Son of God!" Notice the similarity in terminology between this verse and 1 Corinthians 13:12. A glass is an illustration or symbol of the Bible. Paul is saying that a time would come when a perfect mirror would be available—the Bible!

Now, back to 1 Corinthians 13:12. We see through a glass which is imperfect and partial. But one of these days there will be a glass which will be perfect—the Word of God. "Open face" indicates that in the Bible we are able to see a complete picture of ourselves and also a full revelation of the Lord Jesus Christ.

In New Testament times, there were people who had the gift of prophecy. When they preached they couldn't say, "Turn in your Bibles to Romans 8." There was no book of Romans. So the gift of prophecy was needed. They literally spoke the word of God. But preachers today do have the perfect mirror of the Word. The ability of the New Testament prophet is not needed today.

Further, God gave men the knowledge to write the Bible under His inspiration. When the full revelation of Scripture was completed, the gift of knowledge ceased. No one has the gift to write additional Scripture today. What could possibly be added to "that which is perfect"?

Tongues: A Sign Gift

Tongues ceased and there are several reasons why. First, tongues served as a sign to the unbelieving Jews. First Corinthians 14:21 says, "In the Law it is written: 'Through men of strange tongues and through the lips of foreigners I will speak to this people.'" The reference is taken from Isaiah 28:11–12. God would give a judgment sign to the Jews similar to the sign given to them in the days of Isaiah. At that time, God judged Israel. The Assyrians came speaking a language which the Israelites could not understand. As a judgment from God, the Assyrians conquered the Israelites. In New Testament times, early believers spoke tongues as a judgment sign to the unbelieving Jews. What did the Jews say? "They are drunk!" In A.D. 70, the Romans destroyed Jerusalem and burned the temple. Judgment fell. There was no more need for this judgment sign.

Secondly, tongues ceased because it belonged to the infancy period of the church. Look at 1 Corinthians 13:11: "When I was a child, I talked like a child, I thought like a child, I reasoned like a child. When I became a man, I put childish ways behind me." A baby is one of the sweetest things in the world. She begins speaking by using very brief syllables. "Dada." "Mama." Baby talk is cute. I'm reminded of this with my grandchildren. But it wouldn't be cute if a forty-year-old man still said, "dada" and "mama." Baby talk is intended to be a foundation. Eloquent language is built upon baby talk. Paul said, " When I became a man, I put childish ways behind me." "Grow up," he declared. "Put your toys into the toy box and mature in the Christian life." To attempt to go back and pick up something that was intended for the infancy of the church is to go back into immaturity. Paul urged the Corinthians to move on!

Some Closing Statements

I want to wrap up the study of tongues by giving you a summation of the modern tongues movement as I view it. I say this in the spirit of love. I do not mean to be derogatory toward sincere, genuine people who may differ with me. I make these statements on the basis of what I have witnessed in the modern tongues movement.

First, the basic doctrines of the modern tongues movement are in error. The most erroneous of them all is that tongues is an evidence of the baptism or filling of the Holy Spirit. This is contrary to 1 Corinthians 12:13: "For we were all baptized by one Spirit into one body."

Then, 1 Corinthians 12:30 specifically says, "Do all speak in tongues?" The obvious answer is no. Speaking in tongues cannot be the evidence of the filling of the Holy Spirit. If it were, Paul would not have said that all people do not speak in tongues. He did say that all believers are commanded to be filled with the Spirit (see Eph. 5:18). Also, all believers have been baptized by the Spirit (see 1 Cor. 12:13).

In addition, where in the Bible do we find suggestions about how to induce this gift? Nowhere! Those who seek to "prime the pump" have no biblical basis for doing so. When you try to prime the pump, it means there's not much water there! Remember, the Holy Spirit is sovereign. He "bestows gifts as he will."

Second, whenever and wherever tongues appears, it is always hurtful and divisive. Tongues is a source of division and discord. It is always disruptive. A few years ago I had the privilege of leading a young lady to know Christ as her personal Savior. She began to grow quickly in her Christian life. Soon after her salvation, I heard her quote from memory the entire letter of 1 John. I watched her became involved with a group of people in the tongues movement. She became critical of our church and its ministry. Later she abandoned the Christian faith altogether. The last I heard, she was living a sinful lifestyle.

When people are taken away from the main business of witnessing, we should look for the reason. In addition, tongues is no trophy given for the "best spirituality in a church" award! Keep in mind that the church in Corinth was the only New Testament church which had the gift of tongues. Remember also that Corinth was, according to Paul's judgment, a carnal congregation.

Let those who believe in tongues go to churches where the doctrine is believed. It is much better for a person to be open in this matter. If you believe in tongues, declare yourself. Find a church which believes this doctrine. Don't stay in a church where it is not believed and thus become a source of division.

Third, there seems to be no known language spoken in the modern manifestation of tongues. W. A. Criswell points out in his book *The Holy Spirit in Today's World* that the Toronto Institute of Linguistics studied the tongues phenomenon. They concluded that no human language was spoken. Every phonetic sound of the tongues they studied related to a language spoken by the person speaking.

Fourth, none of the great people of God in church history spoke in tongues. D. L. Moody did not speak in tongues. Charles Spurgeon did not speak in tongues. Billy Graham does not speak in tongues. I read a few years ago about a pop singer who has sung in the Las Vegas gambling casinos. He says he has spoken in tongues. Is he more spiritual than the great men of God who have won multitudes to Christ because he has spoken in tongues and they haven't? I think not!

For that matter, we have no evidence that Jesus spoke in tongues! Can you imagine someone asking Jesus today, "Jesus, are you filled with the Spirit?"

He would say, "Oh, yes, I was filled with the Spirit when I was baptized. The Spirit of God descended upon me like a dove."

"Well, Jesus, did you speak in tongues?"

"No, I healed the sick. I raised the dead. I gave salvation to hurting souls. But I didn't speak in tongues."

"Well, then, Jesus, I'm sorry. You aren't filled with the Spirit."

Finally, tongues is not helpful in winning lost people to Christ. In 1 Corinthians 14:16, 17, and 23 Paul discussed the unsaved coming into a Christian worship service. He indicated that if people are speaking in tongues, the unsaved won't understand and will think they have gone into an asylum. Paul made it clear that our priority is to exalt Christ in such a way that Christians can be edified and the unsaved evangelized. This means that Christian worship must be understood by Christians and non-Christians alike.

Paul says in verse 19, "But in the church I would rather speak five intelligible words to instruct others than ten thousand words in a tongue." That is quite a comparison! Ten thousand words. At a normal rate of speaking, that might take ninety minutes. But five words would take just a few seconds. Is there any question what Paul is saying? Five words which are understandable are better than a blizzard of words that no one can understand.

Let me give you five words which are better than ten thousand in an incomprehensible language: "Christ died for our sins." Multitudes of people can be won to Christ with that simple, understandable message. Our priority should be using the tongue we have to witness to the lost without utilizing any other tongue. "O for a thousand tongues to sing, our Great Redeemer's praise," says the hymn writer. He had the right idea!

It seems to me that tongues is a detour off the main highway of the Christian life. What is the function of the Holy Spirit's power? Acts 1:8 can't be missed: "But you will receive power when the Holy Spirit comes on you; and you will be my witnesses."

There is a great hunger in our day for the things of God. The resurgence of tongues shows this. I believe the Spirit of God himself is creating this hunger. Christians of all denominations want something that is real, genuine, and of the Spirit. The deadness and dullness of multitudes of our churches is lamentable. But we must stay away from poor substitutes and seek the real thing.

In some ways the tongues movement is similar to the drug culture. An addict must snort or shoot stronger and stronger drugs. This cycle is repeated in the tongues movement. The thrill of tongues wears off. So the next "high" is being slain in the Spirit. From there, exorcisms or miracles or prophecies or visions provide the emotional thrill. Some "crisis" arises for this person involved in tongues, and the thrill subsides. If something new and more exciting does not come along, the person might begin to fake his "highs." He may go into deep despondency or spiritual decline. Don't let this happen to you.

In his excellent book *The Corinthian Catastrophe*, Robert Gardner recounts an interesting tale. There is a fable about a dog with a bone in his mouth walking across a bridge. He looks over the edge of this low bridge and sees another dog (actually himself) with a bone in its mouth. The bone in the reflection appears bigger and better than the bone he has. Dropping his bone, he reaches for the bone he sees in the calm reflection. He loses the reality he has for a reflection of this reality. Don't sacrifice the reality of the Spirit-filled life for an imitation.

Final Questions Concerning Tongues

1. Which must guide all your decisions about tongues—experience or Scripture?

2. Which should you desire—the best gifts or the least gifts?

3. Which is most important—building up yourself or building up others?

4. Which does a church the most good—an unknown tongue or a simple Bible message?

5. Which is the evidence of the filling of the Spirit—an emotional experience or power to witness for Christ?

6. Which will win more people to Christ—ten thousand words which can't be understood or five simple words which are understandable?

CHAPTER 14

KEEPING IN STEP

Charlie never learned to keep in step. He was in our high school marching band for four years. He played the trumpet. Everyone tried to help him keep in step. Our frustrated band director used to march right beside him in practices. Other members of the band offered their help. But Charlie just couldn't do it. It got to be quite a show every time the band performed. During the annual Pimento Festival, the band would march in the downtown parade, and there was Charlie, out of step, out of time. All the halftime shows for four football seasons featured the same comic mistake. Charlie couldn't keep in step!

It's not like he didn't try. He was always attempting to do better. Sometimes he would skip along trying to get in step. Other times, he would hold his left foot high and hop on his right one, trying to find the correct time to put down the left one. He never found it! He just didn't have a sense of timing.

I have thought a lot about Charlie through the years. In many ways he reminds me of many Christians who try to live the Christlike, Spirit-led life. They want to be in step. They just can't seem to pull it off. They hear the beat; they just can't keep it.

First Peter 2:21 says, "To this you were called, because Christ suffered for you, leaving you an example, that you should follow in his steps." This verse teaches that we are to follow the footprints the Lord Jesus left behind. This does not suggest that we are to attempt to imitate the life of Christ. Keeping in step in the Christian life is done through identification, not imitation. It is not that we live the Christian life by trying to imitate the lifestyle of Jesus. Rather, he lives his resurrected life through us because we have received him by faith. The Christian life is not lived by imitation (trying to be like him), but by identification (identifying with his death, burial, and resurrection).

It is true that Jesus on occasion invited people to follow him. At the beginning of his ministry, Jesus said to Peter and Andrew, "Come, follow me, and I will make you fishers of men" (Matt. 4:19). They left their nets and followed Jesus (see Matt. 4:20). After his resurrection, Jesus said to Simon Peter, "Follow me!" (John 21:19). Now, how does following Jesus become practical in the life of a Christian? How can a believer learn to keep in step with Jesus, the heavenly drum major? I believe the simple answer is found in Galatians 5:16: "Walk in the Spirit" (KJV).

Let's review. When you receive Jesus Christ as personal Savior, the Holy Spirit comes to live in your heart. This is a gift. In turn, the Holy Spirit gives believers a variety of spiritual gifts. These are Spirit-given abilities to serve the Lord Jesus through the Spirit's power. The Bible also teaches that the Holy Spirit wants to produce the graces of the Holy Spirit in and through the life of a believer. What are these graces? These are the Christlike characteristics which the Holy Spirit produces in our daily lives. They make us the person we should be.

The Holy Spirit has a specific role in the life of a Christian, and the Spirit's role in a believer's life uncovers two commands. They are crucial to understanding how to live the Christian life in the power of the Spirit. We have already considered the first of these Ephesians 5:18 commands, "Do not get drunk on wine, which leads to debauchery. Instead, be filled with the Spirit." Each day we are to yield ourselves to the control of the Holy Spirit. We humans don't enjoy surrendering our will. Just observe rush hour traffic! Daily we must surrender our lives to the Spirit's direction and guidance.

The second command, "Walk in the Spirit," comes from Galatians 5:16 and 25 (KJV). Yield your life to the Holy Spirit daily and "walk in the Spirit." This is what the Bible teaches us. We have God's pattern and plan for living a victorious, Christlike life on a daily basis. This is the secret of following in his steps. It is the truth which helps us keep time with Jesus and march in step each day.

Soon after we become Christians and begin to discover the role of the Holy Spirit in our lives, we make a startling discovery. We find that we have all kinds of opposition. A number of enemies will try to keep us from walking in the Spirit. These enemies will hinder our attempts to live the victorious Christian life. There is an infernal enemy—Satan. He works to hinder us in every way possible. There is also the external enemy—the world around us. This includes everything about our culture which is antagonistic to the things of God. The third enemy is perhaps the most formidable and threatening of all. It is the internal enemy. The Bible refers to this internal enemy as "the flesh" or worldly desires.

Galatians 5:16–25 deals with this enemy, the flesh. Verse 16 talks about "the desires of the sinful nature." Verse 17 teaches "the sinful nature desires what is contrary to the Spirit." Verse 19 speaks of "the works of the flesh" (KJV). Something very specific is intended by the use of this term *the flesh.* Material flesh is not really what is meant. At the moment of your physical birth, you receive your material body. This means the blood and the skin and the cells that help you function as a human. You also receive "the flesh." In this sense, the flesh represents the sinful tendencies that become a part of your existence at your birth. All of us were born "in the flesh." Sometimes the Bible refers to this flesh nature as "the old man." Our old man is our old nature. It is our old or natural nature. It is everything our physical birth makes us. We are born in the flesh and we will bear the flesh all the days of our lives.

Then something wonderful happens! We receive Christ as our personal Savior. We are born spiritually (see John 3:1–15). At that moment, we receive a new spiritual nature. Remember that Jesus said to Nicodemus, "The Spirit gives birth to spirit" (John 3:6). The Bible refers to this new nature as the new man. Your new spiritual nature represents everything you can be by the power of the Holy Spirit of God. By virtue of your physical birth, you have an old nature—the flesh. By virtue of your new birth, you have a new nature—the spiritual nature.

Here's the deal! When you receive your new nature, at the time of your spiritual birth, you do not lose your old nature. To be born of the Holy Spirit does not mean the old flesh disappears. Some teach that the old nature may be eradicated or eliminated. If you think this is true, just ask your mate about it! Someone has said that the old nature is born with us, and it will be borne by us all the days of our lives.

The Christian must learn to walk in the Spirit and not fulfill the lust of the flesh, as Galatians 5:16 indicates. To do this, the believer must walk and let the Holy Spirit direct the new nature. This will keep us from giving in to the temptations of the old nature—like becoming angry and yelling at our kids, or saying words or phrases we shouldn't say.

Let's look at the command in Galatians 5:16, "Live by the Spirit, and you will not gratify the desires of the sinful nature." The reference is to living your daily lifestyle. It's living daily in the power of the Holy Spirit. To walk in the Spirit means living for Jesus day by day in the power of the Holy Spirit. This produces victory over the flesh. The only way to overcome the lust of the flesh is to live day by day for Jesus in the power of the Holy Spirit.

A Conflict

A careful look at Galatians 5:17 and 18 indicates that there is a conflict here: "For the sinful nature desires what is contrary to the Spirit, and the Spirit what is contrary to the sinful nature." The word *contrary* means "to be opposite" or "to be in continual opposition." The old *you* and the new *you* don't get along at all. The flesh and the Spirit are mortal enemies. They put up their dukes constantly and fight each another. Civil War? Yes. For Christians, this often feels like an internal Antietam.

What if a spider and a butterfly could be fused together in the same body. Imagine the conflict! The spider nature would be constantly pulling downward to the darkness and dirt. The butterfly nature would be constantly pulling upward to the brightness and the light. This is what happens in the life of a believer. Your old "spider" nature is constantly pulling you back to the things of the world. Your new "butterfly" nature is always pulling toward the things of the Lord—the holy and the good and the pure.

Think about this. One Sunday morning your new nature wants to get up, go to church, hear the word of God, and worship the Lord Jesus. Your old nature fights it. "You are tired," an inner voice says. "You've had a tough week. Don't get up so early. Rest yourself. You deserve a break! Go to the beach or the ballgame." You experience conflict.

The new nature likes to give. Motivations of compassion and love bring a desire to help others. Someone is in need. The new nature wants to give some money to help them. The old nature says, "Oh, you can't afford that. Don't do that. They don't deserve it anyhow." The new nature wants to tithe to the church as the Bible teaches. The old nature says, "No way! They don't need all that money down at the church." The old nature wants to read filthy literature. The new nature says, "This book will pollute your mind. It will paint unclean pictures on the canvas of your memory."

Conflict like this exists in a thousand different scenarios every day of life. High school kids, people in the workplace, and housewives have to grapple with this conflict every day.

Galatians 5:17 confirms that this conflict is going on. Verse 18 says, "But if you are led by the Spirit, you are not under law." There are two basic ways a person tries to overcome the old nature and walk in the power of the Holy Spirit each day. Some people try by imposing rules from the outside. A set of rules, regulations, and guidelines are drawn up. This we call legalism. The Christian who tries to live his life on the basis of observing an external set of rules places himself under the law. The Bible teaches that we have been delivered from this kind of life.

As believers, we are no longer under the law. We are no longer in bondage to the law. This does not mean, however, that we are free to live as we choose. It has been said that the Old Testament had 632 commands that were to be obeyed. The Pharisees were compliance experts. They could click off all 632 items. They drove other people nuts!

To be led of the Spirit is not to be under the law. Victory in the flesh/spirit conflict isn't achieved by following a set of strict external rules. Victory is based on being led by the Spirit internally. The Holy Spirit lives within to guide us. He is there to give us spiritual motivation. He creates desires in us to do what is right and to stay away from what is wrong. Remember, the Christian life is not lived by imposing rules from the outside. It is lived by yielding to the Holy Spirit on the inside.

Let's take a closer look at the word *led* in verse 18. It means "to guide" or "to lead." If you went to an office building for an appointment and you didn't know where to go, you might walk over to a security guard. "Can I help you?" he would ask.

"Yes, I would like to go to office number 1542."

The officer says, "Go down this hall about halfway. Take a left. Take two more rights; then you'll find three elevators. Take the middle elevator. Punch the fifteenth floor. When you get to the fifteenth floor, take a left and go down two or three doors, then take a right and back to the left. You'll be there." I don't know about you, but I have a feeling I might have problems following his directions!

Now get this! What if you entered the same office building for your appointment. You say to the security guard, "I need to go to room number 1542."

He replies, "I'm going that way myself. Just follow me and I'll take you there."

Much more helpful and comforting, wouldn't you agree? The Holy Spirit doesn't just give directions and leave you to find your own way. He says, "You follow me and I'll take you exactly where you ought to go." This is what it means to be led by the Holy Spirit. He is not a director; he's a guide. As we "walk in the Spirit," he will guide us and lead us.

Being led by the Spirit doesn't mean being driven. I feel sorry for many people whose living of the Christian life causes such misery. They feel they are driven like a bridled horse with a ruthless driver holding the reins. In John 10, Jesus beautifully illustrated the Christian life. He drew an analogy to sheep being led by the shepherd. Many beautiful truths emerge from this picture. Sheep recognize and follow the voice of their shepherd. The more touching truth, though, is that "he goes on ahead of them, and his sheep follow him because they know his voice" (John 10:4).

A goat herder drives the goats. But we do not have a goat herder. We have a Shepherd. He goes before us. Our wonderful Shepherd, the Lord Jesus, has placed the Holy Spirit, the Spirit of the Good Shepherd, in our hearts. We follow as he leads us where we should go.

Walking in the Spirit means that you allow the Holy Spirit to lead you rather than your old nature.

A Contrast

Expectations! We learn early in our lives that others have expectations of us. Mrs. Maxwell was my sixth-grade teacher. She was my favorite because she encouraged me to achieve my full potential. She set high goals for me. I remember how good I felt when I performed up to her expectations.

In Galatians 5:19–22, we learn of spiritual expectations. God sets forth expectations for his children that, when followed, produce a fulfilled and fruitful Christian life. What are these expectations? God wants us to "walk in the Spirit." But when we attempt this, a contrast occurs. The contrast is between "the works of the flesh" and the "fruit of the Spirit." Just like Mrs. Maxwell's expectations, if we Christians will try our best to live by God's expectations for us, the fruit of the Spirit will be produced in our lives.

The word *lust* in verse 16 (KJV) refers to those "inner desires of the old nature." I won't discuss each of these vices of the flesh individually. Peterson's paraphrase of the passage captures their meanings for us today.

> It is obvious what kind of life develops out of trying to get your own way all the time; repetitive, loveless, cheap sex; a stinking accumulation of mental and emotional garbage; frenzied and joyless grabs for happiness; trinket god; magic-show religion; paranoid loneliness; cutthroat competition; all-consuming-yet-never-satisfied wants; a brutal temper; an impotence to love or be loved; divided homes and divided lives; small-minded and lopsided pursuits; the vicious habit of depersonalizing everyone into a rival; uncontrolled and uncontrollable addictions; ugly parodies of community. I could go on.[1]

Here, like streams of filth belching up from the sewer of the old nature, is the result of yielding to the flesh. Interesting, isn't it, that these verses are written to Christians? This is a warning. If we allow the flesh to take control of our lives, even we as born-again believers can be controlled by these vices. Becoming a Christian doesn't mean your old nature is gone. It is still very much with you. You have the same potential for sin you always had because you're still human.

Galatians 5:21 also gives us a warning that "those who live like this will not inherit the kingdom of God." If these characteristics are exhibited in your life, this verse says you had better sit up and take notice. You may not be a Christian. But even born-again Christians can yield to the flesh and allow some of these vices to appear in their lives.

Whew! Let's get out of the sewer. Galatians 5:22 is much more positive. This verse mentions the graces or the fruit of the Holy Spirit. Spiritual gifts are shown in what we do. Spiritual graces are displayed by what we are. Nine spiritual graces are listed in this verse. The Holy Spirit produces these in our lives. The verse gives a ninefold description of what life can be like if we walk in the Spirit. This verse actually gives a beautiful picture of the Lord Jesus. As we walk with the Spirit, our day-by-day life becomes very similar to the life of Jesus.

But this doesn't happen all at once. We're talking about a *walk*. The Christian life is not a leap from worldliness to perfection. The Christian life is walk. As you yield your life to the Holy Spirit and walk with him, he begins to produce the fruit.

Keep in mind that the fruit on the tree is the result of what's going on inside the tree. The Holy Spirit dwelling within will produce these kinds of graces. The fruit of the Spirit is not produced by our own efforts, but by the Holy Spirit. Just like an apple tree with ripe apples, we must have the correct amount of sun and water to produce Holy Spirit fruit. The sunlight and the life-giving water come from the Holy Spirit.

The nine graces can be organized into three groups. The first group consists of love, joy, and peace. These show godly fruit. Love—you will love Jesus and God's people and unsaved people. Joy—there will be an exuberance and happiness about your life. Peace—there will be a remarkable peace in your life.

The second group includes patience, kindness, and goodness. These indicate the human fruit. Patience—you will find yourself more patient with people. Remember how Jesus was so patient with his disciples and with sinners? Kindness—you will find you are being kinder to people. You will treat others as the Lord treats you. Goodness—your actions will be more loving and others will notice!

The third group consists of faithfulness, gentleness, and temperance. Your life will manifest these. Faithfulness—you will become more trustworthy and loyal. Gentleness—there will be a more submissive, peaceable spirit about you. Temperance—this is self-control. It is the kind of complete control an athlete has over his body during competition.

All nine graces are produced by the Holy Spirit in your daily walk. They will become more a part of your life, like exercised muscles, as you live for Jesus in the power of the Holy Spirit.

One day I was walking through an apple orchard. I passed an apple tree and noticed it was the saddest apple tree I had ever seen. Its branches were wilted and drooped. I said, "What's the matter with you, apple tree?"

The apple tree said, "I'm sad and miserable."

"What's wrong with you, apple tree? You're in this beautiful apple orchard, and you are lucky because you produce beautiful apples."

"I know I'm supposed to produce apples, but that's just it. I'm trying really hard. I'm squeezing and pushing and shoving. See that little apple up there? That's about all I've been able to produce. Just one little green apple."

I looked at the apple tree and said, "Silly tree, relax! You don't have to work that hard. Just let what's on the inside of you do the job. That will produce the fruit. All you have to do is bear it."

The apple tree said, "Really? Do you mean it?"

"That's right."

I went back to the apple orchard a few days later. Passing by the tree, I noticed it was the happiest tree I had ever seen. There were little apples coming out all over its branches. I said, "How are you doing, apple tree?"

"Oh, I'm so glad you came by and explained fruit-bearing to me. I've just been allowing what's inside of me to produce the fruit on the outside of me. I don't have to work so hard anymore. I just bear the fruit."

A Conquest

Guess what! We've reached the pinnacle! Galatians 5:24–25 brings us to the point of victory in this matter of walking in the Spirit. Verse 24 says, "Those who belong to Christ Jesus have crucified the sinful nature with its passions and desires." The verb indicates something that happened in the past. When was the flesh crucified? Two thousand years ago. Where? On the cross where Jesus died. Have you read Galatians 2:20: "I have been crucified with Christ"? When was Jesus crucified? Two thousand years ago. What about our flesh? It was nailed to the cross too. God says it's been crucified. It's dead. Does this mean we will never yield to worldly desires or works anymore? No, it means we don't have to.

Our flesh was put to death on the cross. This means that we must bring our flesh to the cross on a daily basis. This is what Paul meant when he said, "I die daily" (1 Cor. 15:31 KJV). We must have a daily crucifixion. Every day we must allow the Lord to nail our flesh with all its desires and passions to the place of death.

Does this mean that we will never again fulfill the works of the flesh? No, it means we don't have to. We have a choice in the matter. That's one of the most terrifying conditions of a lost person: not having a choice. When it comes to the passions and lusts of the flesh, the unsaved person is a slave to them. He or she is like a puppet on a string, pulled in all directions by fleshly desires.

But we as believers have victory! Romans 8:12 says, "We have an obligation—but it is not to the sinful nature, to live according to it." This means we don't have to do what the flesh tells us to do. The Christian has options that are not available to lost persons.

Several years ago I saw a dog on a leash in a neighbor's yard. Let's call him Sammy. Sammy was playful and frisky. He would run after anything and everything! If a bird landed nearby, the dog would take off after it. If one of the neighborhood children walked close to the yard, Sammy would take off yelping after her. But the dog was on a leash. When Sammy reached the end of the leash—Bam! The leash would stop him—sometimes quite violently. But Sammy was smart. He got tired of having his neck nearly yanked off. So Sammy learned to stop just before he reached the end of his leash. The leash kept him grounded to the tree.

Then one day my neighbor was in the yard with Sammy. Apparently Sammy didn't realize his leash was off. On this day, when a bird flew by, the dog would take off. But as he reached the usual end of his leash, he would stop. As a child passed, he would dart after the child. But Sammy would stop just short of the length of the leash. The leash was not around his neck, but he had been trained to go no further than the leash allowed. I looked at the dog and said, "Sammy, you remind me of many Christians. They don't understand that the old leash, the flesh, has been dealt with. They are still under the control of the old nature. The flesh calls and they come running."

The Bible teaches in Galatians 5:24 that the flesh, with its affections and lusts, has been crucified. You don't have to do what the old nature tells you to do anymore. You have a new, exciting choice. You can say "yes" to the guidance and leading of the Holy Spirit.

Galatians 5:25 brings the whole idea to an exciting crescendo: "Since we live by the Spirit, let us keep in step with the Spirit." Now you might say, "since we live *in* the Spirit." As saved persons we live in the Spirit. A lost person lives in sin, in the flesh. But a person who has gone through a salvation experience lives in the Spirit. It's all about salvation. Since we are saved, "let us also walk in the Spirit."

In verse 25 (KJV), the word *walk* is used differently. In verse 16 the word *walk* means "to walk around." The idea, as you recall, is to live your daily life. J. I. Packer, in his book *Keep in Step with the Spirit*, points out that the word in verse 25 carries the idea of "walking in line," "holding to a rule," and thus proceeding under another's control.[2] Picture taking one step after another. I believe Packer is right in saying this word could be translated, "Keep in step with the Spirit."

When my daughter Joy was in elementary school, I sometimes drove by the school playground. I occasionally saw her with her class holding to a rope held by her teacher. Joy and her playmates were learning to keep in step by following the teacher. Walking in the Spirit is just keeping in step with the Spirit. Let the Spirit hold the rope, and clasp it with your hand. Step by step by step. Day by day by day. Follow the leading and direction of the Holy Spirit.

How exactly does a person learn to walk? Do you remember? My little grandson was with us during the time he was learning to walk. It's really fascinating to see a baby learn this. How did Jay do it? He didn't go to the library and check out books on walking and read them. His parents did not take him to a special school that specializes in teaching walking. He didn't even go to the shoe store and buy shoes just for aerodynamic walking! One day, with the support and prompting of his parents, he just started walking. That's how you and I learn to walk in the Spirit. Each day we yield ourselves to Jesus. We claim the power and direction of the Holy Spirit. Then we just walk.

Here's how to do it. Each morning have a quiet time. Read your Bible and let the Lord talk to you. Pray and talk to the Lord. As you talk to him in your morning prayer, yield your life totally to the Holy Spirit. Yield your hands to the Holy Spirit. Yield your feet to him. Yield your mind, your eyes, your speech to the Spirit. Turn your life over to his control. Then say, "Oh, Holy Spirit, I don't know where you are going or what you are doing today, but I'm going to walk in your steps." Start your day by keeping in step with the Spirit.

Walking in the Spirit is much like the difference between an automobile and a trolley. Think about how an automobile operates. It works from its own power. A self-contained engine exists under the hood. In the back of the vehicle, there is a tank filled with gasoline. As long as the engine functions properly and you have gas in the tank, you can ride and ride and ride. If you never get a refill, though, sooner or later you will run out of gas and find yourself in a parked car.

A trolley is different. As a boy, I sometimes went to Atlanta to ride a trolley. It was a buslike vehicle that transported people around the city. A trolley doesn't have its own power source. Instead, it has a connecting link to a power line overhead. The trolley doesn't operate under its own power, like a car does. It operates by staying in contact with the power line overhead. As long as the trolley stays in touch with the power line, it keeps moving.

This is what walking in the Spirit is like. You do not operate on your own power. You stay in contact with the power line from above. You live for Jesus each day in the power of the Holy Spirit.

Let's walk in the Spirit today. Let's walk in the Spirit tomorrow. We used to sing a chorus when I was a kid: "Isn't it grand to live for Jesus, isn't it grand? Isn't it grand to live for Jesus, isn't it grand? Isn't it grand to live for Jesus Monday, Tuesday, Wednesday, Thursday, Friday, Saturday, and all day Sunday. Isn't it grand to live for Jesus, isn't it grand?" I would change the song a bit today. Isn't it grand to live for Jesus all day long, every day!

I haven't kept up with Charlie, our misstepping trumpet player in the band. I hope he is making good steps in the walk of life. I really do hope he is in step with God.

Steps to Keep in Step

1. Acknowledge you can walk in the steps of the old life.
2. Claim the truth that your old life was crucified with Christ on the cross.
3. Daily make that death practical in your life by dying to the desires of the flesh that day.
4. Begin each day getting in step with the Spirit.
5. Remember, "The steps of a good man [or woman] are ordered by the Lord" (Ps. 37:23 KJV).
6. As the Holy Spirit leads, keep in step! Keep marching in the Lord's band!

CHAPTER 15

HOLY JEALOUSY? SAY WHAT?

Toys are so different today from what they used to be. Girls don't play with simple dolls anymore. They have to be realistic with authentic burping sounds. Boys don't play with wagons or blocks anymore. Their toys must have machine gun sounds or simulated blood spilling from virtual wounds.

When I was a boy, I really wanted a motorbike. My dad refused my request, citing the dangers. He promised I could use his car when I got my driver's license at age sixteen. I was disappointed.

My friend Bernard got a motorbike for Christmas. I really wasn't happy for him. Actually, I was jealous—so much so that our friendship was damaged. I learned at that early age that jealousy is a dangerous emotion. It can be harmful and destructive.

Holy Jealousy? Say what? Seems to be a contradiction, doesn't it? We don't often think of the two words together. How can jealousy be holy? How can anything holy also be jealous?

Let's complicate the matter even more. Exodus 20:5 says, "For I, the LORD your God, am a jealous God," and Exodus 34:14 says, "For the LORD, whose name is Jealous, is a jealous God." How can God be jealous?

Some jealousy is harmful. Some jealousy is extremely destructive. A husband/wife relationship built on jealousy can produce strife and result in explosive tempers and outbreaks of violence. This is not the kind of jealousy the Scripture refers to in relation to God. There is also a healthy jealousy. This is even true in a husband or wife relationship. Each partner should have a healthy jealousy of the total devotion of the other. No husband or wife wants anyone else to come between him or her. There is a holy jealousy which demands that no one steal the affection of your mate. This is a loving, watchful concern for the welfare of the other.

I had never thought about the Holy Spirit having a jealousy for us until I considered James 4:5. This is perhaps the most unusual verse about the Holy Spirit in all the Bible: "Do you think Scripture says without reason that the spirit he caused to live in us envies intensely?" Most versions of the Bible render the word *spirit* with a little *s*, taking the position that the reference is to the human spirit. However, others regard it as a reference to the Holy Spirit.

A. T. Robertson, one of the greatest Greek scholars ever, asserted that this passage refers to the Holy Spirit. In his discussion of this chapter, he pointed out that there is no Old Testament passage which precisely fits the James 4:5

reference. Robertson said, however, that it might be a poetical rendering of Exodus 20:5. He also said that the general thought is in keeping with Genesis 6:3–5 and Isaiah 63:8–16. According to Robertson, the Holy Spirit is presented in this passage as a jealous lover. He also said the word translated "lusteth" is used in the same sense of Philippians 1:8 where Paul says, "I long for all of you with the affection of Christ Jesus."[1]

The Living Bible paraphrases James 4:5 like this. "The Holy Spirit, whom God has placed within us, watches over us with tender jealousy." I read the verse this way: "The Holy Spirit jealously yearns for the entire devotion of our hearts." The Holy Spirit loves us so much that he desires our total affection and love.

Viewing the Holy Spirit as the jealous lover of our soul reaffirms several truths we have discovered. The Holy Spirit is a person. Jesus referred to him as a person. We also know that the Holy Spirit lives in the hearts of believers. When you receive Christ, the Holy Spirit comes to live inside.

The Holy Spirit is also your Friend. He loves you and he wants the very best for you. He is also concerned that we be completely devoted to the Lord Jesus. The primary role of the Holy Spirit, as I understand it, is to call attention to the Lord Jesus. Jesus specifically said, "He shall glorify me" (John 16:14, KJV). So the Holy Spirit has a holy jealousy. He is jealous of our devotion. He wants it to be given to the Lord Jesus.

Look at the larger setting of James 4:5. Verse 4 deals with the subject of spiritual adultery. "You adulterous people, don't you know that friendship with the world is hatred toward God? Anyone who chooses to be a friend of the world becomes an enemy of God." In a love relationship with the Lord, anyone or anything that comes between the believer and the Lord Jesus constitutes spiritual adultery. The Holy Spirit is a jealous lover. When Christians flirt with this world, the Lord is jealous.

This is holy jealousy. The Holy Spirit is a divine person who loves you far more than you can imagine. He has a holy jealousy for you. He doesn't want you to allow anything to come between your soul and the Lord Jesus Christ.

Some sins, when committed against the Holy Spirit, cause the believer to have a strained relationship with the Holy Spirit. How is sin judged? The seriousness of a sin may be judged by the one who is sinned against. When a marriage partner is guilty of unfaithfulness, for example, the other partner has been sinned against. A broken marriage commitment now exists. The innocent partner is left devastated. In the same way, when we sin we break the heart of the Holy Spirit who loves us.

In this chapter, let's look at two sins against the Holy Spirit that believers can commit. Later we'll look at two sins that unbelievers can commit.

Don't Quench the Holy Spirit

Let's look at 1 Thessalonians 5:19. Remember that this was Paul's first letter to Christians in the city of Thessalonica. In the closing words of this letter, Paul indicated it was possible for believers to sin against the Holy Spirit by putting out the fire of what the Spirit of God wants to do through them. The word *quench* means "to put out a fire." It means "to stifle" or "smother." It may be paraphrased, "Don't suppress the Spirit."

Serving the Lord is one of the great privileges God has given to believers. To enable believers to serve better, the Holy Spirit gives us spiritual gifts. The Holy Spirit provides ministries, or needy places, where these gifts may be used. Then, the Holy Spirit provides us power to serve in these ministries and to exercise these gifts to the glory of God and for the good of others. He then rewards us for doing what he empowers us to do! I've noticed that many ads promote "systems." We see on television a commercial for a carpet care "system" or a skin care "system" for men or women. We could say that the Holy Spirit provides believers a maintenance "system" for spiritual health and happiness. It's beautiful to serve the Lord Jesus in the power of the Holy Spirit.

One beautiful biblical symbol for the Holy Spirit is fire. Regarding Jesus, John the Baptist said, "He will baptize you with the Holy Spirit and with fire" (Matt. 3:11). In the Old Testament, God's Spirit is referred to as "the spirit of burning" (Isa. 4:4 KJV). God's Holy Spirit is like a fire. It burns. It consumes. On the day of Pentecost, when the Spirit of God filled the disciples, "they saw what seemed to be tongues of fire that separated and came to rest on each of them" (Acts 2:3). Yielding to the control of the Holy Spirit can be described as being set on fire for the Lord Jesus.

It is possible, however, for a believer to quench the Holy Spirit. Unlike Old Testament times, believers today cannot lose the presence of the Holy Spirit. He is not withdrawn. But his power can be stifled or smothered. A Christian can render his or her service to the Lord ineffective by suppressing the fire of the Spirit of God. Some Christians put wet blankets of indifference and sin on the fire of the Holy Spirit.

How can a Christian quench the Spirit? What causes Christians to quench the Holy Spirit? In your personal lives, we can say no to his call to serve him. Perhaps God has given you musical ability. You may be quenching God's gift of music by failing to use it for his glory. Perhaps you could sing in your church's choir. Maybe you could play in its orchestra. There may be small group ensembles or even solo work you could effectively use for the Lord. If God wants you to serve him in this way and you refuse, you are quenching the Holy Spirit.

Or God may have gifted you as a teacher. Churches need more teachers. There are young boys and girls who desperately need faithful Christians to teach them the truths of God's Word and the joys of living the Christian life. If you refuse to use your teaching gift, you are quenching the Holy Spirit's fire in your life.

Looking back to the passage in 1 Thessalonians 5, we see many other matters that speak to this point. Verse 16 says, "Rejoice evermore" (KJV). I think we quench the Spirit when we fail to rejoice in the Lord as we should. All of us have burdens. We have an abundant load of problems and cares. If we are not careful, we can dwell on the burdens and forget the blessings. There is so much to rejoice about. Don't quench the fire of the Spirit by failing to rejoice.

Verse 17 says, "Pray without ceasing" (KJV). This does not mean we should pray all the time. It does mean we are to stay continually in an atmosphere and attitude of prayer. Prayer should be as natural to our hearts as breathing is to our lungs. Do you talk to the Lord each day? God is always accessible. His cell phone is always on and he's ready to answer our calls. When we fail to pray as we should, we quench the Holy Spirit.

Verse 18 says, "Give thanks in all circumstances, for this is God's will for you in Christ Jesus." We should be so thankful! Have you thanked God lately for your salvation? Have you thanked him for the Bible? What about your family and friends? Have you thanked him for a good church? When we fail to be as thankful as we should be, we quench the Holy Spirit.

Let's examine now how the Holy Spirit may be stifled in the life of a church. The church in Thessalonica evidently had a problem that was opposite the problem of the church in Corinth. The Corinthian church seemed to have gone overboard emotionally. Some Christians have a tendency to go to extremes. Warren Wiersbe says, "Blessed are the balanced." Churches can also go to extremes. They can get carried away and allow their emotions to override their minds and their judgment. As you read Paul's letter to the Corinthian church, you will notice his efforts to bring them back to a sense of decency and order.

The church at Thessalonica had the opposite problem. It was too stilted. This church had a tendency to stifle the emotional aspects of worship and service to God. Some churches do. The Holy Spirit wants to move with freshness and freedom in a local church. We quench the fire of the Holy Spirit when we do not allow him to do so. I heard about a deacon who prayed, "Oh Lord, if there is a spark among us tonight—Oh, Lord, water that spark!"

Churches all around us are quenching the Spirit. They are failing to reach out to the lost. They have no impact on their communities. Many members are undisciplined, quarrelsome, critical of the preacher, and slack in dedication to the Lord Jesus. Perhaps they seek a church experience on their terms so they remain in control. Firing the preacher is often a solution. Or they seek to attract people by hip-hop culture and music. They might try the tactics of corporate America to revive the church. Some churches try marketing techniques to properly "position" themselves in their community. While it is important to connect with the culture, churches must be careful not to be corrupted by the culture.

Some Christians also quench the Spirit in the lives of other Christians. A young Christian gets excited and pumped up about serving the Lord. Along comes an older Christian who has lost his fire and his zeal for the Lord. "Oh, another tithing campaign," he says. "I've given enough over the years, and this church doesn't know how to administer its funds anyway. I wouldn't give if I were you." A new Christian's enthusiasm can be squelched! Some older Christians are so cold and indifferent in their lives that they are constantly throwing cold water on anyone who has any zeal and excitement for the Lord.

When it comes to serving, we can hurt our jealous lover, the Holy Spirit. We can quench the Spirit. The Holy Spirit will then rebuke us. Perhaps some of us need to ask the Holy Spirit to forgive us. Maybe we need to open the windows of our hearts so the wind of the Spirit can blow in freshness again. Maybe we need to put our souls on the altar so the fire of God can fall upon us again.

Don't Grieve the Holy Spirit

A second command deals with what the Holy Spirit wants to do for us internally. God's Holy Spirit lives in our hearts to separate us from the world. This is sanctification. The Holy Spirit wants to make real *in* you everything Jesus has done *for* you. The Christian experience is intended to produce a Christian life. It involves a complete overhaul on the inside. He wants to cleanse you and change you. The Holy Spirit comes in with dumpsters and begins hauling out the garbage of your old life. Your life begins to show those characteristics which will produce Christlikeness.

It is also possible to hinder the Spirit's work inside us. Ephesians 4:30 addresses this danger. The Corinthian church seemed to have gone overboard emotionally. The Scripture commands, "And do not grieve the Holy Spirit of God, with whom you were sealed for the day of redemption." Did you know it is possible to grieve the Holy Spirit? You can grieve him to the point that he will not be able to do what he wants to do in making you like the Lord Jesus.

The word *grieve* is a very tender word. It means "to make sorrowful." It's a word about love. You cannot grieve someone who does not love you. You can anger an enemy, but you can't grieve him because he doesn't love you. But when you sin against people who love you, you can grieve them.

Job asked one of the most poignant questions in all the Bible: "If you sin, how does that affect him? If your sins are many, what does that do to him?" (Job 35:6). In other words, Job asked if we have ever thought about how our sin affects the Lord? How does he feel when we sin?

Has someone you love a great deal ever done something that hurt you? Remember how it made you feel? Moms and dads love their children with all their hearts. The kids might say something ugly or hateful about them. This cuts the parents' hearts.

I remember hearing the late Dr. Charles Howard, a professor in a Bible college in North Carolina, share a personal experience. One of his daughters had disobeyed, so the family had a meeting. She admitted her misbehavior, and the family agreed on a proper discipline. She would not be allowed to attend some social functions for several days. This was fine with her, until she thought about her plans for the weekend. She became angry and went to her father and said some very hurtful, unkind things. Dr. Howard said her words cut his heart deeply. He sat alone for a few minutes and suffered. In a while, he felt the arms of his daughter clasping his neck. She leaned over and said, "Daddy, I hurt you by what I said, didn't I?"

"Yes, darling, you did." His daughter began to weep and sob.

Then she said, "Oh, I'm so sorry I have hurt my daddy. I'll never do it again."

Some of us need to say that to the Holy Spirit. He loves us far more than any of us could ever love our children. He watches over us constantly. He cares about every detail of our lives. He wants us to become everything he has saved us to become. The Holy Spirit watches our behavior and listens to our words. When we say things we ought not to say or do things we ought not to do, his heart is hurt and he is grieved.

Is there anything in your life hurting the Holy Spirit right now—anything that grieves him? When was the last time you went to the Holy Spirit and said, "Oh, Holy Spirit, I'm so sorry I have hurt you."

The passage around Ephesians 4:30 mentions several sins that grieve the Holy Spirit. Verse 25 says, "Put off falsehood." The Holy Spirit is grieved when we lie. Businessman, have you told a lie today? If so, the Holy Spirit is grieved. As you filled out your income tax, did you lie about something? The Holy Spirit is grieved. Young person, did you cheat on your chemistry exam at school today? Did you look over and take someone else's answer? The Holy Spirit is grieved by your lie.

Verse 26 says, "In your anger do not sin." Verse 31 says, "Get rid of all bitterness, rage and anger, brawling and slander, along with every form of malice." Look at this accumulation of words. Anger—this means boiling, seething anger. Rage—this is that kind of explosive anger that is so destructive. Brawling—this means losing your temper. It's anger to the point of yelling at other people. Slander—this is deep-seated hostility. Bitterness—this means refusal to get rid of the anger in one's heart. It is anger not disposed of—like a bag of garbage rotting in the heat. Settled hostility—this is bitterness, which poisons the inner life (see Heb. 12:15).

Perhaps someone says, "Oh, I have a bad temper. I blow up a lot, but after it's over, that's the end of it." No, it's not all over. It's like firing a shotgun. It's not just the blast. Look at the wounds and bruises left behind. How these sins must grieve the Holy Spirit.

Verse 29 says, "Do not let any unwholesome talk come out of your mouths." The correct shade of meaning for the word translated *unwholesome* is "rotten fruit." It means foul, filthy, dirty speech. What about your language? What about the words you use? Verse 31 mentions slander and malice. If I spent a day with you and went everywhere you went and heard everything you said, would it affect you in any way? Would you change your language? I'm not with you daily, but the Holy Spirit is with you everywhere you go. He hears everything you say. Do your words grieve him?

Think about words of gossip. How gossip hurts people! Remember, the people who gossip *to* you will gossip *about* you. Remember also that the things you seek to listen to will naturally come your way. If you like to hear all the latest rumors and garbage, that's what you'll hear. Do you think gossip grieves the Holy Spirit?

How do we know when we are grieving the Holy Spirit?

First, everything about our spiritual life is affected. You might feel a cold wind of estrangement blowing in your heart. Have you ever hurt someone you love? Your mate? Your mom? Do you remember how it affected your relationship? You were around each other and yet you were not really with each other. A sense of distance existed.

Second, daily devotions are hindered when the Holy Spirit is grieved. You may continue to read your Bible, but it is not as meaningful. Its promises are not as sweet and precious to you. You still pray. But you just can't seem to get connected. Every time you try to reach the Lord, there is a busy signal. Peace is disturbed. Your heart is uneasy. Joy is lost. There is no sense of thrill and excitement in your Christian life. Your service is ineffective and there is no sense of blessing in it. The results are limited at best.

Is any of this true of you? Maybe you need to check your life. There may be something about your behavior that is hurting the heart of the Holy Spirit. He may be grieved. The uneasiness you are experiencing inside may be his way of letting you know that you have grieved him.

What do we do when we grieve the Holy Spirit? Thank God for 1 John 1:9! It is the most-used verse in my Bible. That page in my Bible is the most stained. It says, "If we confess our sins, he is faithful and just to forgive us our sins, and to cleanse us from all unrighteousness" (KJV). When the Holy Spirit makes us aware that we have grieved him, we should go immediately to the Holy Spirit, confess our sin, and forsake it. We must ask God to cleanse us and remove from our lives the source of the problem. Then sweet fellowship with the Holy Spirit can be restored.

Don't Resist the Holy Spirit

Let's turn our attention now to those sins against the Holy Spirit which unbelievers can commit. In Acts 7, Stephen's message is recorded. He spoke to a hostile audience of Jewish unbelievers disturbed by the resurrection of Jesus Christ. They were also disturbed that these early Christians were winning multitudes of new converts. At the climax of his message, Stephen declared, "You stiff-necked people, with uncircumcised hearts and ears! You are just like your fathers: You always resist the Holy Spirit!" (Acts 7:51).

Look at this statement: "You always resist the Holy Spirit." One of the roles of the Holy Spirit is to convict people of sin. The Holy Spirit makes Jesus Christ known to the human heart. Why does the Holy Spirit do this? To make people feel sinful or uncomfortable? No, it is done so they may be forgiven of sins and experience the power and freedom which salvation brings to a broken life.

It is possible, however, for unsaved people to resist the convicting work of the Holy Spirit. What does this mean? The word *resist* means "to strive against." Does this mean an unsaved person is striving against the Spirit? Yes. One way is by opposing the work of God's Spirit in the world. Those who resist the Spirit may do so by standing against everything that is holy and good. For example, some people in areas of government are constantly resisting the Holy Spirit. They favor and promote everything that is immoral and blasphemous. They oppose what is right and good.

The field of education shows the same resistance. Some people fight any effort to have Bible reading in schools. They want no morals or values taught. On the other hand, they promote the teachings of abortion, the use of condoms, and perverted sexual lifestyles. Ironically, these "tolerant" educators are intolerant of anyone who seeks to share the life-changing gospel of Jesus Christ.

In a more personal way, an unsaved person can resist the approach the Holy Spirit makes to their hearts. Remember that Jesus said when the Holy Spirit came, He would convict the world of sin and righteousness and judgment (see John 16:8). The Holy Spirit knocks at the heart's door. He convinces and convicts an unsaved person of his or her need for Christ. But like a thoughtful husband, the Holy Spirit is a gentleman. He will not knock down the door of your heart against your own God-given will. I do not mean this disrespectfully. I say it reverently. If you are determined to do so, God

203

will let you go to hell. But the Holy Spirit wants you to go to heaven. He wants you to experience the joyful Christian life. He wants you to have a full and meaningful life. So don't resist the Holy Spirit.

Genesis 6:3 says, "My Spirit will not contend with man forever." This is a solemn and serious statement. There comes a point when the Holy Spirit gives up on a rebellious heart, and there is no turning back.

The blasphemy against the Holy Spirit should also be mentioned. Matthew 12:31–32 refers to the sin against the Holy Spirit. Jesus said, "And so I tell you, every sin and blasphemy will be forgiven men, but the blasphemy against the Spirit will not be forgiven. Anyone who speaks a word against the Son of Man will be forgiven, but anyone who speaks against the Holy Spirit will not be forgiven, either in this age or in the age to come."

Before this passage is considered, several preliminary statements need to be made. If you are a believer, you cannot commit this sin of blasphemy against the Holy Spirit. A saved person cannot commit this sin. Some people, in great emotional distress, believe they have committed the sin of blasphemy against the Holy Spirit. Their distress and concern about it is positive proof they have not. Evidently, those who have committed such a sin have no concern or care about it. The person who commits this sin cares nothing about the Bible or Jesus. Spiritual things mean nothing to such a person. If you have any desire at all to know Christ, this is evidence that you have not committed this sin.

What exactly did Jesus mean by this sin which he called blasphemy against the Holy Spirit and for which he declared there is no forgiveness? Understand that in verse 31 he promised that all manner of sin and blasphemy shall be forgiven. He said that God will forgive all kinds of sins. We know this is true. For example, David committed many sins, some of them quite serious. He committed adultery with Bathsheba. He murdered her husband Uriah. But David confessed his sins and God forgave him.

Think about Simon Peter, who boasted of his loyalty and commitment, then denied with profanity and curses that he knew the Lord. But Simon Peter confessed his sin and God forgave him.

The apostle Paul said he was a blasphemer. He was also involved in the persecution and murder of Christians. But Paul repented and God forgave him.

But Jesus said there is a sin that a person can commit for which there is no forgiveness. This sin is blasphemy against the Holy Spirit. What does this mean?

God has three witnesses to the human soul calling it to salvation. There is the witness of God the Father. The Jews had heard the witness of John the Baptist. This was the Father's witness to them and they rejected it. Then there is the witness of God the Son. The Lord Jesus came to earth. He walked among us. He lived a perfect life. The Jews saw the witness of the Son, but they rejected him. Now Jesus declared there is one more witness. The Holy Spirit bears witness. He is God's final call to the human soul. After the Holy Spirit, there is no further divine witness. The Holy Spirit is God's final call to the human heart. After he knocks on the heart's door, the final curtain falls and the drama is over.

When a person refuses God's call to salvation through the Holy Spirit, he is saying that he is not interested and that he wants to be left alone. There is no further witness that God can give to the human soul. So as I understand it, the blasphemy against the Holy Spirit is the deliberate, definite choice to reject God's offer of salvation. This is often done with words spoken against the Holy Spirit.

Aaron Burr's name is a black mark on the pages of American history. He betrayed his own country. When he was a college student, a preacher came for a series of revival services on his campus. Aaron Burr came under deep conviction of sin. He struggled with his soul's salvation. But he decided against Christ. Years later Aaron Burr referred back to that time in college when he was under deep conviction of sin. "At that time I made a decision," he said. "I told God—'You leave me alone and I'll leave you alone.' God has kept his word and I have kept mine."

Is there anyone reading this who is close to a decision for Christ? How many times has God been knocking at your heart?

> There is a time, I know not when,
> A place, I know not where,
> Which marks the destiny of men
> To heaven or despair.
> There is a line, by us not seen,
> Which crosses every path;

The hidden boundary between
God's patience and His wrath.
To cross that limit is to die,
To die, as if by stealth.
It may not pale the beaming eye,
Or quench the glowing health.
The conscience may be still at ease,
The spirit's light and gay.
That which is pleasing still may please,
And care be thrust away.
O, where is that mysterious bourn,
By which each path is crossed,
Beyond which God Himself has sworn,
That he who goes is lost.
One answer from those skies is sent,
Ye who from God depart,
While it is called today, repent,
And harden not your heart.[2]

Don't step over the line! Your destiny is at stake.

A boy left home to work in the city. He promised his mom he would go to church on Sundays. The first Sunday his new friends invited him to go horseback riding. Remembering his promise, he refused at first. But then he relented at their insistence. Sunday morning came. As he began his horseback ride with his new friends, he remembered church back home. He could see his parents heading to the home church and remembered his promise. As he approached the middle of town on horseback, church bells invited him to the services. He continued to ride.

As he reached the outskirts of town, the bells grew fainter and fainter. He stopped. He said, "Guys, I come from a Christian home. I promised my mom I would go to church today. I noticed the bells are getting fainter the farther we go. A little more and I'll ride beyond the sound of the bells. Excuse me, but I'm going back while I can still hear the bells."

The bells of the Holy Spirit are ringing in your ears. Perhaps you heard them in childhood. The bells are ringing. As a young person, you heard the bells ringing—"come to Jesus, come to Jesus." Now you're older and wiser.

You can still hear the bells, but they are getting weaker. You may be getting close to the point where you'll never hear the bells again. Come to Jesus while you can still hear the bells! Let God's holy jealousy envelop you today.

Final Thoughts on Your Friend the Holy Spirit and His Holy Jealousy

1. The Holy Spirit is a person, so he can be hurt.
2. The Holy Spirit loves you so much that he has a holy jealousy for you.
3. By things we do or don't do, by what we allow him to do or not to do, the Holy Spirit can be hurt. Be careful—don't hurt the Holy Spirit.
4. If the bells are ringing—listen to the bells!

ENDNOTES

Chapter 1
1. From the song "You've Got a Friend," words and music by Carole King. Copyright © Calgems—EMI Music, Inc., 1971. Used by permission.

Chapter 2
1. From the hymn "Breathe on Me," words by B. B. McKinney. Copyright © 1937 by The Sunday School Board of the Southern Baptist Convention. Used by permission.

Chapter 3
1. From the hymn "Brethren, We Have Met to Worship," words by George Atkins, *Broadman Hymnal* (Nashville: Broadman Press, 1940), 198.

Chapter 4
1. C. L. Salzbugh, *World War II* (Boston: Houghton Mifflin, 1969), 269.

Chapter 6

1. From the song "What a Difference You've Made in My Life." (Archie P. Jordan, © 1977, Chess Music, Inc. Administered by Word Music.)

Chapter 9

1. Billy Graham, *Just as I Am* (San Francisco: HarperCollins, 1997), 318–19.

Chapter 11

1. Compiled from a series of articles from the *Tampa Tribune*, Tampa, Florida, and the *Miami Herald*, Miami, Florida.
2. W. A. Criswell, *The Holy Spirit in Today's World* (Grand Rapids: Zondervan, 1966).
3. From the hymn "It Took a Miracle," words by John W. Peterson, ©1948 by Percy B. Crawford, assigned to Hill and Range Songs, Inc.).

Chapter 12

1. From a series of articles in the *Florida Times Union*, Jacksonville, Florida, August 1997.

2. Ron Dunn, *Will God Heal Me?* (Sisters, Ore.: Multnomah Books, 1997).
3. "Faith and Healing," *Time*, June 24, 1996.
4. *American Legion*, August 1994.

Chapter 14
1. Eugene H. Peterson, *The Message* (Colorado Springs: NavPress, 1993), 400.
2. J. I. Packer, *Keep in Step with the Spirit* (Grand Rapids: Revell, 1984), 11.

Chapter 15
1. A. T. Robertson, *Word Pictures in the New Testament*, Vol. 6 (Nashville: Broadman Press, 1933), 51–52.
2. George W. Truett, *A Quest for Souls* (New York and London: Harper and Brothers, 1917), 370–371.

MORE RESOURCES FOR GAINING A GREATER
SpiritLife

MASTERLIFE
Avery T. Willis
with Sherrie Willis Brown

The phenomenally popular *MasterLife* series is now in paperback! The four six-week courses in the series are all designed to revitalize practicing Christians – enabling them to make Christ the Master of their lives – and to master their own lives by developing a personal, lifelong, obedient relationship with Him.

0-8054-0165-2

EXPERIENCING GOD
Henry T. Blackaby
& Claude V. King

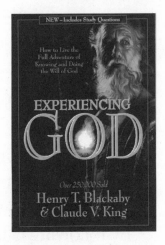

od reveals Himself to each of us in ecial and exceptional ways, so our perception of Him is unique. This emarkable book will help believers ew and revitalize their love for the Lord by seeing His love for us.

Experiencing God is designed to help each of us recognize our own personal relationship with God as He reveals His divine plan and guiding hand to us.

Trade Paper Book   0-8054-0197-0

Available at fine bookstores everywhere.

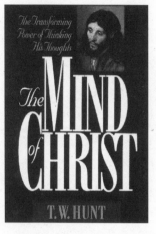
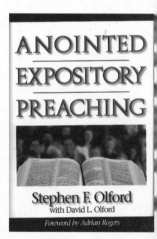